APPLIED MACROECONOMICS

APPLIED MACROECONOMICS

by

CLIFF PRATTEN

OXFORD UNIVERSITY PRESS

1985

Oxford University Press, Walton Street, Oxford OX2 6DP

London New York Toronto
Delhi Bombay Calcutta Madras Karachi
Kuala Lumpur Singapore Hong Kong Tokyo
Nairobi Dar es Salaam Cape Town
Melbourne Auckland

and associated companies in
Beirut Berlin Ibadan Mexico City Nicosia

Oxford is a trade mark of Oxford University Press

Published in the United States
by Oxford University Press, New York

British Library Cataloguing in Publication Data

Pratten, C. F.
Applied macroeconomics.
1. Macroeconomics
I. Title
339   HB172.5

ISBN 0—19—877222—X
ISBN 0—19—877221—1 Pbk

Library of Congress Cataloging in Publication Data

Pratten, C. F. (Clifford Frederick)
Applied macroeconomics.
Bibliography: p.
Includes index.
1. Macroeconomics.   1. Title.
HB172.5P73 1985   339   84—25580

ISBN 0—19—877222—X
ISBN 0—19—877221—1 (pbk.)

Set by Castlefield Press, Northampton
and printed in Great Britain by
Billing & Son. Ltd., Worcester

Acknowledgements

In preparing Applied Macroeconomics I have benefited from a great deal of advice and help. I am especially grateful for the many helpful comments provided by Oliver Hart, Alan Hughes, and Ian McMaster. Referees of a draft also provided numerous constructive suggestions. Mavis Barnett drew successive versions of the graphs and Shani Douglas, Sue Moore, and Ann Mason typed drafts and the final version of the book with their usual efficiency and good humour.

Contents

1
Introduction

The skills for which many economists are employed are those of understanding the operation of the economy and forecasting its development. These skills require a knowledge of economic theory, but theory alone is not enough. They require knowledge of quantitative relationships and information about the operation of institutions. As Alfred Marshall wrote, an 'economist must be greedy of facts'.[1] This book provides an introduction to the demanding task of acquiring and using information in order to test economic theories and understand the economy.

In Britain in 1984 one in eight of the labour force is unemployed. By international standards Britain had a slow growth of output and a rapid rate of inflation during the 1970s. Why has our performance been so bad? Is the answer external shocks to the economy? These occurred during the 1970s, but Britain's growth rate already lagged behind that of other industrial countries during the 1950s and 1960s. Have major macroeconomic relationships been correctly interpreted by economists? Has the British economy been mismanaged by politicians? These are closely related questions. To try to answer them economic theory and facts are used in a two-way process. Facts are used to test theories and to make deductions about the way the economy works.

The economy is complex, and simplified models of it can be misleading. The reactions of households, managers, and investors to events change as they learn from experience, so a search for fixed relationships would be like chasing a mirage, particularly during the turbulent and, for economists, exciting 1970s. The alternative approach used in this book is to assess the durability of major economic relationships and the forces causing relationships to change.

[1] Alfred Marshall, *Principles of Economics*, London, 1890, p. 38.

The book demonstrates the use of statistics and elementary statistical methods to discover how the economy operates. It also illustrates the difficulties and limitations of using statistics to provide answers to questions about the economy.

The book is designed for students familiar with elementary macroeconomic texts who wish to relate their knowledge of macroeconomic theory to the British economy. The stage in the study of macroeconomics at which this applied approach will be useful depends upon the structure of courses. Some directors of studies, including the author, and students, wish to relate theory to data early, and this book makes that possible. Although some knowledge of theory is assumed, theories relevant to the topics examined are outlined to make the book coherent without continual reference to other texts, and to put theories into a testable form.

The book has another purpose. Non-economists are often puzzled by the lack of agreement among economists about the way in which economies operate, and the policy prescriptions they offer. The book provides a guide to the practical operation of the economy and illustrates the difficulty of testing economic theories, a major reason for the lack of agreement among economists.

Paradigms

Many students of economics weary of the presentation of the subject as a battle between the neo-classical/monetarist schools of economists and the Keynesians. Although I have much sympathy with this view, it is not possible to ignore the leading paradigms, and it would not be helpful to do so. The conflicts reflect both a real uncertainty as to how the economy operates and differing views as to how it should be managed; both economists and political parties take the models seriously and are influenced by them. The main elements of the monetarist and Keynesian theories are outlined and tested here, and the reader is provided with data to assess the relevance of the models.

Monetarists and Keynesians emphasize different macroeconomic variables and relationships: monetarists changes in the money supply and their impact on prices and output, and

Keynesians the components of aggregate demand and their determinants. It is possible to describe each of the models and the principal macroeconomic relationships in turn without much back-tracking, but in the earlier chapters some loose ends are left to be taken up in later chapters.

Contents

The Keynesian revolution was a revolt against the traditional modes of thought about the economy, and monetarism was a counter-revolution to reassert them. The classical theory is sketched out in Chapter 1 since it is fundamental to both the main contemporary paradigms. Chapter 1 is included in order to provide non-economists with an introduction to traditional ideas about the operation of decentralized market economies and the Keynesian departure from those ideas.

The post-war development of the British economy is summarized in Chapter 2 in order to quantify the questions about the performance of the economy which are considered later. The oil price shocks were important causes of the deterioration in economic performance, and the size and impact of these shocks are also examined in Chapter 2.

Monetarist theories are outlined, and the links between changes in the money stock and prices and output are tested in Chapter 3. The Keynesian revolution in economic management is outlined in Chapter 4. Keynes's own model in the General Theory, written in 1936, was an essentially fixed-price one: it assumed fixed or near fixed prices because Keynes was not much concerned with inflation at that time. Keynes and the Keynesians, the economists who elaborated Keynes's own theory, developed theories of price determination and inflation which are described in Chapter 5. In Chapter 6 the rate of interest is defined and its relationships with inflation and the demand for money are assessed. One of the key elements of Keynes's model was the consumption function, and in Chapter 7 the stability of the consumption function is considered. Keynes saw investment, the subject of Chapter 8, as the unstable component of aggregate demand. The focus of Chapter 9 is government revenue and expenditure. The balance of payments has constrained the use of

Keynesian policies of expansion, and the nature of this constraint is clarified in Chapter 10. Other constraints on expansive fiscal policies are described in Chapter 11, and the impact of Keynesianism is summarized in Chapter 12.

Monetarism and Keynesianism have surprisingly little to say about the most important feature of any economy, its growth rate. The growth of output can be separated into the growth of output per person employed and the change in employment. The forces determining the growth of output per person are described in Chapter 13. The high level of unemployment is the most serious economic and social problem for Britain in 1984; its causes are summarized and possible solutions are reviewed in Chapter 14. Conclusions about the operation of the economy are summarized in Chapter 15.

Most of the statistics used in the book are for the UK. The primary sources for statistics were *Economic Trends Annual Supplement* (*ETAS*) 1984, and *Economic Trends*, March 1984, for recent data.[2] *ETAS* and *Economic Trends* were used wherever practical so that the source of data would be readily available to readers. The year 1979 was used as a benchmark for statistical purposes; where illustrative statistics are given they are for 1979. Data for later years were not used for this purpose because they were affected by the deepest post-war recession. It was decided not to extend the testing of economic theories to data for other countries, except where the results of using information for other countries affected the interpretation of data for the UK. UK data are sufficient to illustrate the use of techniques of analysis, and if much use had been made of statistics for other countries, institutions in those countries and the problems of interpreting their statistics would have had to be discussed.

The statistical methods employed are elementary. Regression analysis of two variables is used and is outlined in Appendix A which brings together notes about the statistics used and the statistical methods.[3]

---

[2] See Appendix I.1.
[3] See Appendix I.2.

1
Theory

This chapter provides an outline of the origins and basis of the conflicting views about the operation of the macro-economy.

An Exchange Economy

The classical model of a decentralized market economy provides a framework for economic analysis. Either it is accepted as a simplified, but realistic, image of actual economies which is the position of the monetarists, or it is rejected, which is broadly the Keynesian position. The model of a decentralized market economy handed down by Adam Smith and other classical and neoclassical economists has been clarified by general equilibrium theorists. The model is based on the concept of perfect competition, which entails assumptions that decision takers act rationally, there is freedom of movement of resources within the economy, and there is an absence of widespread and persistent economies of scale.[1] Given these assumptions, it is claimed that decisions in a decentralized system are guided by the 'invisible hand' of the market mechanism working through price signals to achieve an efficient equilibrium. This is a state in which the intended actions of economic agents are mutually consistent, and where the allocation of resources maximizes social welfare in the sense that a redirection of resources would make at least one individual worse off.

In 1874 Walras published his mathematical system for displaying the interrelationships within an economy.[2] The Walrasian general equilibrium framework is a system of simultaneous

---

[1] Economies of scale occur where unit costs fall as the scale of production increases.
[2] *Elements of Pure Economics*, translated into English by Williams Jaffe, London, 1954.

equations relating quantities and prices within markets and throughout the economy. It has been used to illustrate the consistency of decentralized decision-making a market economy.

Walras started by narrowing the problem. He first considered a pure exchange economy in which no production takes place, without money, and with time abstracted from the analysis. In this model total market demand for each commodity is obtained by aggregating the demand of all the traders. The excess demand equation for any commodity is the quantity of the good demanded minus its supply, and is a function of its price. Walras investigated the existence and stability of a set of relative prices such that rational individual decisions would result in an overall equilibrium.

For general equilibrium Walras showed that a set of prices is required such that each of the excess demand equations equals zero. The manner of obtaining this set of prices is problematical as the individual traders are assumed to be *price takers*, they take or leave the prices set in the market. Who sets the prices in the market? We may imagine the data required to estimate the excess demand equations being fed into a computer for solution, and traders accepting the equilibrium prices identified in this way. Walras's solution was to posit the existence of an auctioneer who presided over a process of trial and error, of 'groping', towards a general equilibrium solution. This is obviously a theoretical construct. However, it is plausible that within a pure exchange economy it would be in the interests of economic agents to take actions which would move the price structure towards equilibrium by placing goods on the market or withdrawing them, so that the price of commodities for which the demand differs from the supply would change. If market traders grope towards equilibrium in this way there will be delays between an equilibrium being disturbed and a new equilibrium being established.

Walras extended his analysis to an economy in which production takes place and with money.

Production and the Labour Market

Production is integrated into the general equilibrium framework by the inclusion of firms. Firms utilize capital and labour to produce output and maximize the wealth of the agents who own them. Households now maximize their utility through the consumption of commodities and leisure. Households provide labour inputs to firms in return for wages in order to be able to obtain commodities. There are now markets for factors of production, capital, and labour, in addition to commodity markets.

In the short run the marginal product of labour (the extra amount of output obtained by adding another unit of labour) falls as a firm takes on more employees. Profit maximizing firms will increase employment to the level at which the revenue resulting from employing an additional employee equals the marginal cost of an extra employee. Thus the lower the real wage the higher the demand for labour. Individual workers maximize utility by choosing the optimum combinations of work and leisure and the supply of labour is defined as the level of employment forthcoming at a given real wage rate.

Persistent involuntary unemployment is impossible within the Walrasian general equilibrium system. (Involuntary unemployment occurs where some workers are unemployed and there exist jobs yielding a utility to an unemployed worker which exceeds his utility when unemployed, and where the unemployed workers have the same marginal product as those already employed.) All who desire to find employment at the existing level of real wages will do so when the system is in equilibrium. However, there may be some frictional unemployment, employees moving between and searching for jobs. A shock to the economy may result in some unemployment while the economy moves towards a new equilibrium set of prices.

Money

Money can be integrated into the framework as a medium of exchange and a store of value. To obtain a general equilibrium the auctioneer now needs to add to his system an equation for the excess demand for money. One form of equation used is the quantity theory of money, in which money is demanded as some constant proportion of the value of transactions. Assuming a fixed money stock, equilibrium in the money market is obtained with the excess demand for money at zero and the money stock equal in size to the transactions demand. The inclusion of money market equilibrium entails a set of absolute as well as relative prices.

The *neutrality* of money can be illustrated by considering an initial general equilibrium. If the nominal money balances held by agents are doubled, then at the existing level of prices there will be an excess demand for goods and labour, and an excess supply of money. For general equilibrium to be restored all prices will double. Relative prices of commodities and wages for categories of labour remain constant as the absolute price level doubles and the demand for, and supply of, money moves back into equilibrium.

General Equilibrium

General equilibrium analysis demonstrates the formal possibility of an efficient solution to decentralized decision making via the existence of complete markets, including comprehensive futures markets and the auctioneer. (Futures markets are markets where contracts to buy or sell goods, services, or labour, or to borrow or lend money in the future are made.)

Like all models, the general equilibrium model is a simplification of reality. In practice there is no auctioneer, economies of scale are significant in many industries, markets—particularly futures markets—are not complete, and there is uncertainty about the future. General equilibrium theorists accept that their model is not complete, and that the theory of the adjustment of prices and wages once an economy is dislodged from equilibrium is still to be fully worked out.

The price system has a Herculean task to accomplish if it is to achieve optimal allocation of resources. Wages, prices, and particularly the rate of interest, have to be compatible with the achievement of optimal allocation of resources in the future as well as during the current trading period.[3] In a pure exchange economy, agents might grope towards and find an

---

[3] The rate of interest and its determinants are the subject of Chapter 6.

equilibrium structure of prices; in a modern economy where investment and consumption decisions have uncertain results stretching over many years, where futures markets are not comprehensive, and where some prices (including the wages of some groups) are sticky, the practical relevance of the analysis is not self-evident. None the less, many economists explicitly or implicitly assume that the general equilibrium model provides a close enough approximation to reality to provide the best basis for economic analysis and for policy prescriptions. Three broad stances are outlined below; no attempt is made to cover the whole range of views held by economists.

Monetarist View

Monetarism is a counter-revolution to the Keynesian revolution, nevertheless we start by outlining the views of the monetarists. They rest on a Walrasian general equilibrium framework. We concentrate on Friedman's version of monetarism in Chapter 3. Friedman claims that if the monetary authorities operate a policy of increasing the money supply at a steady but moderate rate, this will ensure stable prices, and that in the long run this policy will not result in lower output and higher unemployment than with expansionary fiscal and monetary policies. Friedman has posited a *natural rate of unemployment* which he defines in terms of the Walrasian system: 'At any moment in time, there is some level of unemployment which is consistent with equilibrium in the structure of *real* wage rates'. This 'natural rate of unemployment . . . is the level that would be ground out by the Walrasian system of general equilibrium equations, provided there is embedded in them the actual structural characteristics of the labour and commodity markets . . .'. Starting from a position with unemployment at the natural rate, an increase in the money supply will reduce unemployment, and will put 'upward pressure on real wage rates' and hence prices.[4]

---

[4] M. Friedman, 'The Role of Monetary Policy', *American Economic Review*, March 1968, p. 8.

Keynesian View

Keynes did not accept that the classical model provided a close approximation to reality. 'The characteristics of the special case assumed by the classical theory happen not to be those of the economic society in which we actually live.'[5] In particular the classical theory failed to explain widespread and persistent 'involuntary' unemployment, an obvious feature of Western economies in the 1930s.

An underemployment equilibrium could occur in a state of deficient effective demand, when the two components of aggregate demand in a closed economy, consumption and investment, were not sufficient to utilize the output resources of the economy. Keynes believed his treatment of uncertainty and expectations was the key to his new theory. He noted the separation of decisions to save by households and to invest by managers of firms, and claimed that the level of aggregate demand would not automatically be compatible with full employment.

Keynes argued that investment demand is unstable because it is based on expectations for the future. The future course of events is uncertain so these expectations are likely to be volatile. Suppose there is an adverse movement of expectations; new investment will be thought less profitable, and firms will cut their investment plans accordingly. A counterforce to this would be a fall in the rate of interest which would reduce the cost of investing, but the adverse movement of expectations could operate simultaneously in the financial market. If they did, owners of capital would try to shift the composition of their portfolios of assets towards greater liquidity and away from long-term investment in industry, thus increasing the rate of return required from long-term investments. This increase would create a further disincentive to investment. The attempt to change the composition of their portfolios would increase the demand for money and other liquid assets.

For Keynes the self-adjusting properties of the economy were weak. In brief, consumption, the other component of private domestic demand apart from investment, was not very

[5] J. M. Keynes, *General Theory*, London, 1936, p. 3.

responsive to changes in interest rates. Interest rates might not fall to restore equilibrium. Wages were sticky and, even if they fell, that would not necessarily restore equilibrium because prices would fall in step with wages, and falling prices could affect expectations adversely.

Keynesian economists—the economists who elaborated Keynes's own theory—developed the attack on the reality of the assumptions used by general equilibrium theorists. They emphasized the rigidities in the real economy. Money wages and prices are not responsive to falling demand, firms change output not prices in response to a decline in demand, and technology is not very flexible, so changes in the relative prices of capital and labour brought about by a fall in real interest rates would have little impact on the choices of techniques made by firms or on employment.

New Classical View

The new classical economists claim that 'Keynesian macroeconomic models cannot provide reliable guidance in the formation of monetary, fiscal, or other types of policy'.[6] Keynes emphasized uncertainty and the volatility of expectations. The new classical economists believe that the rational expectations model restores stability to the theory of competitive markets, though they recognize the possibility of shocks causing temporary disturbance and unemployment.

Muth first suggested his rational expectations hypothesis in the following terms: 'Expectations, since they are informed predictions of future events, are essentially the same as predictions of the relevant economic theory'.[7] The basic rational expectations principles, that private economic agents gather and use information efficiently and do not make systematic forecasting errors, are not controversial, but the assumptions the new classical economists add, such as the applicability of the natural rate hypothesis, are not so generally accepted. Some examples will illustrate the new classical approach. It is assumed that the monetarist/general

[6]   Robert E. Lucas and Thomas J. Sargent, *Rational Expectations and Econometric Practice*, London, 1981, p. 316.
[7]   J. F. Muth, 'Rational Expectations and the Theory of Price Movements', *Econometrica*, 1961, p. 316.

equilibrium model of the economy is a true description of the operation of the economy, and that a doubling of the money supply will do no more than double prices. If the government announces that it will double the money supply, rational agents expect prices to adjust. They neither offer nor demand more labour or goods, and they raise wages and prices in line with the money supply. Therefore an increase in the money supply will have no short-term real effects, real income remains unchanged and prices double. Rational agents' expectations are justified and the government fails to alter the real components of the economy. The important implication of these new classical theories is that the output of an economy is not affected by monetary policy even in the short run. However, the new classical economists allow that temporary deviations from the natural level of output and employment will occur if agents misinterpret information. For example, if a government, having operated an accommodating monetary policy, changes its policy and does not accommodate an increase in prices, agents may for a time continue to expect the government to accommodate price rises by increasing the money supply, and they may continue to raise their prices and cause a fall in output.

Another example would be a shock to an economy which creates unemployment. Managers and employees will realize that to restore equilibrium real wages must fall, so managers will cut wages and employees will accept wage cuts until the labour market clears. These examples beg the crucial question whether the monetarist/general equilibrium model does provide a relevant description of how the economy actually operates.

Conclusions

The conflicts between monetarists, Keynesians, and new classical economists cannot be resolved by a priori debate alone. Their predictions have to be tested with actual data for the economy, and it is to this task that we now turn. The problem is not simply one of selecting between theories of how the economy operates. The questions are more subtle. Most, perhaps all, economists would accept that in some measure the general equilibrium model of efficient markets describes many of the forces operating in a modern market economy. Theory and experience also show that there are limits to the smooth operation of economies in practice and that the Keynesian critique of the monetarist, neo-classical, and new classical models provides important insights to the operation of economies. The main practical questions concern the direction and degree of government intervention in an economy. For this it is necessary to assess the effectiveness of each type of government intervention while also pin-pointing the defects of the market system.

General equilibrium theory enables us to conceive of the economic system as a whole. Nowadays it is not so far fetched to envisage a computer model of the economy which reproduces the economic structure and its inter-relationships, so that all the ramifications of a new impulse to the system can be traced. But that stage has not been reached in practice, and the approach used here is far removed from it.

The short cut to practical analysis which developed from Keynes's model and the increased availability of national income data was to summarize the economy in terms of aggregates, national income, consumption, investment, unemployment, the price level and so on, and explain movements of these aggregate variables and the relationships between them. This macroeconomic approach is used in this book, and the limitations and qualifications to the approach are demonstrated in the following chapters.

2

Performance and Shocks

Britain's Economic Performance

Three indicators of economic performance—the rate of growth of output, the rate of inflation, and the level of unemployment—are used in this section to summarize the salient questions about Britain's economic performance.

National income statisticians use the term Gross Domestic Product, GDP, for the total output of the economy. If the value of GDP for each year is revalued in terms of a common set of prices, movements of the volume of GDP, or *real* GDP, can be compared. Diagram 2.1 shows the growth of GDP since 1950[1] at 1980 prices in index form.[2] This index measures movements of the total output of goods and services produced in the economy, and is the single most important macroeconomic statistic; it encapsulates the performance of the economy. Between 1950 and 1980, the index increased from 50 to 100; that is, real GDP *doubled*. The progress of the economy slowed during the 1970s when real GDP increased by only 17 per cent, compared to 29 per cent during the 1950s and 33 per cent in the 1960s.

Diagram 2.1 is drawn on a logarithmic scale. The advantage of this form of presentation is that a constant rate of growth appears as a straight line; on a natural scale it would bend upwards, making it difficult to assess how the growth rate was changing. From 1950 until 1970 there does appear to have been a steady underlying long-term growth rate with cylces around it.

Diagram 2.2 shows the movement of prices measured by the 'GDP deflator': a current weighted index of the home costs of production for the goods and services produced in Britain (with the costs of imports excluded).[3] Between 1950 and 1980 the

[1] See Appendix 2.1.
[2] See Appendix 2.2.
[3] See Appendix 2.3.

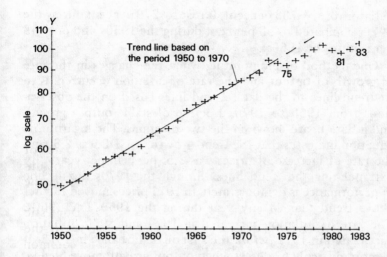

DIAGRAM 2.1   UK index of GDP at 1980 factor cost (1980 = 100).

$$\text{Log}_e \, y = 3.858 + 0.0281t$$

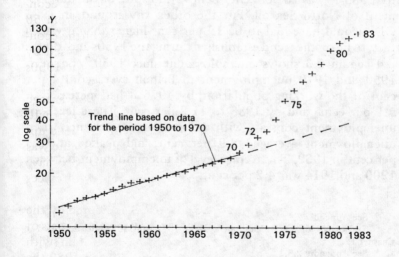

DIAGRAM 2.2   UK index of GDP deflator (1980 = 100).

$$\text{Log}_e \, y = 2.525 + 0.035t$$

deflator rose by 733 per cent. It rose by 279 per cent during the 1970s compared to 53 per cent during the 1950s and only 43 per cent in the 1960s.

One method of pin-pointing when the changes in the rate of growth of output and the rate of inflation occurred, is to fit trend lines to the data. Trend lines based on the observations from 1950 to 1970, a period of stable output growth and inflation, are shown in the two diagrams. The logarithmic equation indicates that the trend growth of GDP was 2.8, and the rate of increase of prices was 3.5, per cent per year.[4] By extrapolating the trend lines through the 1970s the decline in performance is demonstrated. In 1971 prices moved further above trend than in any year during the 1950s and 1960s. The rate of inflation increased in 1974 and 1975. Inflation accelerated in 1971 *before* the first oil disturbance in 1973. It is more difficult to detect when output growth moved below trend. In 1973 output was above the trend set between 1950 and 1970, though it might be argued that this was achieved by government-induced expansion which could not last.[5] Since 1973 output has been below the calculated trend, and by 1983 it was 16 per cent[6] below it, in spite of the development of North Sea oil. Put the other way around, in 1983 GDP would have had to be 19 per cent higher than it was in fact, to be on the trend established during the 1950s and 1960s.

Diagram 2.3 shows unemployment since 1950.[7] Between 1950 and 1970 unemployment in Britain averaged 1.4 per cent of the working population; by 1976 it had increased to 5.1 per cent, and by 1983 to 11.2 per cent. These levels of unemployment contrast with the inter-war experience when unemployment averaged 8.9 per cent, and peaked at 15.3 per cent in 1932. The average level of unemployment between 1900 and 1914 was 4.2 per cent.[8]

---

[4] See Appendix 2.4.
[5] The expansionary policies operated in 1972 and 1973 are described in Chapter 12.
[6] See Appendix 2.5.
[7] See Appendix 2.6.
[8] These figures are based on estimates of unemployment and the working population in C. H. Feinstein, *National Income, Expenditure and Output of the UK 1855 to 1965*, Cambridge 1972.

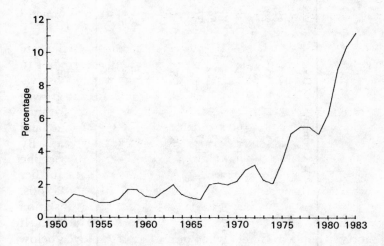

DIAGRAM 2.3 Percentage of the working population who are un-employed.

Source: *ETAS* 1984, col. 5 as a percentage of col. 1.

International Comparisons

A brief international league table, Table 2.1, is shown because it has been Britain's relative performance which has been the focus of economic concern. It was our lagging growth rate during the 1960s which caused disquiet. Growth in all the countries included in the table slowed between the 1960s and 1970s, and the rate of price inflation increased. In both periods Britain's growth was slow by the standards of other advanced countries— a long established characteristic of the British economy—and during the 1970s prices in Britain rose faster than prices in any of the other countries apart from Italy. In 1983 unemployment was higher in Britain than in the other countries.

Diagram 2.4 shows the trend growth of output of OECD countries during the 1950s and 1960s.[9] The trend line based on data for the period 1950 to 1970 is for growth of 4.3 per cent a year, which compares with 2.8 per cent for Britain. Output dipped below trend in 1975. The index of World

[9] See Appendix 2.7.

TABLE 2.1 *An international comparison*[a]
(In performance order)

Growth of Output	Japan	Italy	W Germany	France	USA	UK
GDP (real terms)			(percentage increases)			
1960–70	174	74	57	72	46	32
1970–80	61	36	32	43	33	20

Inflation	W Germany	USA	France	Japan	UK	Italy
GDP Deflator			(percentage increases)			
1960–70	42	34	53	69	51	56
1970–80	66	97	147	100	268	297

Unemployment	Japan	W Germany	UK	France	USA	Italy
			(percentage of the labour force)			
1961–70	1.2	0.8	1.7	1.6	4.6	5.0
1971–80	1.8	2.7	3.9	4.1	6.3	6.5
1983 (Q4)	2.6	7.6	13.1	8.2	8.4	10.0

Source: OECD *Historical Statistics 1960–81*, and *Main Economic Indicators*, April 1984.

[a] National estimates adjusted by OECD to common definitions. Figures for the UK may differ from those in UK sources.

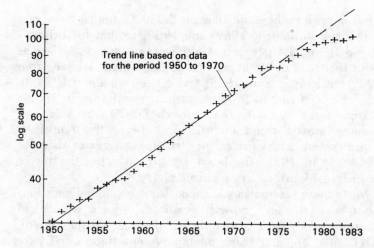

DIAGRAM 2.4   Index of GDP for OECD countries at 1980 market prices, (1980 = 100).

$$\text{Log}_e\, Y = 3.3645 + 0.0427t$$

Sources: *National Accounts of OECD countries* (various issues), *Historical Statistics 1960–81*, and *Main Economic Indicators*, Feb. 1984, by OECD.

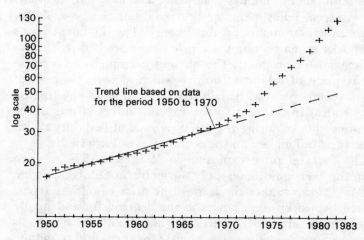

DIAGRAM 2.5   Index of world consumer prices (1980 = 100)

$$\text{Log}_e\, P = 2.792 + 0.034t$$

Source: *Yearbook of International Financial Statistics*, 1983.

consumer prices shown in Diagram 2.5 had a similar trend rate of increase during the 1950s and 1960s to that for Britain's GDP deflator, 3.4 per cent. There were systematic deviations about the trend of World prices;[10] prices increased slowly from 1952, accelerated from 1955, and again from about 1973. In 1983 the departure of Britain's output growth from its 1950–70 trend was very similar to that for the OECD as a whole from its faster growth trend, but the gap between the trend level of prices and actual prices for Britain was greater than for the World in 1982 (the latest year for which estimates of the index of World prices are available).

While these international comparisons beg many questions about why Britain's growth performance was weak, and inflation rapid, they also indicate that the slower growth, faster inflation, and rising unemployment since 1970 were international and not limited to Britain. Explanations of the deterioration in economic performance are unlikely to be limited only to developments within Britain.

The Oil Price Shocks

The term 'shock' implies a surprise, a sudden jolt. If events are foreseen, adjustments and preparations can be made for them and they create less disturbance. The dominant forms of shocks to an economy are price increases and reductions in demand for products. The obvious example is an increase in the price of oil for a country which imports the bulk of its oil requirement, as Britain did at the time of the first oil price shock. In this section the size and direct effects of the oil price shocks during the 1970s are quantified, but at this stage their full impact on the economy is not assessed.

The first oil price explosion in 1973 and 1974 resulted from the exertion of monopoly power by the OPEC countries. The question whether the leap in the price of oil was in part caused by worldwide changes in the demand for and supply of energy is left aside. Whether or not the oil price rise was an exogenous or endogenous change for the World economy, it was an external shock for Britain.

First the size of the oil price shock is measured. Column 1

[10] See Appendix 2.8.

of Table 2.2 shows the price of Saudi Arabian crude oil in terms of American dollars; it fell from $1.93 a barrel in 1955 to $1.3 in 1970. Then between 1972 and 1975 the price increased by 464 per cent. The price of Saudi Arabian oil is fixed in terms of American dollars. The sterling price (shown in column 3 of Table 2.2) is affected by the sterling to dollar exchange rate; between 1972 and 1975 sterling fell relative to the dollar, so the sterling price of oil rose by 536 per cent. By 1979 Britain was nearing self-sufficiency in oil and the second oil price shock forced up the sterling exchange rate, dampening the rise in oil prices measured in sterling. So far the changes have been described in absolute terms, but other prices were rising. For comparison, the GDP deflator is shown in column 4 of Table 2.2 and the price of oil relative to the GDP deflator is shown in column 5. The relative price of oil fell by 60 per cent between 1951 and 1970, then between 1970 and 1980 it rose by 500 per cent. By 1983

TABLE 2.2   *The price of oil* (Saudi Arabian crude)

	$ per barrel	Exchange rate $ to £	£ per barrel	GDP deflator (1980=100)	£ per barrel at 1980 prices
1951	1.71	2.80	0.61	13.1	4.66
1955	1.93	2.79	0.69	15.4	4.48
1960	1.50	2.81	0.54	18.4	2.93
1965	1.33	2.80	0.48	21.5	2.23
1970	1.30	2.40	0.54	26.4	2.05
1971	1.65	2.44	0.68	29.3	2.32
1972	1.90	2.50	0.76	32.3	2.35
1973	2.70	2.45	1.10	34.9	3.15
1974	9.76	2.34	4.17	40.8	10.22
1975	10.72	2.22	4.83	51.9	9.31
1976	11.51	1.81	6.36	59.4	10.71
1977	12.40	1.75	7.09	66.6	10.65
1978	12.70	1.92	6.61	74.3	8.90
1979	17.26	2.12	8.14	84.0	9.69
1980	28.67	2.33	12.30	100.0	12.30
1981	32.50	2.03	16.01	110.3	14.53
1982	33.47	1.75	19.14	117.4	16.32
1983	29.06	1.52	19.12	124.5	15.36

Sources: *International Financial Statistics*, 1983; *ETAS* 1984; and *Economic Trends*, March 1984.

the *relative* price of oil was 7½ times as high as in 1970. These dramatic changes in the price of oil are illustrated in Diagram 2.6.

The main impact effects of the first oil price shock were to speed up inflation and worsen Britain's balance of payments. The effects on inflation are described first.

The Effects on Inflation

The increase in the cost of Britain's oil imports caused by the price rise represented about 4.4 per cent of GDP at market prices in 1972. The method of calculating this estimate is shown in the first five rows of Table 2.3. The increase in the price of oil, tagged on to existing prices and passed on at each stage of production, would have caused the prices of goods and services produced in Britain to rise by 4.4 per cent.[11] The GDP deflator for home costs would not change

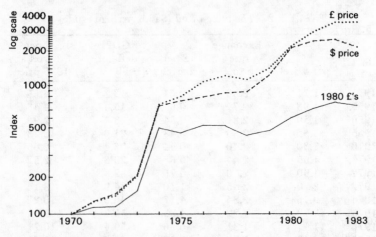

DIAGRAM 2.6   The Price of Saudi Arabian Oil (Indices with
1970 = 100)

Sources: as for Table 2.2.

[11] The increase in the cost of oil imported into Britain would be spread through total final expenditure and would be less than 5 per cent, but the increased price of oil would be tagged on to import prices of goods and services other than oil. So very approximately the final increase in prices would be 4.4 per cent.

at all.[12] Yet between 1972 and 1975, prices measured by the GDP deflator rose by 60.7 per cent and retail prices rose by 57 per cent—by more than they rose throughout the 1960s. Why should the first oil price shock have had such an

TABLE 2.3 *The scale of the first oil price rise*

		Sources
1. Approximate UK net imports and consumption of oil in 1972 (m. tonnes)	100	MDS 1974
2. *Increase* in price of oil per tonne between 1972 and 1975 £	28	Table 2.2 in this chapter (7 bl's to a Tonne)
3. Increase in cost of oil if Britain maintained its imports £bn	2.8	Rows 1 and 2 of this table
4. GDP at market prices in 1972 £bn	63.8	*ETAS* 84 page 4 col. 1
5. Increase in cost of oil as percentage of GDP at market prices	4.4	Rows 3 and 4
6. GDP at factor prices in 1972 £bn	55.7	*ETAS* page 4 col. 5
7. Increase in cost of oil as percentage of GDP at 1972 factor cost	5.0	Rows 3 and 6
8. Imports of goods and services in 1972 £bn	13.8	*ETAS* page 128 col. 2 and page 129 col. 6
9. Increase in cost of oil as percentage of import of goods and services at 1972 prices	20.2	Rows 3 and 8
10. Percentage change in GDP deflator between 1972 and 1975	60.7	*ETAS* Page 4 col. 11
11. Increase in cost of oil as percentage of 1972 GDP at 1975 factor prices	3.1	Rows 3, 6 and 10

[12] The GDP deflator is a measure of *home costs* which would not change if the increase in the price of imported oil was simply passed on.

apparently devastating effect on the rate of inflation in Britain? There was the initial direct effect on prices as the weighted average of prices was raised—this accounted for a 4.4 per cent increase in prices. In addition, prices determined on the basis of a percentage mark-up on costs rose by more than the initial absolute increase in costs. Indirect taxes, such as VAT which are fixed as a percentage of pre-tax prices, caused an addition to prices, and related prices rose. For example, the price of oil is an important determinant of the price of coal, a close substitute for many uses. When the price of oil rose the price of coal followed.[13] Similarly, when the price of oil derivatives, such as plastics, rose, prices of close substitutes such as paper advanced.

If these were the only effects of the oil price increase on the general price level, it would have caused a once for all increase in prices, but would not have generated an inflationary spiral; prices would have risen once by more than the direct effect. Subsequent effects related to the behaviour of wages. The rate of inflation—past, present, and expected—is an important factor in the determination of wage claims and their settlement. The oil price shock which increased prices led to faster wage inflation which again increased prices and wages in an upward spiral. When the sterling exchange rate fell because of the balance of payments effects of the price shock, the sterling price of all imports increased, feeding into the wage-price spiral. These effects of the oil price shock on wages can be described in terms of the natural rate of unemployment. The shock increases the rate of unemployment necessary to prevent wage increases accelerating.

Concern about the impact of oil price shocks on prices is not exclusive to Britain. Some American estimates show that price shocks have large effects on American consumer prices.[14] On the other hand there were no wage and price explosions

---

[13] This implies that the price of coal is influenced by demand and not fixed in relation to costs. By 1970 the price of imported oil was the main determinant of energy prices in Britain. When the price of oil increased, this constraint on the price of coal and miners' wages was lifted.

[14] A. Blinder, *Economic Policy and the Great Stagflation*, New York, 1979. Blinder's estimates show the estimated impact of price shocks continuing over ten years, and the effects on the inflation rate after five years being more than three times the initial impulse.

in Germany after the first oil price explosion;[15] there is no economic law of universal application linking price shocks and wage and price rises. The effects of shocks depend upon the reaction of governments, workers, and managers to them.

The Effects on the Balance of Payments

The other direct effect of an external price shock is on the balance of payments. Here the effect is proportionately much greater. The extra cost of imports of oil caused by the first oil price explosion represented 20.2 per cent of Britain's imports of goods and services in 1972.[16]

The real cost of the increase in oil prices—the extent of the transfer overseas of real resources—is not easy to measure because domestic costs and prices, and prices of exports, rose and offset part of the increase in the prices of imports. One procedure is to take the rise in oil prices in excess of domestic costs measured by the GDP deflator to measure the real cost, but because of the unevenness of the incidence of oil price and domestic cost increases, an arbitrary period has to be selected for the comparison. The first oil price rise was concentrated in time and it is realistic to relate it to advances in other costs over a period longer than that during which the oil price rose. The period from 1972 to 1975 has been used for Table 2.3. Between 1972 and 1975 domestic costs rose by 60.7 per cent, indicating that the real cost of the first oil price explosion to Britain was about 3.1 per cent of GDP. The extra cost of oil imports represented about 3.1 per cent of GDP at factor cost in 1972 revalued at 1975 prices (Table 2.3, row 11).

Britain's economy measured in terms of GDP, grew at a rate of 3.1 per cent per annum during the 1960s. The direct effect of the first oil price explosion was to take out a little more than a year's growth of the economy.[17] This was

[15] The German GDP deflator rose from 100 in 1971 to 106 in 1972, 112 in 1973, 120 in 1974, and 130 in 1975.
[16] The extra import cost of importing the same quantity of oil as in 1972 at 1975 oil prices, as a percentage of imports of goods and services in 1972 (Row 9 of Table 2).
[17] See Appendix 2.9.

replaced later as North Sea oil displaced net imports of oil. In reality the impact on the national income and output was more serious. In terms of Keynesian aggregate demand analysis, the oil price rise transferred income to oil suppliers and reduced demand and output in the industrial countries. The increased payments for oil by consumers in the oil importing countries were not available to buy other goods and services. The transfer of income did not lead to fully compensating increases in demand from oil suppliers or elsewhere, so the oil price rise reduced demand for goods and services produced in Britain and other industrial countries. In terms of general equilibrium analysis, the oil price shock resulted in structural imbalances which required changes in relative prices and a reallocation of resources.

The balance of payments effects of the oil price shocks were crucial. The current balance of payments of the advanced industrial countries (the OECD) and other groups of countries are shown in Table 2.4. Between 1970 and 1973, OPEC countries ran a small surplus on their current account. In 1977, three years *after* the first oil price explosion, the OPEC countries still had a large surplus on their current account, in spite of the increase in imports by the 'high absorbers' among the OPEC countries—oil exporting countries which spent most of the increase in oil revenue on imports.

The effects of the OPEC surpluses turned on the lending policies of the OPEC states and the borrowing by deficit countries. The OPEC surplus would not have been deflationary if it had been offset by other countries expanding demand and by their borrowing extra amounts equivalent to the OPEC surpluses. However, some countries, most notably Germany and Japan, shrugged off the balance of payments effects of the first oil price rise quickly, and did not choose to expand their economies by fiscal and monetary policies or borrow from OPEC countries with surpluses. Meanwhile the OPEC states were reluctant to lend directly to many of the countries with oil deficits. Loans were arranged through Western banking consortia, but there are long-term obstacles to solving oil imbalances by lending to deficit countries. Interest payments on loans add to future deficits and unless OPEC countries increase their imports, or other

TABLE 2.4   Current accounts for major world zones ($bn.)

	Annual average 1970–73	1974	1975	1976	1977	1978	1979	1980	1981	1982	1983
OPEC	4	59½	27	36½	28	–1	65	111	52	–16	–31
OECD	4¼	–26	½	–19	–21	12	–29	–70	–28	–30	–24
Non-oil developing countries	–7½	–26	–31	–19	–13	–26	–39	–60	–76	–65	–45
Other countries	–3	–9½	–18	–13	–8	–12	–8	–9	–10	+3	+4
Discrepancy[a]	+2	+2	+21½	+15	+14	+27	+11	+28	+62	+108	+97

Source: OECD *Economic Outlook*, July 1980 and Dec. 1983.
[a]Includes goods in transit and errors and omissions.

countries increase energy production, or cut consumption of energy, or the price of oil falls, the imbalances grow larger.

Far from increasing demand to maintain output, many countries faced with balance of payments deficits chose, or were forced, to deflate demand in their economies by contractionary monetary and fiscal policies to reduce demand for imports. The inflation sparked by the oil price rise added to pressures for deflation. The effect of deflation was to reduce demand for imports generally, not just imports of oil from OPEC countries with surpluses, so the deflation was transmitted to other countries, many of which had balance of payments deficits already.

Diagram 2.5 has shown how World consumer prices accelerated from 1973. The rate of inflation of World consumer prices increased slowly from about 1965, but there was a change to faster inflation from 1973. Simultaneously growth of world industrial output slowed from an annual rate of 6.8 per cent between 1960 and 1973 to one of 3.2 per cent between 1973 and 1978.[18] The oil price rise was not the sole cause of the acceleration of inflation or slow down of growth of output, but it is not a coincidence that the changes of trend occurred with the first oil price explosion.[19]

Supply Side Effects

The oil price shocks affected the output of an industrial economy in another way, involving changes in relative prices. The increase in the prices of oil and other forms of energy diverted demand from energy intensive products (for example, cars with low mileage per gallon) towards other products and services. Prior to 1973 there was a close relationship between energy consumption and GDP. Since 1973 energy consumption has fallen by about 18 per cent relative to GDP, a qualified indication of the energy saving attributable to the oil price explosion.[20]

---

[18] United Nations *Yearbooks of Statistics*.
[19] See Appendix 2.10.
[20] See Appendix 2.11.

If consumers and firms maintained their total demand in the face of changes in relative prices, firms would have to adapt to meet the new demands. But it takes time to adapt production and there might be a lag during which employment falls. A shock could reduce the potential output of the economy. In a closed economy this effect would not be very serious; firms would adapt.

In practice it is clear that the shocks of the 1970s reinforced other changes creating a requirement for adaptation, technical progress, and trade. Large American cars provide a good example. The oil price rise shifted demand to smaller cars in which Japan had a substantial cost advantage based on a large volume of production, greater experience of building small cars, and lower labour costs. If employment and capacity in America were to be maintained, resources had to be transferred from the motor industry to other industries as well as within individual industries. In the absence of competition from imported cars, more American buyers would have made do with scaled down versions of exisiting models which could be made with the equipment in place, so the rate of adaptation would have been slower.

Increases in the relative price of energy makes processes as well as products obsolete and causes the closure of plants. Again a link exists with imports from energy efficient plants in other countries and reductions in domestic supply.

The supply side effects of the oil price explosions created a requirement for increased investment to facilitate adaptation. In the event profitability, an important determinant of investment, declined in the aftermath of the oil price shocks. In practice, with demand and profitability low, investment fell. It is not possible to separate the demand and supply side effects of the oil price shocks, but they clearly reinforced each other. The demand side effects reduced profitability which slowed investment and adaptation of the economy. The relationship between profits and investment is considered in Chapter 8.

The Second Oil Price Explosion

The second oil price rise in 1979/80, relative to Britain's oil consumption in 1979, represented about 3½ per cent of GDP at market prices. It increased prices, but, in contrast to the first oil price explosion, it did not reduce national income directly by a significant amount because Britain was nearing self-sufficiency in oil. It did result in a transfer of income from the private sector in general to the oil companies and to the government in the form of tax revenue on oil production, so it squeezed real wages. But in the absence of other changes, the government could have reduced other taxes to offset the increase in tax revenue from oil, and maintained real wages. In the event the consequences of the second oil price explosion were harsh for Britain. To understand the reasons for this it is necessary to consider the impact of North Sea oil.

North Sea Oil

UK oil production rose from less than one million tonnes in 1974 to 80 million tonnes in 1980—a level equal to UK consumption of oil in 1980. The development of North Sea oil was not a shock in the sense that it was unforeseen. Plans for its development were in hand from the early 1970s, and it was expected that North Sea oil would reduce the exchange cost of oil. In 1972 the cost of imported oil represented 2 per cent of GDP and 10 per cent of imports. It was expected that North Sea oil would relax the balance of payments constraint on the growth of the British economy. The rise in the relative price of oil greatly increased the impact of North Sea oil.

Diagram 2.7 shows the net imports of fuel (imports less exports) as a percentage of exports of goods for four industrial countries. The oil price rise in 1973/74 doubled the proportion of UK exports required to pay for oil. In 1979/80 the pattern was different; North Sea oil was eliminating net imports of fuel into Britain. Diagram 2.7 also illustrates the massive balance of payments pressures created by the oil price explosions and America's increasing imports of fuel. In 1972 Japan's imports of fuel represented 20 per cent of its exports, by 1980 they had jumped to 53.5 per cent of exports—a large proportion of Japan's exports were required

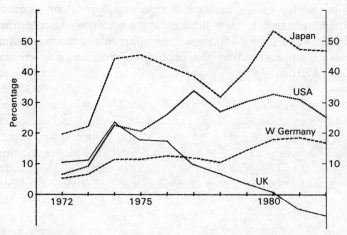

DIAGRAM 2.7   Net imports of fuel as percentage of exports of goods

Sources: OECD country surveys for W. Germany and Japan, *Survey of Current Business*, for the USA, and *MDS* for the UK.

to pay for its fuel imports and were not available to pay for non-oil imports from the countries Japan supplied. Equivalent percentages for the USA were 7 and 33, and for W. Germany 5 and 18. Without North Sea oil Britain's percentage would have risen above 20 per cent. By eliminating net imports of fuel, North Sea oil reduced the supply of sterling which would have been required to pay for oil imports. Other industrial countries had to pay more for their oil, increasing the supply of their currencies. This disparity led to sharp changes in relative exchange rates which are described in Chapter 10. Sterling rose, increasing UK labour and other domestic costs relative to those of countries whose exchange rates were falling against sterling, and put intense pressure on many UK industries trying to maintain their share of world and domestic markets. The pressures increasing sterling were reinforced by the government's monetarist policies which are discussed in the next chapter.

Conclusion

The oil price shocks were significant destabilizing events for Britain during the 1970s. Apart from contributing directly and indirectly to the faster inflation rates prevalent in most Western economies, they slowed the growth of output worldwide. However, they represent only part of the story when it comes to understanding the problems of Britain's economy in the 1970s.

3

The 'Monetarist' Approach to Explaining Changes in Prices and Output

The questions considered in this chapter concern the effects of changes in the stock of money on prices and output. In particular, the 'monetarist' claim that there exists a close link between changes in the money supply and the rate of inflation, is examined.

Monetarism

The monetarist counter-revolution emerged in the late 1950s as an alternative explanation for the operation of an economy to Keynesian demand management. It was led by Milton Friedman, and he claims it originated from the Chicago School's tradition of emphasizing the importance of changes in the money stock for the functioning of the economy. 'Monetarism' is so named because the supply of money plays a central role in both the theoretical and applied studies of the group. To quote Friedman, the statement that, 'money is all that matters for changes in nominal income and for short-run changes in real income' is 'an exaggeration but one that gives the right flavour of our conclusions'.[1] These conclusions can be compared to the view of three Keynesian economists; '. . . we simply do not believe that the achievement of any particular rate of growth of the quantity of money has any clear-cut or predictable implications for the state of the economy'.[2]

The London Business School has been the most influential monetarist school in Britain. The LBS adopted monetarist ideas for its forecasting, and Professors Ball, Burns, and Budd of the LBS have advocated monetarism. However it was the

[1] M. Friedman in R. J. Gordon *Milton Friedman's Monetary Framework*, Chicago, 1974, p. 27.
[2] B. Hopkin, M. Miller, and B. Reddaway, 'An Alternative Economic Strategy —A Message of Hope', *Cambridge Economic Journal*, March 1982, p. 102.

experience of rapid inflation and a more assertive and un-cooperative stance by trade unions, particularly during the 'Winter of Discontent' before the 1979 election, which led to the application of monetarism in Britain. 'Inflation is always and everywhere a monetary phenomenon', Friedman claims. The battle against inflation has been fought with the policies advocated by monetarists.

Friedman's Explanation for Changes in Prices and Output

Monetarists' most influential claim is that there is a direct, albeit lagged, relationship between changes in the money supply and inflation. Put very simply, the idea is that indi-viduals and firms maintain a fixed relationship between their income and money balances. If money balances are increased people will take action—buying other assets and goods and services and restore the ratio of money balances to income. Only in the short-term can output change, claim the mone-tarists, so the increased demand must force up prices.

Friedman' prescription for a healthy economy with low inflation and low unemployment is a steady increase of the money supply, rising at the same or a slightly faster rate than potential output. Sharp increases or decreases in the money supply may initially affect real output and employment, but in the long run, only prices will be affected, all real variables remaining unchanged. How are these conclusions derived?

We begin with the income version of the quantity identity:

$$M \equiv KPY$$

where M is the money supply, Y is a measure of real income, and PY is nominal income, in effect gross domestic product (GDP) at current prices. K is simply the ratio M to PY. Strictly, K is not the reciprocal of the velocity of circulation, V, where V is defined as the rate at which money changes hands, but in practice V is often defined as the reciprocal of K. This definition of V is termed the income velocity of circulation.

$M \equiv KPY$ is an accounting identity. Friedman developed a testable theory of the impact of changes in the money stock on prices and output from it. He claims that the supply of money, M, is an exogenous variable, determined outside the economic system by the central authorities (the Treasury and the Bank of England in the UK). Friedman asserts that the supply of money is, or can be made, exogenous, and that the direction of causation is from changes in M to changes in nominal income, PY, and not vice versa. The realism of this assumption can be questioned as M may expand in response to an improvement in expectations through the credit system, with banks increasing the supply of credit in response to increased demand and themselves creating reserves.

The money supply is balanced by the demand for money from households and firms, which is represented in the identity by KPY. If changes in the supply of money were to cause offsetting changes in K, then the demand for money would not be a stable function of income, and changes in M would have no impact on output or prices. However, Friedman claims that although K may change because of the introduction and spread of new financial practices and techniques of debt settlement such as the credit card, it will not change in response to a change in M, or if it does, the induced change will 'often . . . reinforce'[3] the inflationary or deflationary impact of monetary fluctuations, rather than offset them. If M is increased the velocity of circulation will often increase, not fall, to cancel the effects of the increase in M. Although Friedman initially specifies a demand for money function in terms of a relationship with several variables including human and other forms of wealth, he claims that the demand for money boils down to a stable function of a limited number of variables in particular agents' estimates of their long-run average income, their 'permanent income'.

Transmission Mechanisms

The transmission mechanism through which changes in M affect output and prices is of great importance because it determines the costs in terms of unemployment of using

[3] M. Friedman in R. J. Gordon, *Milton Friedman's Monetary Framework*, Chicago, 1974, p. 27.

monetary policy to stabilize prices. In Friedman's writings
the transmission mechanism is the portfolio adjustment
mechanism. Starting from a position where unemployment is
at the natural level, a rise in M in relation to output will un-
balance the portfolios of assets held by economic agents, and
will create a demand for assets other than money—bonds,
equities, property including houses, and durable goods—as
agents seek to restore the balance of their asset holdings. The
increased demand for these assets will lead to an increase in
their prices. Firms will respond to higher prices for tangible
assets, including the prices of houses and durable goods, by
increasing their *output* and employment. Employment will
rise above its natural level and the rate at which wages rise
will increase. So prices will go on rising and they will rise
to the point at which wealth holders have restored the money
balances in their portfolios to the desired proportion, and
employment has fallen back to its original, natural, level.
The sequence of price changes is for a rise in the price of
assets, then the price of goods, then wages and salaries.
Friedman also writes of holders of money seeking to reduce
their nominal *cash balances* by increasing expenditures, and
this would include other consumer goods besides durables, so
the rise in the price of goods could occur simultaneously with
the rise in asset prices.

The effects of a contraction in the money supply are the
reverse of an expansion. Friedman claims that 'there will be
downward pressure on prices only as a gap emerges between
actual and potential output.'[4]

Expectations play an important role in monetarist models.
Friedman claims that incorrect expectations about the future
rate of inflation will cause the economy to deviate from its
'natural' level of output and employment. If inflation were
anticipated there could be no trade-off between higher inflation and lower unemployment.

A related approach is embodied in the Rational Expecta-
tions/monetarist model of the economy which is outlined in
Chapter 1. With the rational expectations type monetary
transmission mechanism, expectations for prices are based on

[4] M. Friedman, *The Counter-Revolution in Monetary Theory*, IEA, London,
1970, p. 23.

expected changes in M, and changes in expectations lead to changes in actual prices.

An important part of the transmission mechanism in Britain's open economy operates through movements in the exchange rate. An expansionary monetary policy, by increasing net imports (imports less exports) and net lending overseas, will lead to a depreciation of the exchange rate. Agents may anticipate these effects of an increase in M and bring forward devaluation by selling sterling. A lower exchange rate will have inflationary consequences as all imports will be more expensive and that may trigger larger wage claims.

Keynesian economists claim that the transmission mechanism through which an expansionary monetary policy operates is by increasing demand which leads to increases in output and employment. More employment may lead to pressure for increases in wages. Keynesians emphasize the effects of falling interest rates which accompany an increase in the money supply for stimulating investment demand, rather than the effects of increasing asset prices brought about by the impact of an increase in M on asset portfolios. A restrictive monetary policy operates by first reducing demand and hence output, thus creating unemployment which in turn curtails the power of workers and unions to obtain wage increases. Demand is reduced by the policies adopted to reduce the money supply —high interest rates and cuts in the PSBR.[5] Although high interest rates and cuts in the PSBR reduce demand, Keynesians claim that the relationships between changes in these variables and the money supply, and between changes in the money supply and prices and output, are not stable or predictable.

Do the effects of an increase in M depend on its source? The initial impact of the government buying bonds from pension funds to increase M will be on asset prices as the institutions reinvest the proceeds of the bonds in interest earning deposits, equities, and/or property. If the government increases M by increasing its expenditure on goods and services and funding its increased deficit by short-term

---

[5] The Public Sector Borrowing Requirement indicates the extent to which the public sector borrows from other sectors of the economy. It is the excess of current and capital spending by the public sector over its receipts. The public sector comprises central and local government and public corporations.

borrowing, then demand for goods and services will be increased directly. However, Friedman argues that the follow through effects (via the portfolio transmission mechanism) are in aggregate more important than the initial effects, and would be similar whatever the source of the initial increase in the money supply.

The transmission mechanisms in an economy could change. For example, people may be more alert for changes in the rate of inflation after a period of rapid inflation. An isolated burst of growth of M could work through portfolio changes. For repeated large expansions of M the transmission mechanism could work through expectations. Agents seeing an increase in the money supply, or anticipating an increase, may bid up wages and prices.

A Definition of Money

Before testing monetarist theories we require a definition of money. Money has been defined as any commodity generally acceptable in exchange for goods and services or in settlement of debts. Other characteristics of any asset which is to be included as money are that it has a high degree of liquidity, and that it is capital certain. Notes and coins are obviously money, and since the great majority of large transactions in the economy are settled by transferring claims on the banking system (by writing cheques), most measures of money include deposits in bank current accounts. Wider measures of money include other bank deposits, and deposits with other institutions, such as building societies. In terms of liquidity and capital certainty, deposits with banks and building societies are very similar, and both can be distinguished from property, bonds or equities, assets whose realizable value is uncertain.

The definitions of the main measures of the money stock used in the UK are given in the Statistical Appendix 3.1. Criteria which have been suggested for selecting the definition of money to use for statistical work are that the authorities are able to control changes in the set of assets defined as money, and that the demand function for the selected definition of the money stock is stable.[6] For the tests described in this chapter £M$_3$ was used as the best measure of the money supply. It has been the principal measure used by the Treasury and the Bank of England, and Friedman has used this definition.[7] Alternative procedures would be to use a range of definitions of the money supply for each test and account for the differences in the relationships shown, or to use a weighted average of the components of a broad measure of M. The average rate of turnover for each component would be the basis for weighting.

The Evidence

(a) Movements of the Money Supply

The levels of M$_1$, £M$_3$, and PSL$_2$ at the end of 1983 are shown in Table 3.1. The money stock according to the £M$_3$ definition was £104.1 bn. To put the measures of M in perspective they are shown as percentages of GDP, and per capita of the population (including children). £M$_3$ represented 34.6 per cent of GDP in 1983, and £1,848 per capita.

Only in the late 1960s did the movements of the monetary aggregates become a focus of economic policy. The novelty of interest is shown by the official statistical series for the money supply which start in 1963. Table 3.2 summarizes, and Diagram 3.1 shows movements in, the main estimates of the money supply, M$_1$, £M$_3$, and PSL$_2$. M$_1$, the narrow definition of M, has increased more slowly than the wider definitions. The only sub-period when it increased faster than £M$_3$ was from 1976 to 1979. There was some lack of harmony between the growth of M$_1$ and of £M$_3$, but the growth of M according to all three definitions did accelerate between the periods 1967 to 70 and 1970 to 73.

The rapid growth of £M$_3$ in 1972 and 1973 was part of a deliberate policy to expand the economy by the Heath

[6] The criteria are discussed by David Laidler in 'The Definition of Money. Theoretical and Empirical Problems', *Journal of Money Credit and Banking*, August, 1969, p. 509.
[7] Milton Friedman and Anna Schwartz, *Monetary Trends in the United States and the United Kingdom*, Chicago, 1982.

TABLE 3.1   *The money stock at 31st December, 1983*

	£bn.	As a percentage of 1983 GDP at market prices	£ per capita
M_1 of which:	45.2	15.0	802
Notes and coin in circulation	(11.9)	4.0	211
Non-interest bearing sight deposits[a]	(23.9)	8.0	424
Interest bearing sight deposits	(11.7)	3.9	208
£M_3 of which:	104.1	34.6	1,848
Private sector time deposits	(56.6)	18.9	1,004
PSL_2 of which:	169.0	56.2	3,000
Shares and deposits with building societies	(61.2)	20.4	1,086

Sources: *Financial Statistics*, May 1984, and *MDS*, March 1984.
[a] Before any deduction for transit items.

Government. To an extent it was also an unforeseen consequence of 'Competition and Credit Control' introduced in
1971 to reform the regulation of the banking system.[8] The
reserve requirements for clearing banks were reduced and
this enabled them to increase their lending.

One reason for expecting a faster growth of £M_3 than
M_1 during the 1970s is that agents will transfer balances from
current accounts which do not earn interest to interest earning deposit accounts during a period of accelerating inflation.
Deposits in current accounts, but not deposit account balances,

---

[8] The reforms included the removal of quantitative restrictions on bank
advances, the abandonment of the cartel arrangements for fixing interest rates,
and changes in the reserve requirements for banks. The changes are described in
The Bank of England Quarterly, Dec. 1971, p. 476, and by Charles Goodhart in,
'Problems of Monetary Management: the UK Experience', in *Inflation, Depression
and Economic Policy in the West* edited by A. S. Courakis, London, 1981.

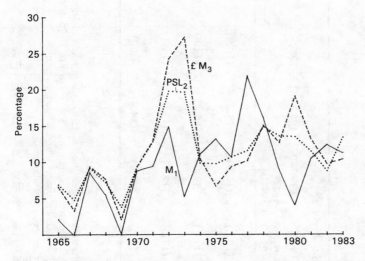

DIAGRAM 3.1   The money supply (Percentage changes between the beginning and end of each year)

Source: *ETAS* 1984, p. 146

are included in M_1; both are included in £M_3 which therefore provides a more reliable guide to the growth of M during the 1970s. Unfortunately for statistical analysis there were simultaneous institutional changes taking place which boosted £M_3 (and PSL$_2$). The release of competition in the banking sector led banks to compete for deposits and raise interest rates for wholesale deposits nearer to their lending rates. These changes and others led to 'round tripping', borrowing and re-lending by commercial companies, which increased bank deposits and £M_3. One purpose of round tripping for companies was to obtain precautionary money balances. Between December 1973 and February 1975, between November 1976 and August 1977, and again from June 1978 until June 1980, banks were penalized if they allowed their deposits to grow rapidly—the so-called 'corset' controls. These controls artificially held down the growth of £M_3 while they operated, as banks developed methods of lending which avoided the controls. When the controls were lifted in 1980 there was some catching-up of £M_3.

TABLE 3.2 *Growth of the money stock*[a]

| | Whole Period 1963–83 | Sub-Periods[b] | | | | | | |
		1963–7	1967–70	1970–3	1973–6	1976–9	1979–81	1981–3
		Year to Year Percentage Changes (Annual rates of change in brackets)						
M_1	443 (8.8)	15 (3.5)	14 (4.5)	42 (12.3)	33 (10.0)	52 (15.0)	17 (8.3)	23 (10.9)
£M_3	735 (11.2)	27 (6.2)	20 (6.3)	66 (18.4)	39 (11.7)	40 (11.9)	35 (16.2)	25 (11.8)
PSL_2	685 (10.9)	31 (7.0)	22 (6.9)	57 (16.1)	40 (11.8)	43 (12.7)	28 (13.1)	23 (11.1)
General Index of Retail Prices[c]	520 (9.6)	15 (3.6)	17 (5.5)	28 (8.6)	68 (18.8)	42 (12.5)	32 (14.9)	14 (6.6)

Sources: *ETAS* 1984, and *Economic Trends*, March 1984.

[a] Money stock at the end of June each year.
[b] The end years of the sub-periods were decided rather arbitrarily. Sterling was devalued in 1967, there was a change of government in 1970, the first oil price explosion occurred in 1973. Economic policy took a new turn in 1976 and sterling started to recover. The second oil price rise started in 1979 and there was a change of government.
[c] Annual averages, which are based on monthly calculation of the index, are compared.

(b)   The Velocity of Circulation

We start by considering the stability of the monetary relationships themselves, in particular the velocity of circulation. The first point to emphasize is the qualifications to any conclusions about the stability of macroeconomic relationships based on statistics for what was a highly unstable decade, the 1970s. It is rather like trying to count stars on a cloudy night; the objects of analysis are difficult to trace anyway.

A key 'monetarist' proposition is that the velocity of circulation is relatively stable. Friedman also claims that changes in the velocity of circulation reinforce the inflationary or deflationary effects of monetary fluctuations, rather than offset them. Here the money stock is related to nominal income—implying that the demand for money is a function of nominal income. Friedman, however, hypothesized that the demand for money is a function of permanent income.

Diagram 3.2 shows the movements of V, the ratio of GDP to $£M_3$[9] since 1965, along with movements of $£M_3$. Between

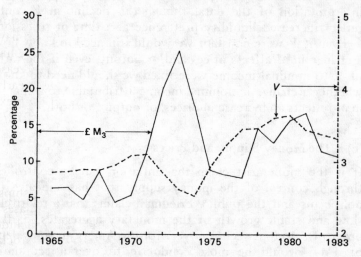

DIAGRAM 3.2   The velocity of circulation and changes in $£M_3$[a].

Sources: *ETAS* 1984, and *Economic Trends*, March, 1984.

[a] See Appendix 3.2.

[9] See Appendix 3.2.

1965 and 1968, V was very stable within the range 2.85 and 2.95, though this implies a fall relative to any rising trend. V rose in 1969 and 1970 by 2.4 and 4.4 per cent respectively. After a further slight rise in 1971 it fell in 1972 and 1973 as the money supply exploded, so that it offset rather than reinforced the change in the money supply. Then V rose and by 1980 it was 28 per cent above the 1965 rate. Since 1980 V has fallen. Monetarists might account for the instability of V during the mid-1970s by the erratic changes in the money stock, particularly the explosive growth of £M_3 between 1971 and 1974. But prior to the distortions of the 1970s, V did increase in 1969 and 1970 after a period of stability. Another explanation is that a rising trend for V between 1970 and 1980 was distorted by the rapid growth of £M_3 between 1971 and 1974, and that this trend reflected faster inflation; agents reduced their money balances relative to their nominal income because inflation was reducing the real value of monetary assets. The decline in V since 1980 coinciding with slower inflation supports this interpretation of the data, though this decline in V could reflect increased liquidity preference at a time of recession.

Even if V were constant we would still need to know how a change in M affects prices and/or output; even if the ratio of M to nominal income were fixed we should need to know whether a change in nominal income attributable to a change in M reflects an increase in prices, or output, or both.

(c)   The Money Supply and Prices

It is the monetarist claim that inflation can be controlled through control of the money supply that has appealed to politicians and the public. Friedman claims that a relatively slow and stable growth of the monetary aggregates, of the order of 3 to 5 per cent per year for the American equivalent of £M_3, would be most conducive to overall economic stability. The actual growth of the money stock in Britain for much of the period from 1963 was far in excess of this, so it is not possible to test Friedman's prescription. What we can examine are the effects of erratic and often high rates of growth of the money supply.

Diagram 3.3(a) shows the relationship between £M₃ and retail prices in the form of presentation used by Friedman.[10] It shows time series of £M₃ per unit of output and retail prices in index form since 1964. For each index the average for the period 1964 to 1983 is set equal to 100, and the index of prices is lagged six months behind the index of £M₃. Changes in £M₃ are adjusted for changes in output to allow for the increase in demand for money required to transact increases in the volume of output and hence income, and for increases in the demand for precautionary balances associated with the increase in income. Friedman's technique of setting the period 1964 to 1983 equal to 100 entails a similar spread of the two indices in the graph. A simpler form of presentation was used for Diagram 3.3(b); 1964 was set equal to 100.

Both £M₃ per unit of output and retail prices rose rapidly during the 1970s. Friedman's presentation 3.3(a), suggests very similar increases for the two variables over the period 1964 to 1983 as a whole. In fact, while £M₃ per unit of output increased by 442 per cent, retail prices rose by 501 per cent and by 11 per cent relative to £M₃ per unit of output. Do the graphs tell us which is cause and which effect? If an increase in the rate of inflation followed an increase in the money supply this would be strong, though not conclusive, evidence of the causal relationship flowing from changes in the money supply to changes in prices.[11] A slow-down in the growth of £M₃ in 1969 was *not* followed by a slowing of price increases, but by faster inflation in 1970 and 1971. Faster growth of £M₃ in 1971, 1972, and 1973 *was* followed by faster inflation.

Diagram 3.4(a) shows the relationship between £M₃ and retail prices in another form. This diagram shows year to year changes in the two variables with no lags. The acceleration of prices *follows* rapid growth of £M₃ from 1972 to 1974, but in 1981 prices decelerated before £M₃. Diagram 3.4(b) shows

[10] M. and Rose Friedman, *Free to Choose*, London, 1980, p. 206.

[11] Friedman acknowledges that changes in one series may precede changes in another series, 'because both are the common result of still other forces and those common forces have a quicker impact on the first than on the second [series]'. *The Optimum Quantity of Money*, London, 1969, 240.

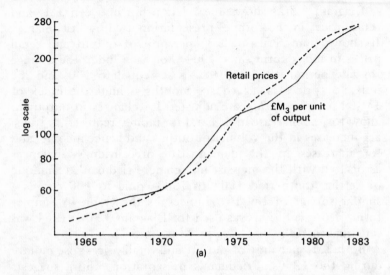

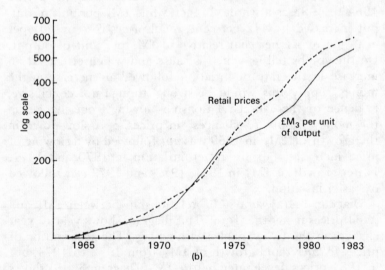

DIAGRAM 3.3   *Indices of retail prices and £M₃*

(a) Graph similar to the one used by Freidman in *Free to Choose*
    (1964–83 = 100)
(b) Alternative presentation (1964 = 100)

Sources: *ETAS* 1984, and *Economic Trends*, March, 1984.

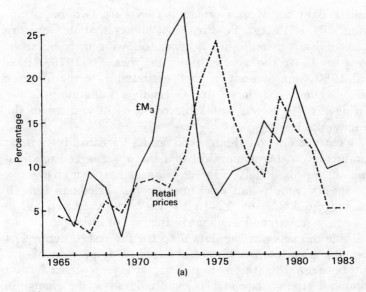

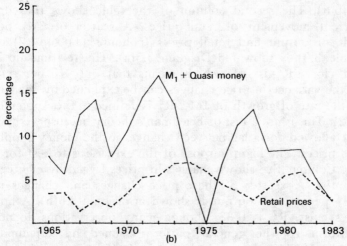

DIAGRAM 3.4   £M₃ and retail prices

(a) UK
(b) Germany

Source: Table 3.3 cols. 1 and 2 (a)
Sources: *OECD*, 'Historical Statistics 1960—81' and *International Financial Statistics*.

similar data for West Germany. There are two important points about this graph. Firstly, it shows that in Germany prices did not increase much faster following three bursts of growth of M; the accelerations in prices in 1973, 1979, and 1980 were at least in part attributable to the oil price rises. Secondly, it shows that Germany's moderate inflation during the 1970s was not achieved by tight control of the money supply.

A more thorough, though still crude, statistical test can be conducted on the assumption that there is a lagged relationship of approximately eighteen months between changes in the money supply and price movements. Friedman himself has suggested a lag of '12–18 months'[12] between a change in monetary growth and a change in the rate of inflation.

Table 3.3 sets out the data used for the test. Column 4 of the table gives the percentage change in £M_3 per unit of output between the start and end of each year, derived from column 1 (the change in £M_3) and column 3 (the change in output). The second column of the table shows the con-current movement of retail prices. A scatter of £M_3 per unit of output and retail prices (columns (1) and (2) of Table 3.3) is shown in Diagram 3.5(a). The relationship is not close. R^2 is 0.1; which means that only 10 per cent of the variance in price changes can be explained by changes in the rate of growth of £M_3. R^2 is defined in the Appendix (P.2). This is not a test of Friedman's theory because we have not allowed for a lag between changes in the money supply and prices. The main purpose of the exercise is to test for a lag. Column five shows changes in prices lagged by eighteen months. A scatter of these price changes and changes in £M_3 per unit of output is shown in diagram 3.5(b). A link does exist, R^2 is 0.38, though many observations do not conform to the general pattern claimed by Friedman. Although £M_3 increased slowly in 1975, prices continued to increase rapidly in 1976/7, and in 1980 and 1981 £M_3 continued to rise rapidly but price inflation in 1981/2 and 1982/3 was slowing. The regression equation indicates that

[12] M. Friedman, The Counter-Revolution in Monetary Theory, IEA, London, 1970, p. 23.

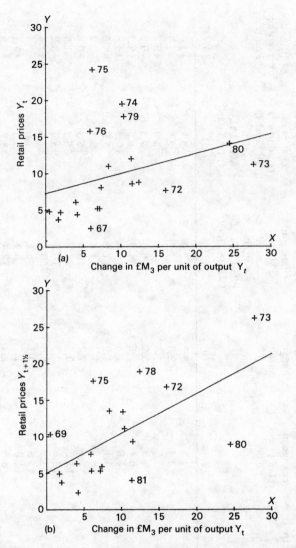

DIAGRAM 3.5 Annual changes in £M$_3$ per unit of output and retail prices.

(a) No lags; $Y = 7.3 + 0.27X$
$R^2 = 0.10$
(b) Retail prices lagged 18 months; $Y = 4.98 + 0.54X$
$R^2 = 0.38$

Source: Table 3.3.

TABLE 3.3   The money supply and prices

	Percentage change in £M$_3$ [a]	Percentage change in retail prices no lag [b]	Percentage change in output [c]	Percentage change in £M$_3$ per unit of output PREDICTED INFLATION [d]	Percentage change in retail prices 18 mnths later ACTUAL INFLATION [e]	Error in Percentage Points [f]
	(1)	(2)	(3)	(4)	(5)	(6)
1964	5.8	4.7	3.7	2.0	3.7	+1.7
1965	6.6	4.4	2.3	4.2	2.3	−1.9
1966	3.3	3.7	1.6	1.7	4.9	+3.2
1967	9.4	2.5	3.2	6.0	5.3	−0.7
1968	7.7	6.1	3.6	4.0	6.3	+2.3
1969	2.1	4.8	1.6	0.5	10.3	+9.8
1970	9.4	8.1	1.9	7.4	5.9	−1.5
1971	12.9	8.6	1.3	11.5	9.3	−2.2
1972	24.3	7.7	7.2	16.0	16.8	+0.8
1973	27.3	11.2	−0.3	27.7	26.2	−1.5
1974	10.5	19.5	0.3	10.2	13.4	+3.2
1975	6.7	24.2	0.5	6.2	17.6	+11.4
1976	9.4	15.8	3.1	6.1	7.6	+1.5
1977	10.2	11.0	1.7	8.4	13.5	+5.1
1978	15.1	8.8	2.4	12.4	18.9	+6.5
1979	12.7	17.8	2.1	10.4	11.1	+0.7
1980	19.1	14.1	−4.3	24.5	8.9	−15.6

1981	13.4	12.0	1.8	11.4	4.0	−7.4
1982	9.7	5.2	2.3	7.2	(5.3)	−1.9
1983	10.4	5.2	3.3	6.9		+0.7
Average	11.3	9.8	2.0	9.2	10.1	Mod. 4.2

Sources: *ETAS* 1984, *Economic Trends*, March 1984, and earlier issues.

a Percentage change in £M$_3$ end of December of the previous year to end of year shown.

b Percentage change in the retail price index from the average of December of the previous year and January of the year shown to December of the year shown and January of the following year.

c Percentage change in GDP at 1980 prices, last quarter of previous year and first quarter of year shown to the last quarter of the year shown and the first quarter of the following year.

d $\left(\dfrac{100 + (\text{col. 1})}{100 + (\text{col. 3})} \times 100 \right) - 100.$

e Percentage change in the retail price index from the average of June and July of the year following the year shown, to the average for June and July of the year after.

f (Col. 5) − (Col. 4).

the response of prices to changes in £M$_3$ per unit of output is less than proportional. The coefficient for X, 0.54 suggests 54 per cent of an increase in £M$_3$ per unit of output is matched in price increases eighteen months later. The distribution of the observations about the line of best fit shows that this is only a very rough guide to the effects of increases in £M$_3$ on prices eighteen months later. The observation for 1973 has a marked impact on the equation shown in Diagram 3.5(b). If this observation is excluded R^2 declines from 0.38 to 0.14, and the coefficient of X from 0.54 to 0.33. However, the effect on prices could be more dispersed than the test allows, starting sooner and/or continuing longer in time than is allowed for here. As Friedman says, 'the relationship is far from perfect'.[13]

Column 6 of Table 3.3 presents the results in another form. It is the 'error' between the change in £M$_3$ per unit of output—the predicted increase in prices—and the actual increase in prices eighteen months later. There are two points of interest: is the error biased in one direction, and how great is the discrepancy. On the first point, the increase in prices is on average under-estimated by 0.7 percentage points. In the late 1970s the error is repeatedly positive, and in the 1980s the errors are negative; the rate of inflation fell despite the earlier rapid rise of £M$_3$. How large is the error? In general, the discrepancy between the two series was large relative to the predicted rate of inflation. The median error was 36 per cent of the change in retail prices but there were exceptions, particularly between 1970 and 1973, when the changes in £M$_3$ preceded faster inflation. Overall the data suggest there are other important influences on the rate of price inflation besides the growth of £M$_3$.

Even if the rapid growth of the money supply in 1972 and 1973 caused rapid inflation, it would be of limited direct interest. Economists do not believe that the growth of the money supply is irrelevant to the inflation rate. Growth of the money supply broadly defined at a rate of, say, 25 per cent a year, must lead to fast price inflation. Even so the effects of rapidly increasing money supply could be very

[13] M. Friedman, *The Counter-Revolution in Monetary Theory*, IEA, London, 1970, p. 23.

interesting. *If* relationships are proportional then extreme observations help to identify the relationships, as the effects on prices of differences between slow rates of change in M may be lost in changes in prices caused by other events. (Friedman makes much use of periods of rapid growth of the money supply to establish a causal relationship between changes in M and prices.) The flaw in this argument is that people's response may not be in proportion to the size of actual or anticipated changes in the money supply. They may react differently to a large change in the money supply and its direct effects, than to a small one. In any case it should be noted that there are additional or alternative explanations for the rapid inflation from 1973 to 1976, the oil price explosion, commodity price rises, and threshold agreements which are described in Chapters 2 and 5.

The lack of a close relationship between £M_3 and inflation following years of moderate growth of £M_3 is of more interest. One possible explanation is that the lag between the growth of the money supply and prices is diffused and variable. Certainly it is plausible that if inflation accelerates, the response to changes in the money supply may speed up as people pay more attention to forecasting the rate of inflation, but if the lag structure changes or evolves it is difficult to test for a relationship using elementary statistical techniques.

New classical economists would expect that the effects of an increase in the money supply would depend upon whether or not it was anticipated. An anticipated increase in the money supply would lead to an increase in prices sooner than an unanticipated increase, but in practice there is no satisfactory method of separating the two types of increase using elementary statistical methods. It is probable that the surge in the money supply in the early 1970s was not foreseen, as it was partly unintended by the government, and it had a lagged effect on prices.

If the view to be tested is that changes in the money stock relative to the change in output are the sole determinants of future price changes, the test disproves the view. Once other forces than increases in M are given realistic roles in influencing price changes, the basis of the exercise as a means of testing the importance of changes in the money stock is untenable. There is a case for deducting current inflation caused by other such forces as the oil price shock as well as the growth of output from the increase in the money supply, before testing for the effects of changes in the money stock on prices in later periods. The justification for this adjustment is that an increase in prices does create a transactions demand for money. There was *not* a substantial increase in the real money supply in 1980 and 1981 to trigger another price explosion which the monetarist rule based on M per unit of output predicted and which did not take place.[14].

The Links in the Transmission Mechanism

Since testing the link between changes in the money stock and prices directly is difficult, it is worth examining some of the links in the chain between changes in $£M_3$ and prices. For example, if the transmission mechanism is one of portfolio adjustment it should be possible to trace it through the movement of asset prices. Diagrams 3.6(a) and (b) show movements of $£M_3$ house prices, and share prices since 1965. The graphs show the percentage changes in the variables each year. Care is needed in interpreting these percentages, particularly for volatile share prices. If share prices fall by 50 per cent during one year, and recover to the initial level in the following year, this will be a 100 per cent increase. This is particularly relevant to 1974 when share prices fell to record low levels in real terms, and to the recovery in 1975.

The movements of share prices and $£M_3$ do not at first glance indicate a relationship. Share prices were very volatile during the period; if they did respond to changes in the money supply it was plainly not the only or main influence. Movements of house prices were more in tune with the changes in $£M_3$, and provide some support for the portfolio transmission mechanism.

---

[14] The change in real $£M_3$ can be obtained from the first two columns of Table 3.3. In 1980 the real money supply increased by 4.4 per cent,
$\left(\dfrac{100 + 19.1}{100 + 14.1} \right) 100 - 100$, and in 1981 by 1.3 per cent.

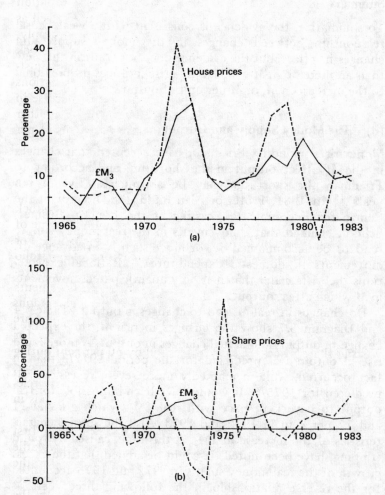

DIAGRAM 3.6

(a) Annual percentage changes in house prices and £M₃.

Sources: £M₃ as for Table 3.3. House prices *ETAS* 1984 and *Economic Trends*, March 1984.

(b) Annual percentage changes in share prices and £M₃.

Sources: £M₃ as for Table 3.3. Share prices *ETAS* 1984, and *Economic Trends*, March 1984.

Summary

To summarize, the evidence is consistent with a weak causal relationship between changes in the money supply and changes in prices, but the evidence does not confirm the view than an increase in M will lead to a rise in prices proportional to the increase in M, or M per unit of output.

(d)　The Money Supply and Output

Monetarists including Friedman have accepted that changes in the M affect output in the short-run, and according to Friedman the short-run 'may be as much as five or ten years'.[15] In 1981, Professor Alan Budd, the Director of the Centre for Economic Forecasting at the London Business School, claimed that, 'movements in the real money supply tend to be accompanied by, or move slightly in advance of, movements in domestic expenditure'.[16] Rational expectations theorists claim that it is only unanticipated movements in M which affect output.

Do changes in real M lead to changes in output? Table 3.4 and Diagram 3.7 show the changes in real M, the expected change in output, and actual changes in output. A more rapid rise in output was predicted for the period 1972/3 than in fact occurred, while a markedly more severe recession was predicted for 1975/6. It would have been impossible for real output to have kept pace with real £M_3 which grew at 11 and 17 per cent in 1972 and 1973. Also the special characteristics of the increase in £M_3 at this time, caused by round tripping, have been noted. It could be argued that the excess growth of the real money supply in 1972 and 1973 accounted for the reverse relationship in the following three years, as economic agents used their excess money balances.

Even excluding the years 1972 to 1977, there does not seem to be a particularly close relationship between changes in real £M_3 and output. It does provide a good indication of changes in output in 1965, 1968, 1971, 1978, and 1980. This

---

[15] M. Friedman, 'The Counter-Revolution in Monetary Theory, IEA, London, 1970, p. 23.
[16] Management Today, May, 1981.

TABLE 3.4   *Changes in the real money stock and changes in output*

	Percentage change in £M$_3$ [a]	Percentage change in deflator for at market prices	Percentage change in real £M$_3$ THE EX-PECTED CHANGE IN OUT-PUT[b]	Percentage change in GDP at 1980 prices, lagged six months THE ACTUAL CHANGE IN OUT-PUT[c]	Error in percentage points (4)−(3)
	(1)	(2)	(3)	(4)	(5)
1965	6.3	5.4	+0.9	+2.4	+1.5
1966	6.4	4.2	+2.1	+1.9	−0.2
1967	4.8	3.1	+1.6	+2.9	+1.3
1968	8.6	3.9	+4.5	+3.7	−0.8
1969	4.4	5.4	−0.9	+1.9	+2.8
1970	5.3	7.5	−2.0	+1.8	+3.8
1971	11.4	9.2	+2.0	+1.6	−0.4
1972	20.1	8.4	+10.8	+5.9	−4.9
1973	25.2	7.2	+16.8	+1.4	−15.4
1974	17.7	14.8	+2.5	−0.5	−3.0
1975	8.9	27.1	−14.3	−0.2	+14.1
1976	8.2	14.9	−5.8	+3.2	+9.0
1977	7.8	13.9	−5.4	+2.6	+8.0
1978	14.6	11.1	+3.2	+2.8	−0.4
1979	12.7	14.4	−1.5	+0.8	+2.3
1980	15.7	19.8	−3.4	−4.1	−0.7
1981	16.7	11.7	+4.5	+1.6	−2.9
1982	11.5	7.3	+3.9	+2.2	−1.7
1983	10.8	5.3	+5.2	+3.2[d]	−2.0
Average	11.4	10.2	1.3	1.8	+0.5 Mod. 4.0

Source: *ETAS* 1984, and *Economic Trends*, March 1984.

[a] £M$_3$ average for year, see Appendix 3.2

[b] $\left(\dfrac{(100 + \text{col. 1})}{100 + \text{col. 2}} \times 100 \right) - 100.$

[c] Average estimate of GDP lagged six months.

[d] Estimate.

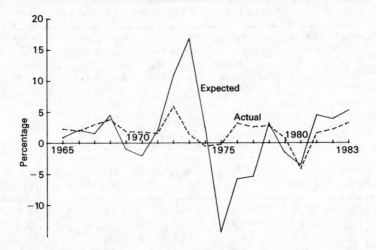

DIAGRAM 3.7   Expected and actual changes in output (year to year
percentage changes)

Source: Table 3.4

does not necessarily indicate causality, but the transmission
mechanisms described earlier point to changes in real M having an effect on output. So far the actual growth of £M_3 has
been considered. If we heroically assume that a steady increase
in the money supply was anticipated at least until the early
1970s, then 1968, 1972, and 1973 would be years of unex-
pectedly fast growth of real £M_3.[17] In 1968/9 and 1972/3
output did expand rapidly.

(e)   Friedman's Phases

We have used annual data to examine monetary relationships.
Friedman and Schwartz used data for half cycles, 'phases',
from their recent published study.[18] The authors conclude
from their elaborate study of changes in the money stock,

[17] One method of estimating the anticipated growth of M is to find a plausible
equation which explains the past growth of the money supply, and assume that
deviations from levels predicted by the equation are unexpected. This approach
could incorporate changes in M in response to cyclical movements of the economy
as anticipated changes.

[18] Friedman and Anna Schwartz, *Monetary Trends in the United States
and the United Kingdom*, Chicago, 1982.

nominal income, prices and output that the results are 'disappointing', but add that they are 'most informative'. The results are disappointing 'because we have not succeeded . . . in giving satisfactory empirical content . . . [to] the division over short periods of a change in nominal income between prices and output'.[19] In brief, they have been unable to establish a consistent short period relationship between changes in the money stock and changes in prices and changes in output.

None the less, they claim thir results are informative. 'For the United Kingdom there seems little if any relation between monetary change and output: a simple quantity theory that regards price change as determined primarily by monetary change and output by independent other factors fits the evidence for the period [since 1871] as a whole.' 'The output series bears little or no relation to any monetary factors, either the quantity of money in the current or prior phases.'[20] Their evidence is summarized in Table 3.5. The data do show a clear relationship between the size of the increase in the money supply (column 1) and the increase in prices (column 2) but this does not tell us which is cause and which effect. The changes in output and low unemployment are not as closely tied to the growth of the money supply, but the rank correlation coefficients show they are both positively related to it. Friedman claims that, 'inflation is always and everywhere a monetary phenomenon', but perusal of the table suggests that fast growth of the money stock and rapid price rises are also phenomenon associated with wars and the emergence of OPEC.[21]

(d)   The Record Since 1979

The Callaghan Labour Government, under pressure from the IMF, did pay lip service to monetary policy after 1976.

[19] M. Friedman and Anna Schwartz, *Monetary Trends in the United States and the United Kingdom*, Chicago, 1982, p. 462.

[20] *Ibid.*, p. 463.

[21] D. F. Hendry and N. R. Ericsson have reviewed Friedman and Schwartz's study and concluded that 'failure by [the authors] to present test evidence pertinent to their main assertions leaves them devoid of credibility', *Monetary trends in the United Kingdom*, Bank of England Panel Paper No. 22, p. 82.

TABLE 3.5   *Money stock, prices, and output*

	Money stock	Prices (percentage increases) (rank order in brackets)[a]	Output	Unemployment
1871–1881	18 (7)	−7 (8)	19 (7)	3.9 (3)
1881–1891	23 (6)	−4 (7)	26 (3)	5.9 (7)
1891–1901	28 (4)	4 (5)	22 (6)	4.6 (5)
1901–1911	16 (8)	3 (6)	18 (8½)	4.9 (6)
1911–1921	162	145	−12	2.3
1921–1931	−6 (9)	−30 (9)	23 (5)	8.6 (8)
1931–1941	59 (3)	31 (4)	40 (1)	9.4 (9)
1941–1951	104	52	16	0.9
1951–1961	27 (5)	47 (3)	28 (2)	1.2 (1)
1961–1971	72 (2)	62 (2)	24 (4)	1.8 (2)
1971–1981	304 (1)	257 (1)	18 (8½)	4.5 (4)
Rank correlation coefficient between rank for money change and rank for variable		0.90	0.15	0.30

Source: Milton Friedman and Anna Schwartz, *Monetrary Trends in the United States and the United Kingdom*, Chicago, 1982; and *ETAS* 1984 for data for 1981.

[a] For purposes of ranking the decades 1911 to 1921 and 1941 to 1951 are excluded because they were most affected by wars.

But it was not until 1979 when Mrs Thatcher's Conservative Government adopted a whole-hog monetarist approach that monetarism was tested in Britain. It is rare for economists to be able to observe the application of theories, yet without too much exaggeration that is what has happened since 1979. Mrs Thatcher has adopted monetarist policies, and is the first post-war Prime Minister to reject any commitment to maintaining full employment. After much difficulty in controlling the money supply in 1979 and 1980 it was brought under control during 1981. By early 1983 the growth rate of £M$_3$ had slowed and prices were rising more slowly than at any time since the early 1970s.

    An important technical economic innovation by Mrs Thatcher's government has been the introduction of a medium-term financial strategy (MTFS). This centred on targets for the growth of the money supply. The aim of the strategy is contained in the following quotation from the 1980 'Financial Statement and Budget Report'; 'Control of the money supply will over a period of years reduce the rate of inflation. The speed with which inflation falls will depend crucially on expectations both within the United Kingdom and overseas. It is to provide a firm basis for those expectations that the government has announced its firm commitment to a progressive reduction in the money supply growth.' The MTFS was intended to provide an anchor for expectations about the future growth of the money supply —a self-imposed substitute discipline for the gold standard.

The following targets were set in the 1980 budget in terms of $£M_3$:

Period	(Target) Growth of $£M_3$ Percentages	Actual growth of $£M_3$ Percentages
March 1980 to March 1981	7–11	19.7
March 1981 to March 1982	6–10	13.1
March 1982 to March 1983	5–9	9.8

The government has no direct control over $£M_3$. One policy adopted by the government to reduce $£M_3$ was to reduce the PSBR by cutting government expenditure. Less borrowing would mean a combination of slower growth of the reserve assets of banks and lower interest rates, and would simultaneously reduce aggregate demand and hence demand for money. The other control available to the government was its influence over interest rates. By allowing interest rates to rise it could reduce borrowing by the private sector. At first the stringent policies imposed by the government to limit the growth of the money supply seemed to have a perverse effect as high interest rates attracted deposits and as the recession forced companies to increase their borrowing.

In the 1982 budget $£M_3$ was replaced as the single target monetary variable. A range of measures was made the focus of control, in 1984 these ranged from a new measure, M_0 (mainly notes and coins in circulation), to PSL_2. It was claimed that this modification to monetary management was in response to the rapid change which the financial system was undergoing. This modification to monetary management again illustrates the arbitrariness of definitions of the money stock.

Mrs Thatcher's experiment has shown that it is possible to reduce the growth of the money supply without the use of direct controls. But the cost has been high. A reduction of the PSBR and the sky-high interest rates required to reduce the growth of the money supply reinforced the recession caused by the oil price rise of 1979 and the development of North Sea oil described in the previous chapter. The obvious remedy for the upward pressure on the exchange rate caused by the oil price rise and North Sea oil was to lower interest rates, the reverse of monetarist policies. In the event output was hit hard and employment even harder. But control of the money supply and the policies applied to achieve that control backed up by world recession have fulfilled money's function as the 'Old Policeman', to use Sir Denis Robertson's phrase.[22]

(g)   Conclusions

Friedman is fond of quoting John Stuart Mill's dictum; 'There cannot . . . be intrinsically a more insignificant thing, in the economy of society, than money, except in the character of a contrivance for sparing time and labour. It is a machine for doing quickly and commodiously what would be done, though less quickly and commodiously, without it: and like many other kinds of machinery it only exerts a distinct and independent influence of its own when it gets out of order.' The review of the evidence shows that in the 1970s it did get 'out of order'. The rapid growth of the money supply was a factor causing and facilitating the galloping inflation which occurred in Britain—monetary policy was itself a source of economic disturbance.

If the objective of the counter revolution was simply to establish the claim of the Chicago School 'that money does matter' it has been accepted by economists, if it was ever in doubt. The simple tests reported in this chapter support the

[22] *Lectures on Economic Principles*, London, 1959.

claim. That M is a factor influencing output and prices is not contested, but the tests used display the looseness of the monetary relationships throughout most of the period since 1963, and the difficulty of predicting the effects of changes in M. The German data are also important—they show that bursts of growth of M do not necessarily lead to rapid inflation, and that tight control of M was not the explanation for Germany's moderate inflation during the 1970s.

In Britain and elsewhere, 'monetarism' became a Saint George with which to fight the dragon of inflation. Contract the money supply and inflation would magically wither away before your eyes. Friedman, at least, realized it is not so easy: 'In the short run, which may be as much as five or ten years, monetary changes affect primarily output.'[23] Behind the monetarist façade there is a fundamentally different approach. At the root of monetarist philosophy lies the concept that markets and competition work; competition and freedom to compete are also the ideals at the root of Conservative ideology. Conservatives claim that from the 1950s Britain became increasingly uncompetitive, Union power removed competition and the notion of fair exchange from the labour market, and incentives were eroded. A policy of contraction brings them back to some markets. It is not merely an anti-inflation device. It is a policy designed to intensify competition for British industry, check wage inflation, expose inefficiencies, force innovation, and improve productivity. There was a need for a new approach to Britain's economic problems, but the monetarist experiment coincided with the second oil price shock and the deepest post-war world recession and exacerbated their harsh effects for Britain, and the world recession was itself intensified by the widespread adoption of monetarist policies.

[23] Milton Friedman, *The Counter-Revolution in Monetary Theory*, IEA, Occasional Paper, 1970, p. 23.

4

Keynesian Demand Management

Management of Aggregate Demand and Unemployment

Keynes's main concern in the *General Theory* was to provide a theoretical basis for policies of economic expansion to bring the economy to full employment. The reasons Keynes gave for rejecting the classical theory have been outlined in Chapter 1 and are not repeated here. 'Laissez-faire' was the dominant economic doctrine in Britain until the 1930s. The responsibility of the Government was to balance its budget, to ensure monetary and political stability. Government intervention would cause price distortions preventing the optimal allocation of resources. The Keynesian revolution drastically altered this view of the Government's role in the economy. The Great Depression and mass unemployment during the 1930s demonstrated the inability of the economy to right itself. Where was the 'invisible hand'? Keynes had already said it did not exist, or was too slow at an aggregate level, and that the Government must take its place.[1]

Keynes introduced aggregate demand, the total demand for goods and services produced within the economy, as the focus for analysis. In his model aggregate demand, made up of consumption and investment, determined the level of output and the extent to which the resources of the economy were employed. The Government could and should control the level of aggregate demand by fiscal and monetary management; this was the mechanism to achieve expansion and full employment. The tenor of Keynes's exposition in the *General Theory* was that most, if not all, of society would gain by bringing the economy to full employment.

---

[1] J. M. Keynes, 'The End of Laissez-Faire', in *Essays in Persuasion*, London 1972. The essay was first published in 1926.

From 1945 until 1979 British Governments accepted responsibility for maintaining full employment. Keynesian economists and governments emphasized the use of fiscal policy and interest rates to regulate the economy, and the budget deficit was treated as a thermostat to control aggregate demand. If forecasts indicated an imminent decline in aggregate demand and an increase in unemployment, the deficit was enlarged by increasing government spending and/ or reducing taxes to stimulate aggregate demand. This was in direct opposition to the traditional Treasury belief which prevailed until the 1930s that the budget should always balance.

Growth

In the *General Theory* Keynes was concerned with the problems of utilizing the capacity of the economy. Keynesian economists developed Keynes's analysis to explain the rate at which the capacity of an economy increases. As in Keynes's account of unemployment, Keynesian theories of growth stressed investment. Investment should be boosted to increase the rate of growth of the potential output of the economy, and Keynesian governments had a firm preference for low interest rates to encourage investment.

Limits on the Expansion of Demand

In practice limits to the use of expansionary economic policies emerged. First, by concentrating on a closed economy in the *General Theory*, Keynes had by-passed the problem of a worsening balance of payments. During the 1950s and 1960s Britain was beset with recurrent balance of payments crises. Expansionary policies are self-defeating if they result in an increase in imports and a balance of payments deficit which necessitates deflation of demand. Balance of payments crises, rather than increasing inflation, were the reason for imposing the 'stop' phases of the cycles. However, by the 1960s it was becoming increasingly evident that the policy instruments, as well as manipulation of the budget, were required.

One proposal for dealing with balance of payments deficits

was to devalue sterling, thereby making imports more expensive and Britain's exports cheaper. Following devaluation in 1967 the balance of payments problems were temporarily solved, but they were to re-emerge. Moreover, devaluation increased prices of imports and contributed to inflation, directly through the impact of higher import prices on the retail price index, and indirectly through the contraction of real income which caused wage-push inflation. An alternative proposal, as yet untried, was the introduction of import tariffs and quotas, advocated by the Cambridge Economic Policy Group and the Labour Party.

Keynes's concentration on a closed economy also by-passed the operation of international financial markets which are particularly important for Britain. The damaging impact of expansionary policies on the balance of payments could be brought forward and/or magnified by speculative movements of currency. Capital account outflows alone could trigger deflation. There was a conflict between maintaining low interest rates and preventing large capital outflows. Britain's interest rates had to be kept at the levels prevailing elsewhere; in particular, they were tied to those in the USA.

Towards the end of the 1970s, North Sea oil relieved the balance of payments constraint, but by then inflation and the threat of inflation had taken over as the arch-enemy of expansionary policies. The initial Keynesian explanation for inflation had been simple. Just as chronic unemployment was the result of a lack of effective demand, so price inflation was the consequence of an excess of effective demand over productive capacity. But in the 1970s unemployment was higher than in the 1950s and 1960s, prima facie evidence that it was not excess demand causing inflation to accelerate. The response of many Keynesians was to focus on cost-push factors causing inflation, particularly the oil price and wage shocks. The policy suggested for dealing with inflation was the use of incomes policies, designed to check the rate of increase of wages, costs, and prices. But incomes policies in Britain have not met with long-term success.

These limits to expansionary policies are reconsidered in Chapter 12; first the components of aggregate demand are examined.

The Components of Aggregate Demand

Table 4.1 shows the components of aggregate demand in 1979, the last year of deliberate Keynesian management of the economy. Columns 1 and 2 show GDP in 1979 at market prices and columns 3 and 4 at factor cost. Market prices are those paid when goods and services are bought. They include indirect taxes and any reduction in prices attributable to subsidies. In these terms, Consumers' Expenditure (C) accounted for 60.9 per cent of GDP, General Government Consumption (G) 19.8 per cent, Gross Domestic Investment (which is made up of investment in fixed assets (I_f) and investment in stocks or stockbuilding (I_s)) 19.1 per cent, and Exports (E) and Imports (M) 28.4 and 28.0 per cent. The proportions of Exports and Imports to GDP show the extent to which the UK economy is interlocked with, and dependent upon, the world economy. G includes only a part of total government expenditure; expenditure on goods and services for the education system, the health service, defence, etc. It excludes investment expenditure by the public sector which is included as Gross Domestic Investment, and transfer payments such as pensions.

Factor costs, which are market prices less indirect taxes and after adding back subsidies, are a better measure of the use of resources. Indirect taxes fall more heavily on consumption so the proportion of GDP going to C is lower in terms of factor costs. None the less, in terms of factor costs, C is still by far the largest component of aggregate demand, accounting for 59 per cent of GDP, and 45 per cent of total final expenditure.

The novel feature of the table is the final two columns which are obtained after deduction of depreciation—the charge by which the cost of fixed assets is charged to income during the life of the assets. This is more meaningful in economic terms. It shows the demands on the net output of the economy, that 8.0 per cent of the net domestic output was invested—added to the capital stock—in 1979. The remainder of Gross Domestic Investment, 12.5 per cent of GDP at factor cost, was required to maintain the capital stock. These estimates are approximate because of the

TABLE 4.1 *The components of aggregate demand 1979*

		At market prices		At factor cost		Excluding capital consumption	
		£ bn.	% of GDP	£ bn.	% of GDP	£ bn.	% of NDP
Consumers' expenditure	C	118.4	60.9	100.4	59.4	100.4	68.7
General government consumption	G	38.4	19.8	35.7	21.1	35.7	24.4
Gross domestic investment							
Fixed	I_f	34.9	18.0 }	34.6	20.5	11.7	8.0
Stocks	I_s	2.1	1.1 }				
Exports of goods and services	X	55.2	28.4	53.0	31.3	53.0	36.3
Total final expenditure		248.9	128.0	223.6	132.3	200.7	137.3
Less imports of goods and services	M	54.5	28.0	54.5	32.2	54.5	37.3
Gross domestic product		194.4	100.0	169.1	100.0		
Net domestic product						146.2	100.0

Source: *National Income and Expenditure*, 1983 Edition, Table 1.1.

difficulty of measuring depreciation. Private consumption took nearly 69 per cent, and government consumption 24 per cent of net output. Gross data, rather than estimates of net GDP, are commonly used for analysis and are used in later chapters, partly because of the difficulty of estimating depreciation, which is affected by the rate of technical progress, scrapping, and capacity utilization.

5

Wages and Prices

The Record

The 1970s will be remembered as the decade of rapid inflation. Although there was concern at the time, the price inflation of the 1950s and 1960s was moderate and stable; the average year to year increase in retail prices was 4 per cent, and the cycles about the average were gentle. This chapter focuses on the causes of the rapid inflation during the 1970s.

Movements of prices, wages, and profits since 1965 are recorded in Table 5.1, and for a longer time span in Diagram 5.1. The choice of measure of wage movements, wage rates or earnings, is considered in the Appendix.[1] Between 1970 and 1980 retail prices rose by 261 per cent, wage rates by 346 per cent, and real wage rates by 24 per cent. Cause and effect flow in both directions between wages and prices. Wages are an important component of costs, so changes in wages lead to changes in prices, while the rate of increase of prices affects wage claims. Diagrams 5.2 and 5.3 illustrate these links. Diagram 5.2 tests whether there is a relationship between an increase in prices and an increase in wages during the following year. Large wage increases between 1974 and 1975, 1975 and 1976, and between 1979 and 1980 did follow large price increases.

The equation shown in Diagram 5.2 indicates that annual wage increases are made up of two components, a constant increase of 5.96 per cent, plus 58 per cent of the percentage increase in prices the previous year. If prices rise by 10 per cent between year one and year two, then wage rates increase by 5.96 + 5.8 = 11.76 per cent between year two and year three. The price equation shown in Diagram 5.3 indicates that prices rise by 1.52 per cent, plus 74 per cent of the

[1] See Appendix 5.1

TABLE 5.1 *Prices, wages, and profits*

	Retail price index	Index of basic weekly wage rates	Index of average earnings	Real wage rates[a]	Real earnings[b]	Price deflator for imports	Profits as percentage of GDP[c]
	(Year to Year Percentage Increases)						
1966	3.9	4..6	6.6	0.7	2.6	1.6	14.2
1967	2.4	3.9	3.5	1.5	1.1	1.2	13.9
1968	4.8	6.6	7.8	1.7	2.9	11.1	13.7
1969	5.4	5.3	7.9	−0.1	2.4	2.6	14.1
1970	6.3	9.9	12.1	3.4	5.5	6.6	13.0
1971	9.4	12.9	11.2	3.2	1.6	4.0	13.2
1972	7.3	13.8	12.9	6.2	5.3	2.7	13.8
1973	9.1	13.7	13.5	4.2	4.0	23.7	13.5
1974	16.0	19.8	17.8	3.3	1.6	42.6	10.7
1975	24.2	29.5	26.5	4.3	1.9	14.0	9.3
1976	16.5	19.3	15.5	2.4	−0.9	22.1	9.3
1977	15.9	6.6	10.2	−7.9	−4.8	14.2	12.2
1978	8.3	14.1	14.5	5.4	5.7	2.9	13.0
1979	13.4	15.0	15.6	1.4	1.9	7.7	11.1
1980	18.0	18.0	18.8	0	0.7	10.0	9.8
1981	11.9	10.2	12.9	−1.6	0.9	5.7	9.4
1982	8.6	6.9	9.4	−1.6	0.6	5.1	9.5
1983	4.6	5.6	8.4	0.9	3.7	n.a.	n.a.

[a] $\left(\left(\frac{100 + \text{Col. 2}}{100 + \text{Col. 1}} \right) - 100 \right)$

[b] $\left(\left(\frac{100 + \text{Col. 3}}{100 + \text{Col. 1}} \right) - 100 \right)$

[c] Gross trading profits arising in the UK of Industrial and Commercial Companies (*ETAS*, p. 172 (Col. 3 and for 1966–9 Col. 4)) as a percentage of GDP at factor cost. Gross trading profits exclude stock appreciation and profits on North Sea oil activities and are before deduction of depreciation or taxes. See Appendix 5.2.

Sources: *ETAS* 1984, and *Economic Trends*, March 1984.

percentage increase in wages. If wages increase by 10 per cent between year one and year two, prices would rise by 1.52 + 7.4 = 8.92 per cent between the same years. The R^2 for the first equation is 0.26, so it provides only a very rough

DIAGRAM 5.1   Retail prices and wage rates (year to year percentage increases)

Sources: as for Table 5.1

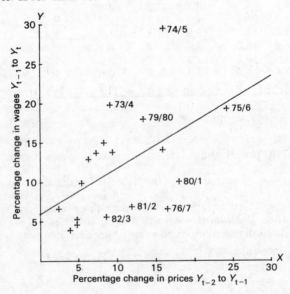

DIAGRAM 5.2   Wage Rates and Retail Prices (1966 to 1983)

$$Y = 5.96 + 0.58X$$
$$R^2 = 0.26$$

Sources: as for Table 5.1.

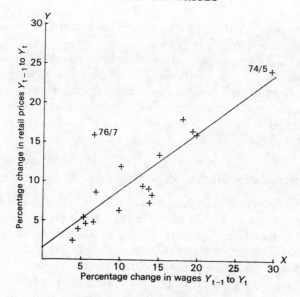

DIAGRAM 5.3   Retail prices and wage rates
(1966 to 1983)

$$Y = 1.52 + 0.74X, R^2 = 0.71$$

Sources: as for Table 5.1

indication of changes in wages.[2] The R^2 for the second
equation is 0.71, indicating that 71 per cent of the variance
in price increases can be explained by the variance in wage
increases. A caveat here is that cause runs in both directions,
increases in prices may trigger increases in wages between
the same years.

The operation of incomes policies affects the relationships.
The three outlying observations in Diagram 5.2, 1973/4,
1974/5 and 1976/7, were all affected by these policies.
Threshold agreements, which are described later, increased
wage settlements in 1974, and the social contract reduced
wage settlements in 1976 and 1977. The years 1980/1 to
1982/3 lie below the line fitted to all the observations. This
is compatible with the high levels of unemployment at this

---

[2] The equation suggests that price increases were not fully compensated by
increases in wages in the following year. However, part of the effect on wages may
be lagged by less and/or more than the lag allowed in this exercise, so it cannot
be concluded that a price-wage-price spiral is damped.

time limiting the extent to which price rises could be recouped
in subsequent increases in wages.

These links between increases in prices and increases in
wages mean that a continuation of rapid inflation once
started is easy to explain. In this chapter, therefore, we
concentrate on the causes of the initial accelerations in
inflation between 1970 and 1971, 1973 and 1974, and
between 1978 and 1979.

The Determination of Prices and Wages

The initial Keynesian explanation for inflation evolved from
Keynes's analysis of effective demand. Inflation occurs when
demand exceeds the potential output of the economy as
shown in Diagram 5.4(a). The difference between aggregate
demand and potential output at full employment is termed
the 'inflationary gap'. At full employment the excess demand
leads to a bidding up of prices, or wages and prices. The
analysis implies an asymmetric response to an increase in
demand—up to full employment only output rises, past full
employment only prices rise—as shown in Diagram 5.4(b).
This sharp dichotomy did not apply in practice during the
1950s when prices rose at levels of unemployment above
those regarded as full employment during the early post-war
period, but which were appreciably lower than Keynes himself envisaged as full employment. One explanation for prices
rising before full employment is the emergence of bottlenecks for the supply of certain goods and services, a possibility
which Keynes foresaw.

This Keynesian explanation of price determination implies
a price elastic supply of goods and services up to full employment, or the emergence of bottlenecks. Whatever other
explanation is offered for price determination, it must be
stressed that Keynes's model in the *General Theory* of
demand fluctuations leading to output changes, requires
prices to be fixed or not very sensitive to demand. If this is
not the case, increases in demand will be dissipated in price
rises.

A second Keynesian approach to price determination
emphasizes the importance of wage (and salary) costs in

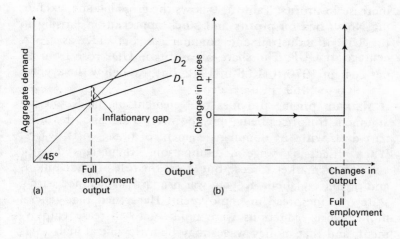

DIAGRAM 5.4

(a) An inflationary gap   (b) Price and output responses to
                                              demand increases

total home costs. During the 1970s income from employment
(including income from self employment) averaged nearly 70
per cent of total home costs. The argument has two parts:
a description of the way prices are related to costs, and an
explanation of wage determination. Surveys indicated that
many firms set their prices equal to unit costs plus a percentage profit margin—hence the term 'cost-plus pricing'. It
was suggested that profit margins were determined by con-
vention and that firms did not change prices in response to
cyclical changes in demand by changing their profit margins.
This departure from profit-maximizing behaviour has never
been convincingly explained. None the less, the conclusion
that product pricing has been passive in accelerating inflation in Britain in the 1970s is persuasive. Profits which are
shown as a percentage of GDP in Table 5.1 were not buoyant.
The statistical problems involved in measuring profits are
outlined in the Appendix.[3] Here we use one indicator of
profits which shows that at an aggregate level profits did not
rise ahead of wages—wage inflation was not triggered by an

[3] See Appendix 5.2.

increase in profits. Table 5.1 shows the gross income, excluding North Sea oil profits and stock appreciation, arising in the UK of industrial and commercial companies as a percentage of GDP. The share of profits in GDP rose from 13 per cent in 1970 to 13.8 in 1972, but was below the average for 1966 to 1969, 14.0 per cent.

Mark-up pricing provides one element of the Keynesian argument for prices being unresponsive to demand; the other part deals with the dominant element of home costs, wages. When discussing wage determination, Keynesians do not emphasize 'market forces', but stress the role of trade unions and organized labour. Keynes was primarily concerned with a state of widespread unemployment. He argued that general money-wage reductions were unlikely to increase employment, and that money wages may be inflexible at high levels of unemployment. One explanation for this is that workers are strongly 'relative wage conscious'—they are concerned with their wage relative to other groups, as well as the absolute amount. Wage bargaining is decentralized and not simultaneous, so each group of workers will be reluctant to accept a money wage cut as they have no guarantee that others will follow.

The Phillips Curve

A path-breaking attempt to quantify the relationship between increases in wage rates and unemployment was published by Professor A. W. Phillips in 1958[4]. He tested the application to wages of the economic law that when the demand for a commodity or service is high relative to the supply of it, the price is expected to rise. He tested whether the pressure of demand for labour, measured by unemployment, accounted for movements of wages. He found an empirical relationship between changes in wage rates and the level of unemployment —the Phillips curve— based on data for the period 1861 to 1913. Data for the periods 1913 to 48 and 1948 to 57 also fitted the original curve well.[5] The curve is reproduced in Diagram 5.5(a); the rectangle shows that with unemployment

[4] A. W. Phillips, 'Unemployment and Money Wage Rates', *Economica*, 1958. Phillips included changes in unemployment and prices in his analysis.
[5] See Appendix 5.3.

at 1.9 per cent, wage rates rise by 3 per cent, which would be compatible with constant wage costs per unit of output if labour productivity were rising at 3 per cent a year, a realistic target. At 1 per cent unemployment, wage rates rise by 8.7 per cent. A feature of the Phillips curve which coincided with Keynesian perceptions of wage determination was the near inflexibility of wages at high levels of unemployment; the rate at which wage rates fall increases very little at unemployment levels above 5 per cent. Data for the 1960s shown in Diagram 5.5(b) did not contradict the Phillips curve, though the increases in wages in 1967, 1968 and 1969 were above the levels predicted.

The Collapse of the Phillips Curve

The relationship between wage increases and unemployment for the 1970s is shown in Diagram 5.5(c); the increases in wage rates were greatly in excess of the predicted increases. The three periods of accelerating inflation cannot be explained by lower unemployment leading to faster increases in wages.

The experience of the 1970s signalled the end of the Phillips curve trade-off between the rate of increase of wages and the level of unemployment, but it was not surprising. Price inflation had been recognized as a factor influencing wage increases. In his original 1958 paper Phillips suggested that a 'factor which may affect the rate of change of money wage rates is the rate of change of retail prices . . .'. But he argued that this 'will have little or no effect . . . except at times when retail prices are forced up by a very rapid rise in import prices . . .'. R. G. Lipsey, who worked with Phillips on the same research project, discovered that for the period from 1923–39 and 1948–57 the most important variable for estimating changes in money wages was the rate of price increases, not unemployment. He concluded that 'there is a strong feed-back from price changes to wage changes with a great deal but not all of the rise in wages being attributed to wages chasing prices'.[6] Lipsey also commented that the 'fitted relation (the Phillips curve) may not be a very good guide

---

[6] R. G. Lipsey, 'The Relation between Unemployment and the Rate of Change in Money Wage Rates in the United Kingdom, 1962–1957. A Further Analysis', *Economica*, 1960, p. 31.

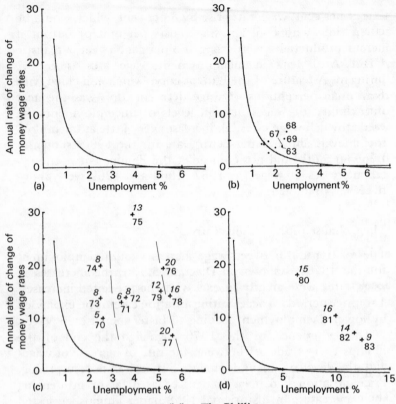

DIAGRAM 5.5   The Phillips curve

(a) The Phillips curve; $Y + 0.9 = 9.638x^{-1.394}$.
(b) The 1960s.
(c) The 1970s[i]
(d) The 1980s (Different scale on X axis).

[i] The figures in italics are the average rates of inflation in the previous two years.

to the relation between changes in wage rates and the level of unemployment if unemployment were to remain substantially unchanged for a long-time'.

Phillips had noted the importance of cost of living adjustments. There were sharp falls in wages in 1921 and 1922, much greater than would be expected from the Phillips relationship, and he attributed these to the automatic cost of living adjustments in wage bargains which were common at that time. In 1974 and 1975 'threshold agreements', introduced in the later stages of Heath's incomes policy, meant that increases in retail prices triggered increases in wage rates.[7]

Did movements of import prices trigger faster inflation during the 1970s? Diagram 5.6 tracks the movements of retail prices, earnings, wage rates, and unit values of imports of goods. The impact of increasing import prices on wages would be expected to operate via increases in retail prices. The sharp post-devaluation rise in import prices in 1968 was followed by a step up in the rate of increase of retail prices, and, after a lag, by an acceleration in wage rates and earnings in 1970. An acceleration of wage rates and earnings in 1974 followed the explosion of import prices in 1973 and faster increases in retail prices. The acceleration of wages increases in 1978 followed rapid increases in import prices in 1976 and 1977. For the three main episodes of accelerating inflation there is also evidence of wage rates and earnings accelerating ahead of retail prices, whether or not the increases in wages were triggered by earlier increases in import prices.

Real Wage Resistance

The expansion of the public sector and the increases in taxes during the 1960s generated the idea that taxes could have effects similar to increasing prices on wages. When bargaining, workers consider their after-tax income and ignore any improvement in the services provided by the government. The CEPG contends that wage bargainers focus on real post-tax wage increases. Post-tax earnings rose slowly in 1969, the year prior to the steep change in wage rate increases. Large increases in 1972 and 1978 were not, however, followed by any tailing-off of wage rate increases in the following years.[8]

What are the implications of wage claims based on

---

[7] In November 1973, the limits set for pay increases during the following year were £2.25 a week or 7 per cent, with a limit of £350 per annum, plus 40p a week for each 1 per cent rise in the retail price index above 7 per cent.

[8] See Appendix 5.4.

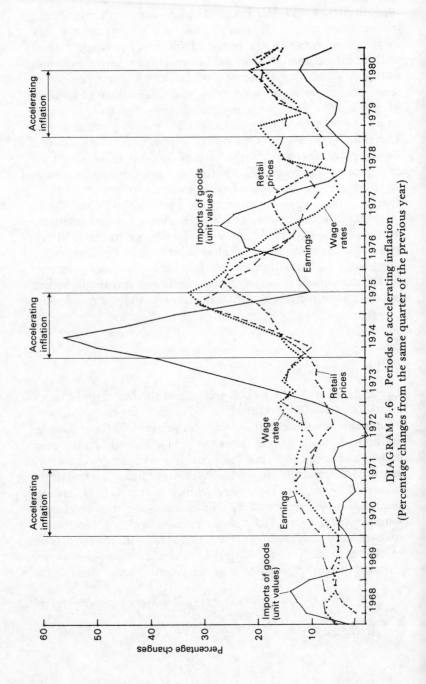

DIAGRAM 5.6   Periods of accelerating inflation
(Percentage changes from the same quarter of the previous year)

aspirations for maintaining or increasing real wages?[9] If unions have a target real wage increase of, say, 4 per cent while the economy can provide 2 per cent, then the outcome will be spiralling inflation as unions bargain for larger and larger money wage increases to get their target real wage. Temporarily, inflation may lead to increases in real wages at least for some groups because there are lags before increases in costs (wages) work through to prices, and not all incomes may keep pace with inflation. But the lags in the adjustment of prices are likely to shrink if rapid inflation persists.

Theories of real wage resistance have employees aiming to maintain or obtain a moderate increase in their real wages. But why should they stop there? During the 1970s some groups of workers were aiming for substantial improvements in real pay. The only reason why the actual average real increases were small was that real wages were limited by the productive capacity of the economy.

The Keynesian perception of highly monopolistic labour markets lends itself to instability and a range of wage rate increases compatible with a given level of unemployment. If the price of oil leaps, it is not difficult to explain continuing inflation as powerful groups of workers vie with each other to maintain and increase real incomes.

The Natural Rate of Unemployment

Friedman's explanation for the collapse of the Phillips curve went to the root of the relationship. He claimed that it contained 'a basic defect'—the failure to distinguish between nominal wages and real wages—and that Phillips presupposed 'a world in which everyone anticipated that nominal prices would be *stable* . . . whatever happened to prices and wages'.[10] Friedman and Phelps developed the 'expectations —augmented Phillips curve' which models this insight.

The expected rate of inflation certainly changed between the 1950s and 1970s. The process could have occurred in

[9] Wage bargains could be made in terms of real wages by indexing wages to changes in retail prices, but such agreements are not common.
[10] M. Friedman; 'The Role of Monetary Policy', *American Economic Review*, Vol. 58, 1968, p. 8.

this way: after many years of stable or near stable prices in peace time, agents may expect recent rates of inflation at, say, 3 per cent to continue. If inflation increases to 6 per cent agents will gradually revise their expectations of inflation, first to 4 per cent, then to 6 per cent. If they act on these revised expectations when setting wage claims and prices, inflation will further accelerate. If inflation accelerates to 12 per cent expectations may adjust more rapidly, and at some point agents may begin to extrapolate the acceleration of prices rather than form their expectations by averaging past rates of inflation. If inflation rises from 3 to 6 to 12 per cent, they may expect it to go on rising to 24 per cent, and this change of expectations may again trigger faster and larger increases in wages and prices. Thus faster inflation during the 1970s could be explained by changes in expectations.

Friedman starts his description of the natural rate hypothesis with a subtle change to the shape of the Phillips curve as shown in Diagram 5.7(a). In contrast to the Phillips curve, prices fall at high levels of unemployment.[11]

Friedman then presents a family of Phillips curves, each one corresponding to a 'particular anticipated or perceived rate of inflation'. Here it is assumed that productivity does not change, that wages are the only costs, that initially expectations are for zero inflation $p^e = 0$, and that unemployment is at the natural rate, U_N in Diagram 5.7(b). If for some reason unemployment falls below U_N to A, employees will aim for and get wage increases of 3 per cent. But prices will also rise by 3 per cent, and the expected rate of inflation will rise from zero to 3 per cent. The economy will move to a new short-run Phillips curve because of this change in expectations. In the next round of negotiations, wages will increase by 6 per cent, and so on. If the method of forming expectations switches to extrapolating the rate of change of prices then the process will speed up. While unemployment is below the natural rate, inflation will accelerate. If unemployment moves above U_N the reverse process will apply; wages will fall and they will fall at an increasing rate until employment

[11] For example, with unemployment at 15 per cent the Phillips curve predicts wages will fall by 1 per cent, implying prices fall by about 3 per cent, if labour productivity is increasing.

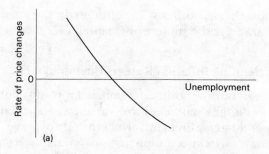

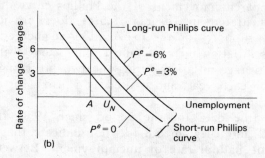

DIAGRAM 5.7

(a) Friedman's version of the Phillips curve[i]
(b) The expectations-augmented Phillips curve

[i] *Inflation and Unemployment*, IEA Occasional Paper 51, London 1977.

reverts to U_N —the natural rate. The long-run Phillips curve is vertical. Friedman argues that the short-run trade-off between inflation and unemployment was only achieved by 'fooling people' with a rate of inflation faster than expected, and that this could not persist. In the long-run price expectations are fulfilled so that there is no trade-off between inflation and unemployment. Rapid inflation may even increase the natural rate by distorting price signals and result in a backward-sloping long-run Phillips curve.

The natural rate hypothesis begs a number of questions. Can employees increase wage settlements simply because they revise upwards their expectations of the rate of inflation? Do labour markets clear in the long-run? What is the duration of the lags in the process? In this chapter the empirical validity of the hypothesis is considered; the operation of labour markets is the subject of Chapter 14.

Non-Accelerating Inflation Rate of Unemployment

The natural rate hypothesis is much more difficult to test than the Phillips curve. Two variables, expectations for inflation and unemployment, affect the rate of wage increases, and estimates of expectations are not available from official sources. Also, the natural rate may be shifting.

The apparent movement of the Phillips curve during the 1970s illustrated in Diagram 5.5(c) does provide some statistical support for the expectations-augmented Phillips curve. As inflation increased the Phillips curve drifted outwards. (Average inflation during the two preceding years is shown for each year, and is used as a proxy for expected inflation.)

Plainly the data for the period since 1950, shown in Table 5.2 and Diagram 5.8, do not indicate that there is a constant natural rate of unemployment. Between 1951 and 1954, and again between 1956 and 1960, wage rate increases slowed with unemployment below 2 per cent. Yet in the 1970s wage rates accelerated at higher levels of unemployment. The data are compatible with a changing natural rate.

It is not possible to estimate the natural rate of unemployment from aggregate statistics. NAIRU (the non-accelerating inflation rate of unemployment) can be estimated from data of the kind shown in Diagram 5.6 and Table 5.2. Estimates made for America indicate a NAIRU of about 5 per cent in the 1960s. What of UK experience? During the 1950s and 1960s NAIRU may have been less than 2 per cent as wage increases were not accelerating; by 1979 it appears to have been more than 5 per cent as wages increased sharply between 1978 and 1979. Experience of decelerating wage increases after 1980 indicates a NAIRU at about 10 per cent unemployment.

The natural rate theory predicts that when unemployment is above the natural rate wage rates will fall. Average wage rates have not fallen in Britain in spite of unemployment

TABLE 5.2   *Unemployment*

	Unemployment %	Year to Year percentage increase in wage rates	
1950	1.4	1.8	
1951	1.1	8.5 ⎫	
1952	1.5	8.4 ⎪	
1953	1.5	4.5 ⎬	Decelerating
1954	1.2	4.3 ⎭	wage increases
1955	1.0	6.9	
1956	1.1	8.0 ⎫	
1957	1.3	5.0 ⎪	"
1958	1.8	3.6 ⎬	
1959	1.9	2.6 ⎭	
1960	1.5	2.6	
1961	1.4	4.2 ⎫	"
1962	1.8	3.6 ⎭	
1963	2.1	3.7	
1964	1.5	4.8 ⎫	"
1965	1.3	4.3 ⎭	
1966	1.4	4.6 ⎫	"
1967	2.1	3.9 ⎭	
1968	2.3	6.6 ⎫	"
1969	2.2	5.3 ⎭	
1970	2.4	9.9	
1971	3.1	12.9	
1972	3.3	13.8 ⎫	"
1973	2.3	13.7 ⎭	
1974	2.3	19.8	
1975	3.6	29.5 ⎫	
1976	4.8	19.3 ⎬	"
1977	5.1	6.6 ⎭	
1978	5.0	14.1	
1979	4.7	15.0	
1980	5.8	18.0 ⎫	
1981	9.0	10.2 ⎪	"
1982	10.4	6.9 ⎬	
1983	11.2	5.6 ⎭	

Source: *ETAS* 1984, and *Economic Trends*, March 1984.

having been above 10 per cent for three years since 1981. The Phillips curve based on historical data also conflicts with the idea of there being a natural rate of unemployment above which wages will fall steeply.

One approach to reconciling the natural rate theory with

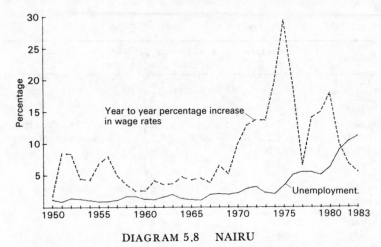

DIAGRAM 5.8   NAIRU

Sources: *ETAS* 1984, and *Economic Trends*, March 1984.

experience is to assume there are long lags before agents adapt their expectations for inflation and/or they recognize their power to increase income in conditions of full employment. Also changes in the composition of the labour force towards a higher proportion of youths and women may have increased the natural rate between the 1960s and 1970s when measured as a percentage of the total labour force. Monetarists claim that increases in social security benefits and increases in taxes relative to income during the 1960s and 1970s eroded the incentive to work. It is very unlikely that changes in the composition of the labour force or incentives contribute very much to the explanation of the acceleration of inflation during the 1970s. The evidence is considered in the Statistical Appendix and Chapter 14.[12]

Other Explanations for Rapid Inflation

The 'economic' approach to explaining the collapse of the Phillips curve in the early 1970s, as described so far, is not comprehensive; there were political changes as well. Unions were confident of their power. The Wilson government in the 1960s had co-operated with the unions, and, after initial frigidity, Mr Heath tried the same tack. Decades of low

[12] See Appendix 5.5.

unemployment increased the confidence of unskilled workers, so the scene was set for confrontation over shares in the national income. Paradoxically this occurred at the time when the economic forces which had elevated the power of the unskilled were ebbing away, for reasons we describe in Chapter 14 when we deal with unemployment.

During the 1970s the future rate of inflation was difficult to forecast. In these circumstances unions may focus on the claims made by other unions—estimate what other unions will claim and settle for—and set their own claims at similar levels. As wage settlements are the main determinant of price rises this procedure may be close to guessing the rate of inflation.

Wiles has suggested one non-traditional explanation for the 'new gale' of wage demands which swept through the economy during the 1970s. The 'communications revolution which, making everyone instantly aware of everything . . . sharply increased the amount of envy and imitation in the world, and reduced the number of things that are sacrosanct. We . . . moved from wage claims based on the actual situation in the trade through claims based on concessions made elsewhere in the economy to claims picked out of the air—an air ringing with, for instance, foreign wage claims'.[13] The development of television was a decisive change in communications; during the 1950s and 1960s transmission spread through the country, and by 1970 90 per cent of the population were equipped to receive at least BBC 1 and ITV. A similar development occurred in other industrial countries. Television provides a much more vivid impression of events than radio.

Wage bargaining is a two-sided process, and the management side did not resist the pressure for higher wages in the 1970s. The causes of this weakness included the high cost of resisting strikes but were also political. There was no political consensus to resist wage claims, and politicians sometimes undermined resistance in the private sector or gave way to wage claims in the public sector. In Germany employers banded together more effectively than in the UK. Resort to

[13] P. J. Wiles, 'Cost Inflation and the State of Economic Theory', *Economic Journal*, 1973, p. 378.

industry-wide lock-outs by employers in Britain might have exacerbated political tensions. An economic factor which may have influenced some managements was that UK wages were low by European standards, and some firms with high productivity by British standards could afford to meet wage claims.

The importance of management resistance to wage claims has been demonstrated by Mrs Thatcher. Since 1981 firm resistance to wage claims in the public sector has reduced wage inflation in that sector while market forces have reduced wage increases in the private sector. The extent to which a firm policy on wages by employers in the private sector could reduce wage inflation in the absence of high unemployment is not clear, but German and Japanese experience suggests it is very important.

Conclusions

What conclusions can be drawn about the causes of the wage and price explosions of the 1970s? The natural rate hypothesis does not *explain* events during the 1970s, though revised expectations for inflation may have played a part; the decisive causes of rapid inflation were the social and political developments. For reasons given in Chapter 2, both oil price rises were also important in propelling inflation, but the acceleration in wage increases preceded the first oil price rise. In 1978 wage rates rose rapidly and the 'Winter of Discontent' (1978/9) set the seal on further large increases in wage rates before the second oil price rise. The 'Barber boom', fuelled by monetary expansion, other commodity price rises, and the threshold agreements in the later stages of Heath's incomes policy were factors which greased the path for faster inflation caused by social and political developments.

Our conclusions about the relationship between unemployment and the rate of wage increases are that:

(a) The two variables are negatively related. Experience of high unemployment during the 1980s has again shown the effect of high unemployment to reduce the rate at which wages increase. If money is the 'Old Policeman' for the economy, then unemployment is the Old Policeman's baton.

(b) The average levels of money and real wages do not necessarily fall even with unemployment levels above 10 per cent.

(c) It is not possible to make firm predictions from statistics of the effects of lower levels of unemployment on the rate of wage increases.

One qualification to the approach used in this chapter is its macroeconomic nature. Other explanations for changes may emerge from a study of events at a more disaggregated level. Although aggregate profits were not buoyant in the 1970s, some companies were very profitable. House prices rose early in the inflation and this led to wage increases in the building industry. Incomes policies disturbed differentials particularly between the public and private sectors. However, we believe these are secondary rather than fundamental explanations.

6

Interest Rates

Introduction

Shackle summed up his survey of 'the Nature and Role of Interest' with the comment, 'interest can appear . . . as the pivot of the entire economic system' and it 'seems to reign over the theories of employment, of money, of growth, of the general price level and of the balance of payments'.[1]

What determines the rate of interest? In brief, the rate of interest is the price paid for loans of money, and is determined by the supply of, and demand for, money. To explain changes in the rate of interest the forces affecting the supply of, and demand for, money and other assets have to be traced. In this chapter the relationships between the rate of interest and inflation, yields on other assets, and the demand for money are analysed. The relationships between the rate of interest, saving, investment, and the PSBR are considered in later chapters.

Definition

The pure long-term rate of interest has been defined as 'the rate that is paid to a borrower of unimpeachable solvency for a loan of indefinite duration'.[2] The yield on Consols or other long-term Government bonds is usually taken as a measure of this rate of interest. In recent years the question of payment of nominal interest by the British government has never been in doubt (the risk of default has been non-existent).

It is traditional to speak of 'the rate of interest', but when economists use the term they have in mind a whole spectrum of interest rates depending on the duration and solvency of

[1] G. L. S. Shackle 'Recent Theories Concerning the Nature and Role of Interest', *Surveys of Economic Theory*, London, 1965.
[2] J. R. Hicks, *Critical Essays in Monetary Theory*, Oxford, 1967, p. 85.

loans. In practice one, or a small number of interest rates, are used to represent the spectrum of interest rates. Table 6.1 and Diagram 6.1 show the movements of long and short-term interest rates in nominal terms. Long-dated government bonds are used as an indicator of long-term interest rates, and the Treasury Bill yield as an indicator of short-term rates. In

TABLE 6.1 *Interest rates* (%)

	Short-term interest rate[a]		Long-term interest rate[b]	Real short-term interest rate[c]
	average (1)	range (2)	(3)	(4)
1963	3.7	3.4–3.8	5.4	+1.8
1964	4.6	3.8–6.6	6.0	−0.1
1965	5.9	5.5–6.7	6.6	+1.4
1966	6.1	5.6–6.9	6.9	+2.3
1967	5.8	5.3–7.7	6.8	+3.2
1968	7.1	6.6–7.7	7.6	+0.9
1969	7.6	6.8–8.0	9.1	+2.7
1970	7.0	6.9–7.7	9.3	−1.1
1971	5.6	4.3–6.9	8.9	−2.8
1972	5.5	4.3–8.5	9.0	−2.0
1973	9.3	7.1–12.9	10.8	−1.8
1974	11.4	11.2–12.4	14.8	−6.8
1975	10.2	9.5–11.7	14.4	−11.2
1976	11.1	8.6–15.0	14.4	−4.1
1977	7.7	4.5–12.1	12.7	−3.0
1978	8.5	5.9–11.9	12.5	−0.4
1979	13.0	11.6–16.8	13.0	−4.1
1980	15.1	13.4–17.0	13.8	+0.9
1981	13.4	11.6–16.6	14.8	+1.2
1982	12.0	9.0–14.0	12.9	+6.5
1983	9.8	9.0–11.2	10.8	+4.4
Averages				
1963–72	5.9		7.6	+0.6
1973–83	11.0		13.2	−1.7

Sources: *ETAS* 1984, and *Economic Trends*, March 1984.

[a] Treasury bill rate; the range relates to rates on the last Friday of each month.
[b] Bond rate—the yield on long dated (20-year) British Government bonds.
[c] The method of calculating the real rate of interest is described in footnote p.92.

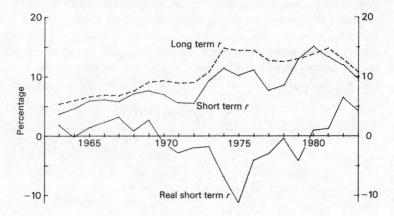

DIAGRAM 6.1   *Interest rates*

Source: Table 6.1.

1963 the long-term rate was 5.4 per cent; it rose to 14.8 per cent in 1974 and stayed near that level through the rest of the 1970s. Short-term rates averaged out lower than long-term rates, but fluctuated more. An indication of the fluctuations in short-term interest rates during the years is shown in column (2) of Table 1.

Real and Nominal Rates of Interest

It is important to draw a distinction between the nominal and real rates of interest. Table 6.1 and Diagram 6.1 show the real short-term rates of interest. This is the nominal short-term interest rate adjusted by the rate of inflation during a year.[3] From 1970 until 1979 it was *negative*. Holders of Treasury Bills were receiving negative real interest; inflation more than wiped out the nominal interest. This rate is gross, many investors pay tax on their interest income, so the

[3] The rate of inflation was calculated by comparing the general index of retail prices for December at the end of each year and January of the following year with the index for the same two months a year earlier. Where x is the nominal rate of interest and y the percentage rate of inflation, the real rate of interest is

$$\left(\left(\frac{100 + x}{100 + y} \times 100\right) - 100\right).$$

negative, post-tax, real interest they received was even lower than the real short-term rate shown in the diagram.

Short and Long-term Interest Rates

Short-term interest rates were below long-term rates during the period 1969 to 1978. In 1980 they were higher. Generally long-term interest rates are higher than short-term rates. One explanation is that the markets are segmented; some investors cannot lend long term. Also if the rates were the same, more investors would prefer to lend short-term to have greater liquidity, and borrowers would borrow long-term to secure their funding and to avoid the costs of rearranging loans, so the long-term rate would move above the short-term rate. If investors expect interest rates to rise in the future, then the short-term rate will be below the long-term rate. Some investors will prefer to make short-term investments and re-invest long-term when the expected fall in bond prices occurs, and some long-term borrowers may borrow in advance of their requirements and lend the proceeds of the loans short-term. The demand for loans will be weak during a recession (as in 1975) and so interest rates—particularly short-term rates—will be low. If the central authorities are holding down the exchange rate, as in 1977, domestic short-term interest rates must be kept low to check the inflow of funds.

Interest and Inflation

The direct cause of the increase in *nominal* interest rates during the 1970s was faster inflation. If interest rates are below the expected rate of inflation, agents will buy inflation proofed assets instead of holding monetary deposits, bills or bonds, reducing the demand for money and the supply of loanable funds. In 1982 the government made inflation-proofed bonds, whose value is linked to the retail price index, generally available to investors. If the expected rate of inflation rises, investors will sell fixed-interest bonds and buy index-linked bonds until the expected return on the former has risen to match the expected return on the index-linked bonds. Prior to the introduction of index-linked bonds there were no assets which provided a guarantee of inflation proofing. However, property fulfilled this function in a rough-and-ready way; commercial property in the eyes of pension-fund managers and houses for private investors. If a gap developed between interest rates and the *expected* rate of inflation, agents would try to buy more property. In practice the increase in demand for property was slowed by uncertainty about future interest rates, the lumpiness of property investment, the cost of buying and selling property, and the capital uncertainty and illiquidity of property. If the gap between expected interest and inflation rates was large, agents might buy consumer goods in advance of their requirements rather than hold interest-earning deposits, etc., in spite of the inconvenience of storing products, the possibility of deterioration, and, for some products, changes in fashion. Agents knowledgeable about financial and commodity markets speed up this process of adjustment between expected inflation rates and intererest rates by borrowing to buy commodities and other assets. Rapid inflation was the proximate cause of high interest rates, but the primary causes of high interest rates must be traced to the causes of inflation—for monetarists increases in the money supply.

We have not shown an estimate of the *real* long-term rate of interest in Table 6.1 or Diagram 6.1, for in order to know what investors and borrowers perceive to be the real long-term rate of interest we need to know their expectations of the long-term rate of inflation. We have no direct estimate of these expectations, but we can estimate them by using the long-term rate of interest itself.

Investors have a choice of investments. Pension and Life Assurance Funds—the main acquirers of long-term bonds—choose between investment in bonds, equities of companies, and property.[4] During the inflationary 1970s, property investment had the best record. The rental income from property investments, combined with the capital appreciation, exceeded the return on other types of investment. Rents and capital values, particularly on prime shop properties, more than kept pace with inflation.

If we assume that fund managers reckoned that the rents

---

[4] Since 1979 they have been free to invest overseas without penalty, so their effective range of choice has increased.

and values of prime shop properties would keep pace with inflation and acted upon it, we have a benchmark for estimating their expectation of the long-term rate of inflation. They would trade property for bonds until the difference in yields approximated to the rate of inflation they expected.

An Example

In 1979 the average annual yield on prime shop properties let on leases with rent reviews at three or five year intervals was 4.2 per cent. The average yield on long-term government bonds was 13 per cent. The difference in yields was $\left(\left(\frac{113.0}{104.2} \times 100\right) - 100\right)$, 8.4 per cent, and this was the long-term rate of inflation expected by fund managers. Fund managers investing in long-term bonds yielding 13.0 per cent expected a compound real return of 4.2 per cent, the same as on prime shop properties.[5]

Diagram 6.2 shows the expected long-term rate of inflation calculated in this way[6] and the actual short-term rate of inflation. The roughness of these estimates of the expected rate of inflation must be emphasized, but they suggest the expected rate of inflation was persistently below the actual short-term rate and moved up behind the actual rate of inflation. Investors did not foresee galloping inflation, and when it occurred they did not expect it to continue indefinitely. Also the decline in the expected rate of inflation in 1982 was lagged behind a fall in the actual short-run rate. The evidence supports the view that agents adapt their expectations to past changes in variables, but not slavishly; they did not project the galloping inflation of the mid-1970s. It seems unlikely that other agents in the economy anticipated the acceleration of inflation better than investors. This is evidence that changes in expectations in the mid-1970s were *not* the cause of accelerating inflation.

Relative Yields

Investors bring the expected yields on different investments

---

[5] See Appendix 6.1.
[6] See Appendix 6.2.

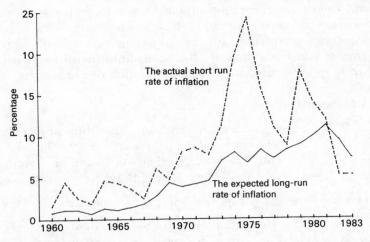

DIAGRAM 6.2   The expected long-run rate of inflation and the
actual short-run rate.

Sources: The sources of the data and method of calculation of the
expected long-run rate of inflation are described in the text and Statistical Appendix, 6.1 and 6.2. The actual short-run rate of inflation is
the year to year change in retail prices.

into balance by selling investments with lower than average
expected yields and buying investments with higher than
average expected yields. The expected real long-term rate of
return on shop properties and bonds is influenced by the
expected returns on other investments, mainly investments in
offices, warehouses, factories, and the equity of companies.
The expected profitability of companies and the return on
equity investments depends upon a number of inter-related
factors including expectations for the growth of the UK
economy. If the economy grows rapidly, profits and dividends
will also increase rapidly.

It is expected *future* returns which determine *current*
yields on different assets, and *past* performance is very
important for determining these expectations. Firstly, what
happened in the past is fact, whereas what will happen in
the future is unknown; it is therefore tempting to rely on
facts. Advertisements by unit trusts which display their past
record and mention future possibilities and uncertainty

only briefly, are evidence of this balance. Secondly, professional investors who are guided by the past and conventional views, and are proved wrong by events, may not be penalized for their errors, but those who try to unravel the future may have more difficulty justifying their stance if their views prove to be mistaken.

In 1981 there was a spectrum of current yields,[7] starting with shop properties yielding 3½ per cent, offices 4¼ per cent, equities 5½ per cent, and long-term bonds 14.8 per cent. Changes in relative yields reflect changes in expectations. In a closed economy where the money supply is fixed and does not respond to demand, there is no way investors can instantaneously change their aggregate holdings of real and financial assets. If one investor is to sell an asset, a house, say, he has to find a buyer willing to swop money for the house. If investors reduce their expectations of the future return on investments in companies, that will lead to an increase in current yields on those securities as the prices of the securities fall, but a reduction in yields on some other assets including bank deposits.

Security Yields since 1970

Diagram 6.3 shows the movements of yields on securities since 1970. The changes in the yields on bonds reflect changes in the prices of the bonds. Changes in yields on equities reflect changes in share prices and dividends; unlike interest on existing bonds, dividends are not fixed. Similarly yields on property are affected by changes in rents as well as changes in the value of property. The diagram shows sudden increases in the current yields on bonds, equities, and property in 1974 — when the values of many assets collapsed. During 1974, profits were squeezed by increased wages, the effects of the first oil shock, and the government's failure to index-link company taxation.[8] Once prices of securities fell there was some panic which reinforced the fall and pushed up current yields on property and equities.

[7] Yields are the income in the latest year as a percentage of the market value of the investment.

[8] Only in November 1974 did the government effectively exempt stock appreciation from Corporation Tax.

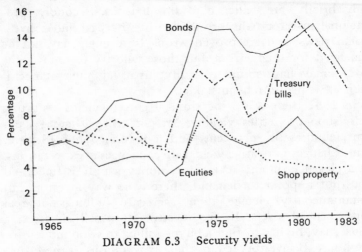

DIAGRAM 6.3   Security yields

Sources: *ETAS* 1984, and *Economic Trends*, March 1984. The source of estimates of yields on shop property are given in the Statistical Appendix, 6.2.

During the 1970s shop rents kept pace with inflation, but dividends on industrial shares lagged because of the squeeze on profits. From 1965 to 1972 current *yields* on equities were below those on shop property, but by 1978 the relationship had been reversed. Investors had extrapolated the better performance of shop property to the future, and increased their demand for shop properties.

Another feature of the pattern of yields during the 1970s was the increase in interest rates relative to the yields on equities and shop property. Although the *current* yields on equities and shop property were below interest rates, the future dividends and rent increases were expected to balance this difference. These changes in yields, caused by changing expectations of inflation, were masked for a time by the financial crisis in 1974.

Overseas Investment

Freedom to invest overseas adds another element of control and volatility for UK securities. Short-term assets, such as interest-earning deposits in Britain and overseas, are close substitutes for some investors; consequently short-term interest rates (adjusted for expected exchange rate changes) move closely. America, the dominant Western financial market, sets the pace for short-term rates.

Diagram 6.4 shows British and American short-term interest rates during the 1970s. British rates were above American rates, reflecting the higher rates of inflation in Britain which, other things being equal, imply that sooner or later sterling will be devalued against the dollar. In fact the difference in interest rates *circa* 1975 was surprisingly small given the much faster rate of inflation in the UK. In 1981, when inflation was falling in Britain and the Government would have liked to reduce interest rates, high American

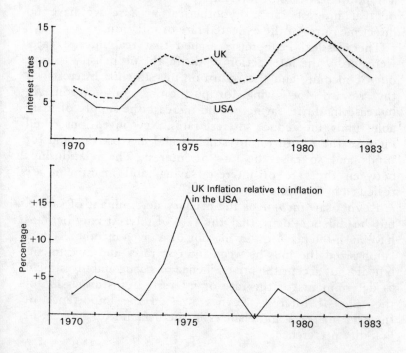

DIAGRAM 6.4   British and American interest rates (Treasury Bill rates)

Sources: *Economic Trends* 1984, and *Surveys of Current Business*, various issues.

rates impeded this. The Government would have had to accept a further fall in sterling. In theory Britain can have lower interest rates than America. The sterling/dollar exchange rate would fall to a point where the expected appreciation of sterling would compensate for lower interest. In practice, a fall in the exchange rate may cause wages and prices to rise in Britain, and agents may expect the fall in the exchange rate to continue and thereby exaggerate it.

The Real Rate of Interest

So far *relative* interest rates and yields have been examined in the context of financial markets. Here we consider the economic forces which determine the real rate of interest— a hypothetical rate of interest representative of the spectrum of real interest rates; hypothetical because we have no direct measures of the expected rate of inflation.

The classical economists argued that real interest rates were set by the inter-action of thrift, the propensity to save out of income, and the return on investments. Interest was the 'reward' for saving—for postponing consumption. An increase in thrift, saving, would increase the supply of loanable funds and reduce interest rates. New inventions could increase the return on investments and increase demand for funds and so raise the rate of interest. The relationships between the rate of interest, saving, and investment are reviewed in Chapters 7 and 8.

Keynes saw *income* as the primary determinant of saving, but he did not 'deny that the rate of interest may perhaps have an influence'[9] on saving out of a given income. Keynes emphasized the link between interest rates and investment, but did not accept the pre-eminence of saving and investment as determinants of the rate of interest. In his discussion of the rate of interest, Keynes stressed the importance of financial markets and changes in the demand for money, or liquidity preference.

The Keynesian Demand for Money Function

Keynes identified three reasons for wanting to hold money.

[9] *General Theory*, p. 178.

Firstly, the transactions demand—money required to settle current transactions: the amount of money held for this purpose would be a function of nominal income, and was expected to be relatively stable. Second was the 'precautionary' motive, stemming from the need 'to provide for contingencies requiring sudden expenditure ...', and money's property of being the least risky of a range of possible wealth storing assets in the absence of inflation.[10]

The third function of money was to act as a bridge between the present and future. In an uncertain world without comprehensive futures markets, money holdings may be an imperfect substitute for taking positions in futures markets. This demand for money for 'speculative' purposes depends upon the expected development of the economy and the distribution of expectations among agents. In Keynes's argument it was a function of the difference between the current rate of interest and the expected rate. Keynes believed expectations to be volatile, so he saw this component of the demand for money as unstable.

Let us suppose that the government is able and does control the total stock of money. Then it will be true that a *desire* for more liquidity cannot be satisfied; it will simply lead to a higher interest rate. Nevertheless, there is a mechanism whereby an increased desire for money for speculative purposes *can* be satisfied. As the rate of interest goes up, investment and income fall. When income falls, the amount of money demanded for *transactions* purposes falls. Hence, more of a fixed money stock is left over to fulfil the speculative demand.

Keynes also questioned the effectiveness of a reduction in interest rates to maintain employment in the face of increasing thriftiness or a fall in the expected return on investment. Keynes claimed that there might be some limit to, or drag on, the fall in interest rates—a liquidity trap. The hypothesis has contemporary echoes. Rapid inflation during the 1970s has made owners of assets cautious about accepting low yields on bonds during the 1980s, which is a factor impeding the

---

[10] During periods of inflation, non-interest earning forms of money depreciate. Precautionary and speculative balances are likely to be held in interest-earning forms of money and will be excluded from narrow definitions of M.

fall in long-term interest rates. In 1983 the rate of inflation was 5 per cent and bond yields averaged 11 per cent. If inflation stays at 5 per cent or less as the government claims it will, the real long-term rate of interest will be 6 per cent or more, which is high by historical standards. Since 1973 companies have not borrowed much by issuing long-term bonds because they have been reluctant to enter into commitments to pay high nominal rates of interest far into the future. Instead they have borrowed short-term funds and arranged medium-term loans at floating rates that are tied to short-term rates.

The Demand for Money

Monetarists claim that the demand for money is a stable function, with permanent income the main explanatory variable; Keynesians' claims imply that it is not a stable function of income.

The relationship between money and nominal income (not permanent income) in another guise—the velocity of circulation—was considered in Chapter 3. During the 1970s V was not stable, so the demand for money was not a stable function of nominal income alone. Here movements of the inverse of V and the long-term interest rates are tracked. We consider whether the instability of the demand for money relative to nominal income during the 1970s was attributable to movements of interest rates. The Keynesian perception is that investors have some notion of a normal rate of interest. If the actual interest rate moves below that rate, they will choose to hold money because they expect interest rates to rise and bond prices to fall. When interest rates rise, the cost of holding money in non-interest earning forms of money instead of other assets increases, and, *ceteris paribus*, the expectation that the next movement of interest rates will be downward, increases. We relate the demand for money to the long-term rate of interest between 1964 and 1983. The relationships outlined lead us to expect that there is an inverse relationship between the two variables. In fact there are practical reasons for expecting the relationships to be complex. During the 1970s investors' expectations of the nominal long-term rate of interest certainly changed. Also, interest rates on deposit accounts which are included in £M_3 were rising, so the differential advantage of holding assets other than money was not necessarily increasing as interest rates rose.

Diagram 6.5(a) shows the relationship between the ratio of the money stock to GDP (M/PY) and the long-term rate of interest (r). What do the facts say? Figure 6.5(a) shows there is a reasonable correlation, which is improved when the years 1973 to 1975 are removed (6.5(b)). (During the excluded years there were large monetary disturbances.) But interestingly we also observe that M/PY was drifting *steadily* over this period: the trend line in Figure 6.5(d) confirms this. It is therefore possible that the correlation of 6.5(c) is due to the demand for money and r drifting *independently*; probably, faster inflation raised r, and innovations in methods of debt settlement, and faster inflation, led to economies in money holdings.

Liquidity Preference

One source of instability for the demand for money envisaged by Keynes was that many investors would attempt to liquidate their holdings of financial assets if there were a worsening of expectations about the future. Investment by institutions, particularly pension funds and insurance companies, now forms a much larger fraction of overall investment than it did during the 1930s. Their investments during the 1970s are summarized in Table 6.2. The Table provides no evidence that these institutional investors collectively liquidated their holdings. The institutions did not hold on to and neutralize part of the stock of money which would otherwise be available to finance transactions. In aggregate their acquisitions of short-term assets are a small proportion of the total.

There is an exception to these broad conclusions. In 1974 acquisitions of short-term U.K. assets formed half of the net acquisition of assets by the financial institutions. Share prices fell to record low levels in real terms in 1974. However,

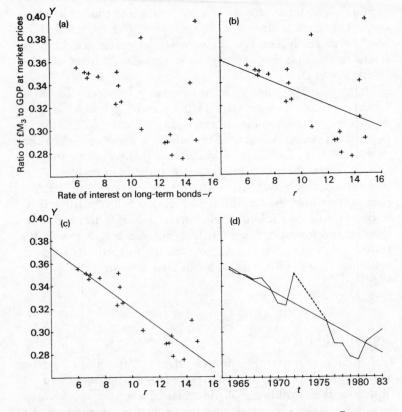

DIAGRAM 6.5   The Demand for Money and Interest Rates

(a) All observations
(b) All observations; $Y = 0.38 - 0.005r$; $R^2 = 0.19$.
(c) 1973–5 omitted; $Y = 0.41 - 0.009r$; $R^2 = 0.83$.
(d) A time trend (1973–5 omitted); $Y = 0.36 - 0.004t$; $R^2 = 0.82$.

the move to increase liquidity by institutions was a symptom as well as a cause of the financial crisis of the time; other causes were the 'Barber boom', the oil price shock, the dilatory adjustment of the tax system to account for inflation, strikes, and political uncertainty.

A recent example of increased liquidity preference occurred in May 1984. There were steep declines in share prices. The *Sunday Telegraph* of 27 May 1984, reported the following statement by the chief executive of the 'Prudential

TABLE 6.2   *Net acquisitions of assets by financial institutions £bn.* [a]

	Total	Cash and balances with banks in the UK	All short term UK assets	British Govt. securities	UK company securities	Overseas company securities	Land, property, and ground rents
1970	1.7	n.a.	0.3	0.1	0.8	n.a.	0.3
1971	2.1	n.a.	−0.1	0.9	0.9	n.a.	0.3
1972	2.7	n.a.	0.4	0.3	1.6	n.a.	0.3
1973	3.0	n.a.	0.5	0.5	0.9	n.a.	0.5
1974	3.3	n.a.	1.6	0.2	0.2	n.a.	0.7
1975	4.7	−0.2	−0.5	2.5	1.5	n.a.	0.7
1976	6.0	0.2	0.05	3.0	1.3	n.a.	1.0
1977	7.1	0.3	0.1	3.3	1.8	n.a.	0.9
1978	8.6	0.5	0.8	3.9	1.7	n.a.	1.1
1979	11.5	0.2	0.8	5.2	2.2	0.6	1.2
1980	12.5	0.05	−0.2	4.7	3.0	2.0	1.8
1981	14.6	0.8	1.1	4.8	3.0	2.4	1.8
1982	14.0	0.7	0.9	3.2	3.6	2.7	1.8
Holdings of assets at the end of 1980	119.2	2.9	5.8	28.9	44.4	7.0	21.9

Source: *Financial Statistics*, May 1984, Feb. 1981, and earlier issues.

[a] Superannuation funds and the general and long-term funds of insurance companies.

Portfolio Managers', the country's largest investment institution: 'Our strategy is now to let the cash build up . . . there has been a massive change of sentiment'. If a few large institutions adopt this strategy the result is likely to be a fall in bond and share prices, which may cause the institutions to reverse their policy and to re-enter the market.

The institutions do vary their acquisition of assets, to some extent in response to the changing availablility of different types of security. The size of the funded PSBR and new issues by companies play a part in these changes. A source of instability related to liquidity preference could occur if investors altered the valuation of different types of security. The changing yield structure shown in Diagram 6.3 suggests that changes of this sort do occur. One possibility is that the relative valuation of industrial equities could be depressed and lead to a freeze on new equity funding of industry. It has been argued that equities were undervalued in the 1970s. However, sources of finance apart from new issues of shares were available to companies, particularly bank finance. Many British companies were not highly geared and could substantially increase their borrowing from banks during the 1970s. Also, if investors depress some asset prices they inflate others, which may lead to investment.

Hyman Minsky has re-emphasized another source of instability in the financial system: waves of credit expansion and deflation. He claims that during booms firms make more use of debt financing, households and firms cut their cash and liquid asset holdings relative to their debt, and banks increase their loans. Credit expansion increases the money value of assets and justifies further borrowing, but involves a process of increasing the ratio of debt to real assets which cannot continue indefinitely. The boom falters and turns to crisis, and credit contraction sets in.[11] Lending to property companies in the early 1970s, which escalated following 'Competition and Credit Control', and the 1974 secondary banking crisis, illustrates this process. Lending to developing countries in the late 1970s, and the international banking crisis in 1983, is another example.

[11] *John Maynard Keynes*, by Hyman Minsky, New York, 1976, Chapter 6.

Control of Interest Rates

The government, acting through the Bank of England, 'controls' interest rates by open market operations. But it cannot control *both* interest rates *and* the growth of the money supply independently within the present arrangements. For example, if the government wishes to make short-term interest rates rise, the Bank of England attempts to 'keep money short in the market . . .'.[12] Higher interest rates reduce borrowing and hence the money supply, though in practice the short-term results can be perverse. Thus the money stock grew rapidly in 1980 and 1981 *in spite* of high interest rates (Diagram 6.5). The recession at first increased borrowing by companies to meet redundancy payments and other losses. High interest rates themselves increased borrowing by some agents who could not meet interest payments without further borrowing. Also, some borrowers may have been slow to realize that interest rates were going to remain at high levels, so postponing the effects of the increase in interest rates.

In the long term there are also limits to the government's control. If a government pushes down interest rates, this will lead to faster growth of M. If this leads to faster inflation nominal interest rates will rise for the reasons given earlier. There are also links between the government's borrowing requirement and interest rates, which are examined in Chapter 11.

Some Keynesians believe that the links between increases in M and prices are weak, and, within limits, they would not be concerned about the rate of increase of M. They advocate that the authorities use their control interest rates to maintain the exchange rate at a target level.

During the 1960s the authorities issued directives to banks limiting their lending, particularly for speculative purposes. Such controls allow the authorities increased scope for lowering interest rates to increase demand. Keynesians point to the costs of maintaining stable financial markets in the absence of controls, and the repeated cuts in the PSBR which

[12] Evidence of the Chief Cashier of the Bank of England to the Radcliffe Committee. Report of the Committee, *HMSO*, 1959, p. 122.

have been made to avoid financial crises and higher interest rates. The case against such controls is that they fail in the long-term because other institutions displace banks by borrowing and lending funds. If the government tries to plug such attempts the controls become messy; if they do not, the controls discriminate and are unfair to banks.

Money Supply and Interest Rates

Keynesians expect an increase in M to lead to a fall in interest rates and an increase in aggregate demand for goods and services. If the supply is increased the price will fall. Diagram 6.6 shows that short-term interest rates fell in 1971 when M began to rise more rapidly, but that a rise followed. Keynesians could argue that the rise in interest rates was caused by faster inflation from 1973, but that this was not attributable to the increase in M, and that the real rate of interest fell. Monetarists contend that the increase in M led to faster inflation.

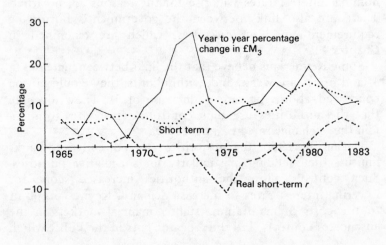

DIAGRAM 6.6   Changes in £M$_3$ and interest rates

Sources: *ETAS* 1984, and *Economic Trends*, March, 1984.

Conclusions

Shackle's comment about the rate of interest 'as the pivot of the ... economic system' was referred to in the introduction. In this chapter some relationships between this key variable and other variables have been examined. In later chapters the relationships between consumption, investment, the PSBR, and interest rates are considered, but already it has been shown that this instrument for bringing about adjustment in the economy is affected by a number of forces. If inflation occurs, or may occur, in the future there is uncertainty about the level of the long-term interest rate, and after a period of rapid inflation real long-term interest rates can get stuck at historically high levels. Interest rates ruling overseas, particularly in the USA, also influence interest rates in Britain. These factors must hinder the movement of interest rates to maintain equilibrium within the UK economy at a high level of employment.

Consumption and the Savings Ratio

Introduction

In a simplified Keynesian framework, income is the sum of consumption and saving. In practice, for national income accounting the economy is divided into four sectors—the personal, companies, Government, and overseas sectors. Consumption is then related to personal disposable income (PDI), a part of total income. The main sources of personal income in 1979 are shown in Table 7.1; they are wages and salaries, income from self employment, rents, dividends, interest, and national insurance benefits. The main deductions from personal income to generate PDI are direct taxes and national insurance contributions.

In this chapter we focus on personal savings, the residual after deducting consumption from PDI, as a percentage of

TABLE 7.1   *Personal disposable income in 1979*

		£bn	% of TPI
Income before tax			
Income from employment[a]		114.8	67.8
Income from self-employment		15.3	9.0
Rent, dividends, and net interest[b]		18.0	10.6
National insurance benefits		21.0	12.4
Total personal income (TPI)		169.3	100.0
less:			
UK taxes on income	21.7		12.8
National insurance contributions	11.5	33.4	6.8 19.7
Total personal disposable income		135.9	80.3
less Consumers' expenditure		118.4	69.9
Balance — *Saving* by the personal sector		17.5	10.3
Saving as a percentage of PDI		12.9	

Source: *National Income and Expenditure*, 1983.

[a] Including employers' national insurance contributions.
[b] Including imputed rent of owner-occupied dwellings.

PDI (the nominal savings ratio). The nominal savings ratio for 1979 was estimated to be 12.9 per cent in 1983. If saving is a stable function of PDI, then so is consumption, which is by far the largest component of aggregate demand. Changes in the savings ratio have important implications for both output and employment. A Keynesian government wishing to regulate aggregate demand must forecast the savings ratio in order to set its expenditure and taxes at levels compatible with the level of aggregate demand it seeks.

We start by showing that in Britain there has been an increase in the nominal savings ratio since 1950, and that the ratio has fluctuated. Theories which might explain the increase and the fluctuations are outlined and then tested. The saving of the other sectors of the economy is outlined in the Statistical Appendix.[1]

The Savings Ratio 1950–82

The nominal savings ratio since 1950 is shown in Diagram 7.1. Two features emerge clearly from the diagram; there has been an upward trend in the savings ratio, along with pronounced cyclical variations. Between 1950 and 1954 the savings ratio averaged 2.8 per cent (that is to say, savings represented 2.8 per cent of PDI); between 1978 and 1982 it averaged 12.5 per cent. It is possible to split the thirty-year period into four stages. From 1950 to 1961, the savings ratio rose, and the rise was faster in the last two years of this period. Between 1961 and 1971, it fluctuated around a steady average of about 8 per cent. From 1972 the savings ratio again increased, but since 1980 it has fallen. Upon these underlying trends is superimposed a cyclical pattern.

The UK post-war experience of a rising savings ratio is not universal. For the United States there is no evidence of a rising savings ratio, either historically or since 1950 (Diagram 7.2).

Estimates of the Savings Ratio

Estimation of the savings ratio requires compromises of

[1] See Appendix 7.1.

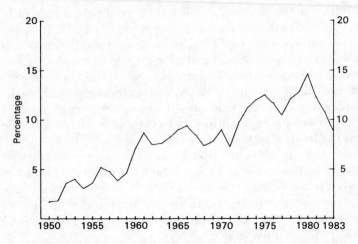

DIAGRAM 7.1   Savings as a percentage of personal disposable
income UK

Source: *ETAS* 1984, and *Economic Trends*, March 1984.

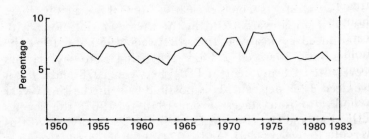

DIAGRAM 7.2   Savings as a percentage of personal disposable
income USA

Source: *Survey of Current Business*, various issues.

principle. The first problem concerns the definition of the
personal sector. In addition to households, official statisticians
include unincorporated businesses, non-profit making bodies,
and trusts in the personal sector. Ideally unincorporated
businesses would be combined with companies in a business
sector and be excluded from the personal sector. Inclusion of
business in the personal sector means that PDI and personal

savings include stock appreciation and are calculated before any deduction is made for depreciation of business assets.

A second qualification to the nominal savings ratio as an indicator of households' saving concerns the measurement of income. On a theoretical level, income is defined as the amount a consumer could consume while maintaining his wealth intact, so capital gains and losses would be included in both income and saving. They are excluded from the definition of income used by statisticians. Inflation causes losses in real terms on financial assets. In this chapter inflation is treated as a factor influencing nominal savings. The choice of nominal savings rather than real savings (savings after providing for gains or losses on financial assets caused by inflation) as the basis for analysis follows the method used for the compilation of official statistics and the procedure used by forecasters.

A third definitional problem concerns the boundary between purchases of goods for consumption and for use as capital equipment. In practice, acquisitions of houses are treated as capital transactions, and all other expenditure by households on goods and services as consumption. Plainly cars and other durable goods are capital goods for households; it is the services derived from these goods which are consumed.

The estimate of savings in national income accounts are calculated as a residual. That is to say, anything left out of PDI after all recorded expenditures have been deducted is counted as savings. In practice the initial estimates of savings are subject to substantial amendment. This is not surprising since savings are calculated as a balance between two large aggregates, personal income and expenditure, which are revised as Census and other data become available. An example of the effects of revisions is shown in Diagram 7.3. The general pattern of changes of the savings ratio is not altered, but from 1955 the revised estimates show a lower savings ratio.

Theories of Consumption and Savings

The theories which could explain movements in the savings

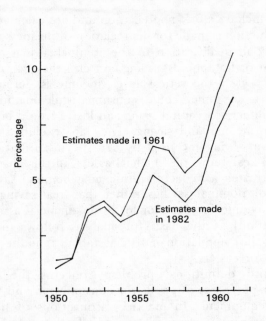

DIAGRAM 7.3   Estimates of savings as a percentage of PDI

Sources: *MDS* 1961, and *ETAS* 1982.

ratio are now outlined. The pre-Keynesian explanations for saving focused on traditions, the distribution of income (an unequal distribution increased saving), the rate of interest, and wealth. The rate of interest was the reward for post-poning consumption:'. . . a fall in the rate of interest will generally lower the margin at which a person finds it just worth while to give up present pleasures for the sake of those future pleasures that are secured by saving some of his means'.[2]

In the *General Theory*, Keynes wrote that, 'The funda-mental psychological law . . . is that men are disposed, as a rule and on the average, to increase their consumption as their income increases, but not by as much as the increase in their income.'[3] This proposition does not imply that a greater proportion of income will necessarily be saved as real income

[2] A. Marshall, *Principles of Economics*, London, 1890, p. 195.
[3] *General Theory*, p. 96.

increases. But Keynes also wrote of the reasons which 'will lead, as a rule, to a greater proportion of income being saved as real income increases'.[4] The security and flexibility that accumulated savings (wealth) provide may make saving the equivalent of 'superior' or luxury goods, and mean that the savings ratio will increase as real per capita income rises.

Historical evidence showing long-term stability of the savings ratio in the USA prompted American economists to revise Keynes's theory of the consumption function. Duesenberry, Friedman, and Modigliani and Brumberg set up hypotheses which could explain a constant long-run savings ratio compatible with rising income. Duesenberry suggested that the amount consumed out of current income would be affected by the previous peak of income, and that saving depended on relative income. As average income rose consumption increased at roughly the same rate, but at any one time those with a high income, relative to their social group, saved proportionately more than average.

New Theories of the Consumption Function

The new theories of the consumption function developed by Friedman and Modigliani and Brumberg during the 1950s were built on the idea that individuals whose income fluctuates will try to even out their consumption. Instead of saving being a sort of superior good, saving is for the purpose of consumption-spreading. Under Friedman's Permanent Income Hypothesis (PIH) individuals form an expectation of their long-run (or permanent) income. Keynes's 'fundamental law' of consumption applies to permanent income, not the fluctuating level of current income. If all changes in income are foreseen, the difference between current income and the permanent level of income is saved. This theory provides an explanation for pro-cyclical fluctuations in the savings ratio around a constant level. For example, when actual income rises above the permanent level the difference will be saved. An important question concerns the way individuals arrive at an estimate of their permanent income, and how they revise this estimate over time. Friedman proposed an 'adaptive'

[4] *General Theory*, p. 97.

or 'error-learning' method of expectation formation, whereby estimates of permanent income are revised to incorporate new information, including changes in actual income. Anticipated deviations of income from expected income will be saved. Windfall or unexpected changes in income will influence consumption if they change expected permanent income. Friedman claims that the transitory components of income which include anticipated temporary changes in income and measurement errors as well as windfalls, are not correlated with consumption.

Friedman treats consumer durables as capital goods which contrasts with the official definitions of consumption and saving. Friedman includes durables in the asset portfolios of households. Changes which cause people to increase their estimates of their permanent income will lead to increased demand for the services obtained from consumer durables and to purchases of consumer durables. Friedman writes, 'is not the timing of the replacement of durable goods and additions to the stock of such goods likely to some extent to be adjusted so as to coincide with windfalls?'.[5] If income rises, expenditure on durables is likely to rise. If expenditure on durables is volatile, saving as defined for official statistics will fluctuate more than saving defined so that consumer durables are treated as capital goods.

Modigliani and Brumberg's life-cycle hypothesis suggests an individual will determine his consumption in order to smooth consumption over his life-time; saving and acquiring assets during his working life and disposing of them during retirement. This hypothesis is also compatible with a constant long-run savings ratio, but changes in the structure of the population and/or changes in the rate of growth of real income can change the savings ratio. An increase in the proportion of young people who save and less elderly dissavers will increase saving. A decline in the rate of growth of real income which does not affect asset values will reduce the saving of young savers, but not affect the dis-saving of the elderly. In practice, a slower rate of growth may be accompanied by declines in the value of assets which will reduce dis-saving by the elderly.

[5] M. Friedman, *A Theory of the Consumption Function*, London, 1957, p. 28.

Inflation

Until the 1970s inflation was seen as a factor which could *reduce* the savings ratio. If people expected prices to rise they would bring forward consumption to take advantage of lower prices. During the 1970s as both inflation and the savings ratio rose, theories were advanced to explain why inflation could lead to an *increase* in saving. The most convincing explanation is that households base their decisions about consumption and saving not on their money income alone, they deduct some capital losses from their income. In particular they deduct the reduction in the real value of monetary assets caused by inflation. Although the effects of inflation cancel out in aggregate—the gains made by borrowers are offset by the losses incurred by the lenders or depositors—inflation could affect the savings ratio. Gains and losses on loans between households cancel out. (This applies where some households deposit money with banks or building societies and these institutions lend the deposits to other households.) But the personal sector is a substantial creditor of the government sector—past governments have borrowed and issued bonds and national saving securities in exchange. Most of these claims on the government are fixed in nominal terms, and their real value is eroded by inflation. The exceptions are index linked bonds. This means households lose and the government sector gains from inflation, and households may save a higher proportion of their income to rebuild their wealth in real terms.

The argument can be put another way. All interest receipts and payments are treated as income in the national income accounts. In practice, a proportion of money interest payments during a period of inflation are a repayment of capital, not income. The public realizes this and considers this interest as capital not income.

There is a further twist to this argument; as inflation reduces the real value of the government's debts to the public, it is simultaneously reducing future taxes in real terms. If households take account of this reduction, if they explicitly or implicitly estimate their future tax liabilities and treat the discounted value of the taxes as a liability when estimating their wealth and permanent income, then inflation would be neutral. The loss on the real value of bonds and national savings would be offset by the reduction in expected future taxes. There would be no effect on consumption/saving decisions, unless the marginal propensity to consume out of permanent income of those who gain from inflation, whose tax liabilities are reduced, differs from those who lose, those who hold bonds, etc.[6]

Other links between the savings ratio and inflation have been suggested:

(a) There may be a lag between changes in income and changes in consumption. If consumption during a quarter is related to money income in the previous quarter, then a simultaneous acceleration in wages and prices will lead to a fall in real consumption in the quarter following the acceleration, and a rise in the savings ratio. Money incomes and savings will have risen but real consumption will have fallen.

(b) The uncertainty created by a high and unstable rate of inflation could cause people to save more. The degree of uncertainty is difficult to quantify and may not be tied to the inflation rate in a simple linear relationship.

(c) The personal sector includes businesses, and stock appreciation during periods of inflation may boost savings.[7]

(d) Unexpected inflation favours debtors and harms creditors, so it tends to favour the young who borrow to buy houses and who may have a high propensity to save. The marginal propensity to save of the creditors could be lower than for debtors.[8]

The Consumption Function

Analytically, we can divide changes in the savings ratio between those attributable to movements *along* the consumption function (caused by changes in income) and shifts of the consumption function itself. If the consumption function is of the form shown in Diagram 7.4(a), then savings will

---

[6] These relationships are analysed by Robert J. Barro, 'Are Government Bonds Net Wealth?' in *Journal of Political Economy*, 1974, p. 1095.

[7] Stock appreciation is described in note 5.2 in the Statistical Appendix.

[8] See Appendix 7.2.

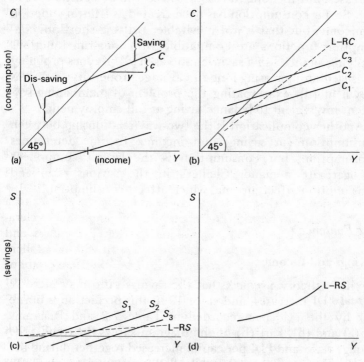

DIAGRAM 7.4   The consumption function

rise with income, the marginal propensity to consume is constant, while the average propensity to consume falls and the average propensity to save (the savings ratio) will rise.[9]

An alternative development is shown in part (b) of the diagram. Here it is assumed that the relationship between consumption and income shifts through time. There are short-run consumption functions which drift upwards, perhaps in response to the development of new consumer goods and services and/or with the trend increase of income. As income oscillates about its long-term trend, savings and the savings ratio change. If the long-run consumption function is as shown in (b), then savings will increase as income

[9] The marginal propensity to consume, c/y, is the proportion of a small change in income which is consumed.

increases, but the long-run savings *ratio* will be constant (as in (c)). So far consumption has been treated as a linear function of income, but that is not inevitable. Drifting short-run consumption functions are compatible with long-run functions implying an increasing savings ratio as in (d). Keynes probably envisaged an increasing long-run average propensity to save as shown in (d)—exacerbating the problem of maintaining sufficient investment to balance saving at full employment.

Another complication is the two-way relationship between consumption (or saving) and income. Income determines consumption, but consumption is the largest component of aggregate demand. Changes in the savings ratio and consumption affect income, which affects consumption.

The Evidence

Savings and Income

Keynes's theory predicts that the savings ratio may increase as real PDI increases, and since 1950 this prediction is borne out by the evidence recorded in Table 7.2 and Diagrams 7.5(a) and (b). Part (b) of the diagram shows the trends; the savings ratio and PDI per capita increased together during the 1950s. During the 1960s while PDI continued to grow the savings ratio fluctuated around 8 per cent. From 1972 the savings ratio increased again to a peak of 14.6 per cent in 1980, but since 1981 it has fallen to about 9 per cent in 1983.

To test whether the relationship is causal, whether changes in PDI lead to increases in the savings ratio, the year to year changes in PDI and the savings ratio were examined. The test works by observing whether larger than average increases in PDI are associated with larger than average increases in the savings ratio. Diagrams 7.6(a) and (b) do suggest a causal relationship. The savings ratio rose in years when real PDI per capita was increasing rapidly; 1960, 1972, 1973, and 1978, and fell in 1976, 1977, 1981, and 1982 when PDI per capita fell. An equation was fitted to the scatter of data for the years 1960 to 1973, only 14 observations. Later years were omitted because the purpose of the exercise was to check whether experience after 1973 was similar to earlier

TABLE 7.2 *The savings ratio*

	The nominal savings ratio %	Year to year change in the savings ratio[a]	PDI per capita at 1980 prices (1980 = 100)	Year to year % change in PDI per capita	Change in retail prices[b]	Real short-term interest rate
	(1)	(2)	(3)	(4)	(5)	(6)
1963	7.6	+0.1	67.4	+4.2	1.9	+1.8
1964	8.2	+0.6	69.4	+3.1	4.7	−0.1
1965	9.0	+0.8	70.7	+1.9	4.4	+1.4
1966	9.4	+0.4	72.0	+1.7	3.7	+2.3
1967	8.5	−0.9	72.6	+0.9	2.5	+3.2
1968	7.4	−1.1	73.6	+1.4	6.1	+0.9
1969	7.8	+0.4	74.0	+0.5	4.8	+2.7
1970	9.0	+1.2	76.7	+3.6	8.1	−1.1
1971	7.3	−1.7	77.4	+0.9	8.6	−2.8
1972	9.7	+2.4	83.9	+8.5	7.7	−2.0
1973	11.2	+1.5	89.5	+6.7	11.2	−1.8
1974	12.0	+0.8	88.8	−0.8	19.5	−6.8
1975	12.5	+0.5	88.8	0.0	24.2	−11.2
1976	11.7	−0.8	88.2	−0.7	15.8	−4.1
1977	10.5	−1.2	86.8	−1.6	11.0	−3.0
1978	12.1	+1.6	93.2	+7.4	8.8	−0.4
1979	12.8	+0.7	98.6	+5.8	17.8	−4.1
1980	14.6	+1.8	100.0	+1.4	14.1	+0.9
1981	12.3	−2.3	97.6	−2.4	12.0	+1.2
1982	10.8	−1.5	97.2	−0.4	5.2	+6.5
1983	8.9[c]				5.2	+4.4

Sources: *ETAS* 1984, and *Economic Trends*, March 1984.

[a] In percentage points.
[b] The change in prices is between the beginning and end of each year.
[c] Estimated.

experience. That the equation of the line has a constant term −0.49 means that the savings ratio falls by half of one percentage point in a year in which PDI per capita does not change. In a year when PDI per capita changes, the savings ratio changes in the same direction by 34 per cent of a percentage point for each one per cent change in PDI per capita. In years when the growth of PDI per capita is more than 1½ per cent the savings ratio rises.

There are important deviations from the relationship; in

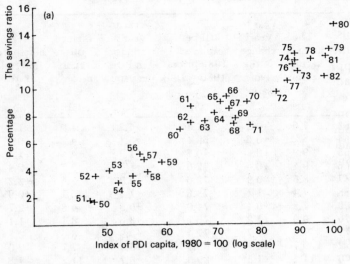

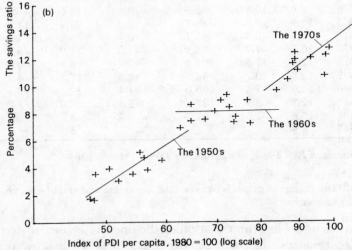

DIAGRAM 7.5   The personal savings ratio and personal
disposable income per capita at 1980 prices

(a) Scatter diagram.
(b) Free-hand trends.

Sources: as for Table 7.2.

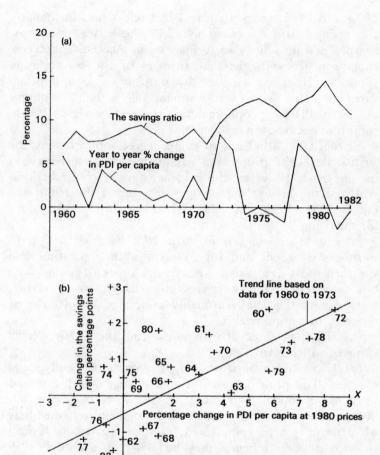

DIAGRAM 7.6   The savings ratio and year to year percentage
                changes in PDI per capita

(a) Time series.
(b) A scatter diagram; $Y = -0.49 + 0.34X$.

Sources: as for Table 7.2.

1974 and 1975, years when real PDI fell or was unchanged, the savings ratio rose, and in 1980 the savings ratio rose sharply despite only a small increase in income. The exceptions conflict with the new theories of the consumption function. If savings is for the purpose of consumption-spreading, the savings ratio should fall with a *temporary* decline in PDI, as people maintain the previous level of consumption out of a lower income.

Keynes's hypothesis is to some degree supported by the British data –the proportion of income saved increased as income rose. However, the evidence reveals contradictions. Why did the savings ratio stop rising during the 1960s and fall in 1981, 1982, and 1983? There are other explanations for the rising British savings ratio:

(a) The low savings ratio *circa* 1950 was a reaction to shortages of goods and forced saving during war-time and the early post-war period when many types of goods were not available to buy or were rationed. The rising savings ratio during the 1950s probably contained an element of recovery to a normal level.

(b) The high rates of inflation during the 1970s were a cause of a high savings ratio.

(c) There were institutional, demographic, and social changes. The principal institutional change was the spread of pension funds. This increased the level of committed saving as the proportion of the population who were members of pension schemes increased, though a part of saving through pension schemes may be offset by a reduction in other forms of saving. Net saving through life assurance and superannuation schemes increased from 5.7 per cent of PDI between 1963 and 1968 to 7.5 per cent between 1976 and 1981.[10] The importance of pension funds and life assurance is shown in Table A.7.2 in the Appendix. Equity in pension funds and life assurance were the largest group of financial assets held by the personal sector—£89 bn in 1980. Changes in population structure are another factor influencing the savings ratio. Children are expensive and may cause a fall in income as well, so less children during the 1970s were probably shifting the consumption function in the direction

[10] Source: *Economic Trends*, November 1981, p. 116.

of increased saving. An increase in the proportion of married women in the working population could have increased the savings ratio. On the other side, the increasing proportion of the elderly in the population probably reduced it.

(d) Rising unemployment during the 1970s reflects the slow growth of output and hence income, and so some effects of rising unemployment on saving could be incorporated in the effects of changes in PDI. However, unemployment may generate separate effects on the savings ratio and this is more likely when unemployment rises above what has come to be considered as the 'normal' level. The fear of becoming unemployed may be proportionately greater and may trigger an increase in the savings ratio. Also, unemployment increases uncertainty, which is another reason to hold back from consumption expenditure and to save. Unemployment is shown in Diagram 7.9; it rose from 1974 to 1977. The importance of unemployment in increasing the savings ratio may be questioned because the savings ratio fell in the 1980s , while unemployment continued to rise, but simultaneously slower inflation may have reduced the savings ratio and could conceal the effects of higher unemployment.

Permanent Income Hypothesis (PIH)

Conventional tests of the PIH relate savings to an average of current and lagged income. A simple test of this sort is described in the Statistical Appendix,[11] but the test does not provide an improved explanation of movements of savings. Nevertheless, events during the 1970s can be reconciled with the PIH. Agents' perceptions of their permanent income may have been affected by the recession, rising unemployment, and in 1974 and 1975, falls in share and property prices which are described below. Agents' expectations of the growth of their income in the future may have fallen and led them to save an increased proportion of their income.

Saving and Inflation

The nominal savings ratio and the rate of inflation moved together during the 1970s, though not in precise year to

[11] See Appendix 7.3.

year synchronization. Diagrams 7.7(a) and (b) show the evidence. Earlier it was shown that, relative to changes in PDI per capita, 1974 and 1975 were exceptional years. They were also years of rapid inflation and this could explain why savings did not fall back when PDI per capita fell.

Taking account of the effects inflation has on the value of monetary assets held by the personal sector has a dramatic effect on the measurement of the savings ratio for the sector. It has been estimated that the real savings (after allowing for real losses on monetary assets and gains on monetary liabilities) were negative during the 1970s.[12] The erosion of the real value of financial assets described earlier seems a powerful reason for the link between saving and inflation, but the other explanations for a relationship between inflation and saving may have contributed.

Earlier it was noted that the effect of inflation on the wealth of the personal sector was neutral if people took future real tax liabilities into the reckoning. Faster inflation did lead to increased saving, and this suggests that people do not fully discount future reductions in real taxes.

Saving and Interest

The expected real post-tax (net) rate of interest is a measure of the incentive to postpone consumption and the disincentive to borrowing—negative saving. Diagram 7.8 shows the savings ratio and the real *gross* short-term rate of interest. (The rate of tax payable on interest income varies with the tax position of recipients.) The savings ratio *rose* during the 1970s while real interest rates were low or negative. This relationship could be explained by agents making errors when forecasting future real rates of interest; they may have over estimated the rates, or the factors which were increasing savings swamped any of the effects of low and negative real interest rates to reduce saving.

[12] *Bank of England Quarterly*, June 1981, p. 234.

Personal Sector Saving	1967–69	1970–72	1973–75	1976–78
average ⎰Nominal	1.3	1.9	5.1	7.8
£bn ⎱Real	−0.3	−1.4	−4.6	−0.5

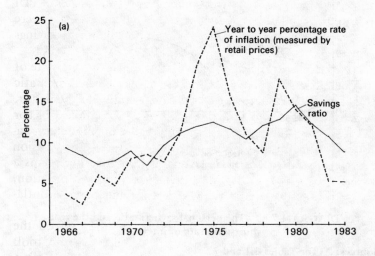

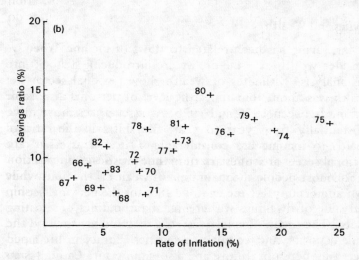

DIAGRAM 7.7   The savings ratio and the rate of inflation

(a) Graph.
(b) Scatter diagram.

Sources: As for Table 7.2.

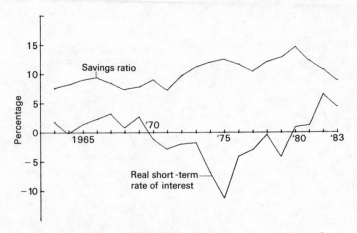

DIAGRAM 7.8   The personal savings ratio and the real
short-term rate of interest

Sources: As for Tables 6.1 and 7.2.

Saving and Wealth

So far, saving has been related to flows of income. When we consider wealth as a factor, we are introducing a stock into the analysis. Estimates of wealth show personal sector net wealth was about four times the level of personal disposable income between 1975 and 1979. As asset prices move quite substantially from year to year, the shifts in the ratio of wealth to income are considerable. (The net assets of the personal sector are summarized in the Statistical Appendix.[13])

For most people the main item of wealth is the house they own and occupy. At the end of 1980, for the personal sector, the value of dwellings was greater than holdings of financial assets. The main financial assets are building society and bank deposits, and company securities. Equity in life assurance and pensions funds are also important. Capital gains from owner-occupied houses are generally not realized, though people may increase their mortgate or other borrowing in response to an increase in the value of the property, and increase their consumption expenditure.[14] Similarly, an

[13] See Appendix 7.4.
[14] It is claimed that the appreciation of house prices in the USA was a factor contributing to the fall in the American savings ratio at the end of the 1970s.

appreciation of assets held by life assurance and pension funds is not spendable, but it may influence saving out of other income and borrowing.

Information about the movement of share prices is readily available, and one index is shown in Diagram 7.9. During the 1970s share prices were very volatile, and between 1972 and 1974 they slumped. One response of households to the fluctuations may be to even out the changes in values by considering a moving average of values when deciding on expenditure. However a sharp change in values like that in 1974 is likely to affect expenditure immediately, and have effects over a time span of several years, or even more. This makes for great difficulty in assessing the full impact of changing asset prices on consumption. There is some indication of the expected inverse relationship with saving. Earlier, the high savings ratio in 1974 was noted, the year in which share prices (and the prices of many other assets) plunged.

Share prices in real terms fared very badly during the 1970s, while savings increased. One reason why share prices did not keep pace with inflation was the decline in the share of profits in GDP which was described in Chapter 5. Diagram 7.6(b) shows that the savings ratio fell faster than 'expected' given the fall in PDI in 1981 and 1982. One explanation for the fall in the savings ratio between 1981 and 1983 was the slower rate of inflation. Another factor could be rising share prices. Changes in wealth attributable to changes in asset prices can be very large in relation to changes in income. Personal disposable income increased by 6.7 per cent between the middle two quarters of 1982 and 1983, equivalent to an increase of £12.5 bn at an annual rate. Between June 1982 and June 1983 the value of the financial assets held by the personal sector, including the sector's equity in insurance and pension funds, rose by £108 bn. (This increase included acquisitions of assets, as well as increases in values of existing holdings.) The date are compatible with changes in asset values having a muted impact on consumption.

Saving and Borrowing

Borrowing to finance consumption is negative saving. If

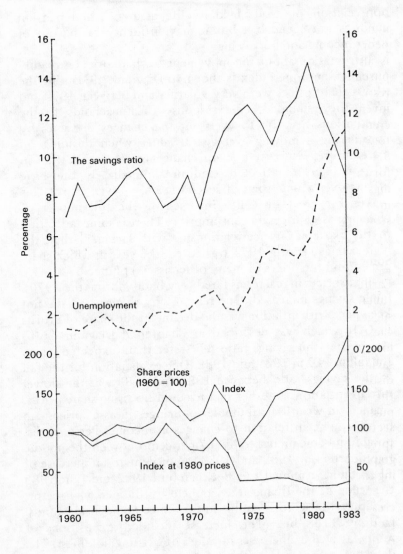

DIAGRAM 7.9 The savings ratio, unemployment, and share prices[a]

[a] The index of share prices is the FT index of ordinary share prices which is published in *ETAS* 1984. Indices of share prices based on wider ranges of shares indicate less sharp falls in share prices in real terms between 1963 and 1983.

borrowing increases, this reduces the savings ratio. Borrowing by consumers is a function of income—as income rises people can increase their commitments to repayments. It is also affected by changes in the official regulation of hire purchase deals and bank lending, such as the release of restrictions which occurred in 1972 and 1982, and the invention and development of new methods of providing credit. Borrowings swung from 8.0 per cent of PDI in 1972 to 3.3 per cent in 1974 and 2.4 per cent in 1975, and back to 5.4 per cent in 1979.[15] The borrowing spree in 1972 brought forward consumption and could explain the rise in the savings ratio in 1974 and 1975, but the low levels of borrowing in 1974 and 1975 may also reflect uncertainty caused by strikes, political changes, and high unemployment.

Some Conclusions

Earlier we distinguished between shifts of the consumption function and movements along it. The evidence described suggests that the major shifts in the savings ratio have been caused by shifts of the consumption function. Abnormally low savings immediately after the war led to increasing savings during the 1950s. Faster inflation and economic disturbances were responsible for the increased saving during the 1970s. An important mechanism by which inflation pushes up savings may be eroding the value of personal sector financial assets. Throughout the post-war period the spread of pension funds and, possibly, in the 1970s, demographic changes contributed to increased saving—again shifting the consumption function.

The idea of the savings ratio slowly rising with increasing real income is appealing, though there are other factors which can explain events during the post-war period. A qualification to the emphasis on the importance of inflation and increasing PDI as influences on the savings ratio is that personal sector saving in the USA did not rise much during the 1970s.

An explanation for the cyclical pattern of the savings ratio

[15] Source: *Economic Trends*, November 1981, p. 116. Borrowing for house purchase is excluded.

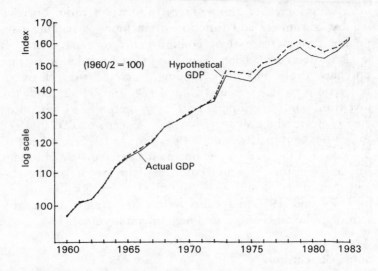

DIAGRAM 7.10   A comparison of actual GDP and counter-functional GDP with the savings ratio maintained at a constant 7.8 per cent[a].
(The average for 1960/62)

[a] The method of calculation is described in the text, and the Statistical Appendix 5.5.

was provided by the permanent income and life cycle hypotheses. However, the predicted pro-cyclical pattern did not apply consistently. In 1974, 1975, and 1980, when the economy was moving into recession, the savings ratio rose instead of declining. Uncertainty and fear caused by the recessions, with increasing unemployment and collapsing share prices in 1974, may have increased savings in these years. This increased the severity of the recession.

The importance of movements of the savings ratio is illustrated in Diagram 7.10, which shows the hypothetical track of GDP if the savings ratio had remained at the value it averaged between 1960 and 1962, and its actual path. These calculations are based on the implausible assumption that, had the savings ratio been different, there would have been no changes apart from the direct effects on domestic output and imports.[16] The largest adjustment was for 1980;

[16] See Appendix 7.5.

GDP would have been 2.8 per cent higher if the savings ratio had been at the 1960/2 level.

What can be concluded about the stability of the savings ratio and the consumption function? The savings ratio has shown considerable fluctuations as well as trend changes. This does not necessarily indicate that saving cannot be predicted. If saving behaviour were well understood then fluctuations could be predicted by examining the determinants of savings. But while *ex-post* explanations of the movements in the savings ratio can be provided, it is the case that *ex-ante* these fluctuations were not foreseen. The conclusion must be that saving and consumption are hard to predict, and the post-war consumption function was not as stable as Keynes hypothesized in the 1930s.

8

Investment

Keynes emphasized the volatility of investment and its importance for explaining fluctuations in demand. In addition, asset accumulation through investment has been seen as crucial for growth. The experience of the 1970s suggests that both these concepts require modification.

Definitions of Investment

Fixed investment is a heterogeneous total, comprising housing and business investment in both the public and private sectors. Fixed investment, or gross fixed capital formation, as defined for National Income purposes and shown in company accounts, is not the same as total investment in the future by companies. Most expenditure on Research and Development (R. & D.) and marketing is excluded. So also is the training of employees. In 1983 ICI's expenditure on R. & D.[1] was £276m—equal to 76 per cent of its world-wide fixed investment and 144 per cent of its fixed investment in the UK. GEC is coy about its expenditure on R. & D. in its published accounts, but the company's expenditure on R. & D. exceeds its investment in fixed assets. Siemens, the German equivalent of GEC, which employed 212,000 people in Germany in 1983 (equal to 4 per cent of the UK labour force in manufacturing) was less shy than GEC about its R. & D. expenditure. It spent about £900m in this area in 1982/3, twice its capital expenditure and equal to about 18 per cent of R. & D. performed by industry in the UK.[2] R. & D., together with marketing, are important elements of investment expenditure, since they involve the design and promotion of exclusive and better quality products. With these caveats, aggregate

[1] Includes expenditure on technical service.
[2] The estimate is given in Siemens's published accounts.

investment as defined for National Income purposes is now considered.

Movements in Investment Expenditure

Gross fixed investment increased in absolute terms, and as a proportion of GDP through the 1950s and 1960s. Between 1950 and 1954 it averaged £15.2 bn at 1980 prices, and increased to £35.7 bn a year between 1965 and 1969. Investment as a percentage of GDP (both at current prices) rose from 13.7 to 18.4 per cent over the same period. This relationship is shown in Diagram 8.1. The percentage reached a peak of 20.2 in 1974 and had fallen to 15.2 by 1983. Investment since 1970 is shown in Diagram 8.2. In terms of 1980 prices, total gross fixed investment was at a level very similar in 1983 to what it was in 1970. The distinction between gross and net investment was drawn in Chapter 4. The capital stock and depreciation, the annual charge for the depletion of the capital stock, were increasing during the 1970s, so net fixed investment, which is also shown in Diagram 8.2, tailed off dramatically, from £19.8 bn at 1980 prices in 1970, to £8.5 bn in 1982.

Total investment can be analysed in three ways: its division between the private and public sectors, by type of assets, and by industry group. Movements in private and public investment since 1970 are shown in Diagram 8.2. There has been a substantial increase in private fixed investment since 1970. From 1976 public investment fell very sharply, from £17.1 bn to £11.7 bn in 1983 at 1980 prices.

Fixed investment by type of asset is summarized in Diagram 8.3. Investment in plant and machinery was the most buoyant, and is the element on which the rate of return during the early years in use should be relatively high.[3] The initial rates of return on buildings are generally lower because they have a longer life over which to earn a return, partly because they are not made obsolete by technical progress to the same extent as machinery. Investment in housing fell markedly in the late 1970s.[4]

[3] See Appendix 8.1.
[4] Throughout this chapter the terms 'houses' and 'housing' are used, rather than the term 'dwellings' used for the national income accounts. Housing includes flats and blocks of flats.

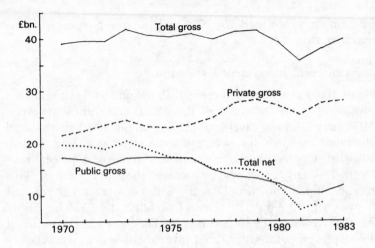

DIAGRAM 8.1   Fixed investment as a percentage of GDP
at current prices.

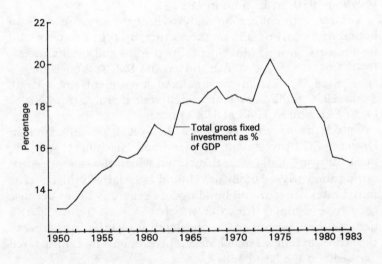

DIAGRAM 8.2   Fixed investment at 1980 prices

Sources: *ETAS* 1984, and *Economic Trends*, 1984.

Investment by industry group since 1970 is shown in Diagram 8.4. One striking feature is the importance of investment in the service sector of the economy; it now represents nearly half of total gross investment. Gross investment in manufacturing industries has been volatile, falling sharply in the recessions of 1974/5 and 1979/81, and was still falling in 1982. In this chapter, fixed investment in manufacturing, housing, and services are considered in some detail; space precludes analysing investment in all sectors.

An International Comparison

From an international perspective, the UK has had a low investment and high consumption economy (Table 8.1). Gross fixed investment in the UK as a percentage of private and public consumption, averaged 22.1 per cent in the 1960s and 23.1 per cent in the 1970s, lower than any of the other leading industrial countries apart from the USA. There is an evident association between higher rates of growth and higher investment. What is not clear from the statistics is the extent to which investment causes growth.

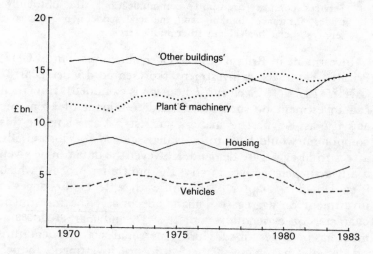

DIAGRAM 8.3   Gross fixed investment by type of asset
(at 1980 prices)

Sources: *ETAS* 1984, and *Economic Trends*, 1984.

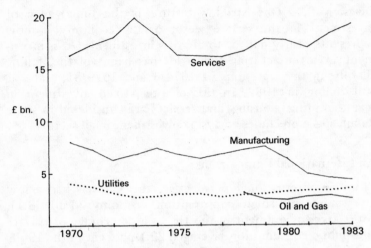

DIAGRAM 8.4   Gross fixed investment by industry group[a]
(at 1980 prices)

Source: *National Income and Expenditure*, 1981 and 1983.

[a] Excluded sectors: agriculture, forestry, and fishing, mining and quarrying, construction and housing.
[b] Services comprise transport, communications, the distributive trades, insurance, banking and financial services, miscellaneous services, social, health, and other public services.

Investment in Britain has been a small component of GDP. Private sector fixed investment represented 15 per cent of GDP in 1979 (13 per cent if housing is excluded). How then can investment be such a crucial determinant of economic activity as Keynesian analysis suggests? Variations in this component would have to be violent indeed to substantially affect total aggregate demand. However the data can be given a different perspective. Firstly, the multiplier process, which is explained in Chapter 11, magnifies the effects of changes in investment on aggregate demand. Secondly, the investment character of expenditure on R. & D. and market development has been described. Thirdly, personal sector expenditure on durables has many of the features of investment, though it is classified as consumers' expenditure. These expenditures might move in a similar way to fixed investment.

TABLE 8.1 *Growth and investment in leading industrial countries, 1960–1980*

	1960s		1970s	
	Average annual rate of growth 1960–70 %	Gross fixed investment as % of public and private consumption 1960–69 (av.) %	Average annual rate of growth 1970–80 %	Gross fixed investment as % of public and private consumption 1970–79 (av.) %
Japan	10.6	49.3	4.9	51.6
West Germany	4.6	35.0	2.8	30.5
France	5.6	30.1	3.6	30.5
Italy	5.7	28.2	3.1	25.9
UK	2.8	22.1	1.8	23.1
USA	3.9	22.4	2.9	22.6

Source: OECD, *Historical Statistics, 1960–81.*

The Determinants of Investment

Firms invest to make profits. The inducement to invest occurs where the expected return—the flow of extra profits—from an investment exceeds the cost, the interest cost of the funds used to acquire the investment. This was the basis of Keynes's theory of investment, and it did not diverge from earlier theories of investment. There are aggregation problems when moving from the microeconomic, or firm, level to macroeconomic analysis. An individual firm may take the supply prices of investment goods as fixed and not affected by the orders it places, but aggregate demand for investment goods may affect their prices.

The modern approach to investment theory is to examine the determinants of firms' 'desired' stock of capital goods and the adjustment of the capital stock through investment. In fact firms do not calculate a desired capital stock and then decide upon their investment. Managers consider investment projects within a capital budget constraint, and past and expected profits are important determinants of the budget constraint.

The Accelerator Theory

One approach to modelling investment at an aggregate level is the accelerator model, which relates additions to the capital stock to changes in output (GDP):

$$I_t = \alpha(Y_{t+1} - Y_t)$$

where I_t stands for additions to the capital stock in the current year, Y_t for income in the current year, and Y_{t+1} for income in the following year. Additions to the capital stock are a function of the expected change in demand, and hence output and income. This relationship is based on technical relationships; the number of machines and factory and warehouse space are assumed to bear a fixed relationship to output. If demand is expected to increase, firms will install more machines etc. to be able to meet demand. Replacement investment is assumed to occur regularly and automatically. This assumption may be realistic during periods of steady expansion, but does not apply during a deep recession. Firms

have flexibility when deciding on most replacement investment, and many decisions on replacement are linked to
investments which are designed to expand capacity or introduce new techniques. (Firms are more likely to replace equipment when they can made use of an expansion of capacity.)

In practice future output is not known in advance, and the
accelerator relationship is recast in terms of current or past
output.

$$I_t = \alpha(Y_t - Y_{t-1})$$

The idea here is that current and past changes in output
provide a guide for expectations of future changes in output;
businessmen extrapolate recent experience.

In practice there are lags between decisions to invest and
investment expenditure—it takes time for managers to make
decisions, to get planning permission if required, to obtain
information about machinery and tenders, to place con-
tacts, and commission and take delivery of capital equipment.
So a more realistic relationship would be:

$$I_t = \alpha(Y_{t-1} - Y_{t-2})$$

In practice the lags vary from months to several years,
according to the type and size of investments, so the lags
are distributed in time and vary between industries.

Plainly the level of output in relation to past levels of
output or capacity affects the impact of an expected change
in output on investment. If output is far below capacity,
firms will not need to invest to produce increased output. A
slightly more sophisticated approach to modelling investment, the 'Capital Stock Adjustment Mechanism', allows for
the existing capital capacity. This states that additions to the
capital stock are related negatively to the size of the existing
stock of capital equipment, as well as positively to the level
of output:

$$I_t = a\,Y_{t-1} - b\,K_{t-1}$$

Where K_{t-1} stands for the capital stock at the end of the
preceeding period, and a and b are constant coefficients.

The expected rate of return on new investments cannot
be measured or estimated directly from macroeconomic
data, and the return on new investments may be different

from the average return or profitability of existing investments. The appeal of accelerator-type models is in their use for forecasting, because the data for past output and the capital stock are available. We can illustrate some limitations of these models by considering fixed investment in manufacturing industries during the 1970s.

Investment in Manufacturing Industries

Investment in manufacturing formed 18.6 per cent of total gross fixed investment, and 9.5 per cent of total net fixed investment in 1979. In retrospect, the main conundrum of the 1970s is not to explain fluctuations in manufacturing investment, but to explain why it held up as well as it did in the face of a bleak domestic and international economic climate.

A simple illustration of the relationship between *gross* fixed investment in manufacturing, and output of manufacturing, is shown in Diagram 8.5(a) for the period since 1955. Movements of the two series are similar; output and investment increased, stagnated, and then fell. Investment lurched around these trends. There is some evidence of changes in investment lagging about a year behind changes in output (Diagram 8.5(b)). But the striking feature of Diagram 8.5 is the stability of gross investment in manufacturing during the 1970s, in contrast to the complete collapse which might have been expected in circumstances of stagnating, then declining, output. In this *limited* sense, investment in manufacturing was buoyant.

The accelerator theory is not cast in terms of *gross* investment, which is shown in Diagram 8.5; it concerns changes in the capital stock. This is not necessarily the same as net investment, gross investment less depreciation. Depreciation is an estimate of the depletion of the capital stock attributable to its use in a year, the amount which has to be set aside to replace the capital stock. Depreciation may not be matched by the withdrawal of machines from use, or a decline in their productivity in the same year.

Net investment (net of depreciation) in manufacturing, which is not shown in Diagram 8.4, did fall away as output stagnated, from £1.8 bn in 1974 to £1.3 bn in 1979, and to —£1.8 bn in 1983 at 1980 prices. If the accelerator is treated as a relationship between net investment and output, then the expectation of very little investment with stagnant output was met. The implication is that the gross investment which occurred was mainly replacement. But there is more to the maintenance of gross investment in manufacturing during the 1970s than this; firms were not simply replacing the capital stock as it wore out. Diagram 8.5(c) shows estimates of the growth of the gross fixed capital stock during the 1970s.[5] The ratio of the capital stock to output increased even faster than the gross fixed capital stock as output fell.

Investment for manufacturing industry groups is shown in Table 8.2. Can the buoyancy of investment be explained at a less aggregated level? The Table shows investment in 1975, and the change in investment between 1974/6 and 1980/82. Investment in the iron and steel industry fell by 77 per cent, while the output of the industry fell by 33 per cent—a larger fall than was sustained by any other industry group. The textile industries, with a 25 per cent fall in output, cut investment by 55 per cent. The industries which increased investment were coal and petroleum, chemicals, vehicles, and paper, printing and publishing. Output of chemicals increased marginally, and output of the other three industries fell. The apparently perverse relationship between output and investment in the coal and petroleum industry group may be explained by investment related to North Sea oil refining and processing, and politically determined investment in the coal industry. In the motor industry, investment has remained high despite falling output because of the fierce international competition. Firms are forced to improve products and reduce costs by large investments, or are forced into bankruptcy. Also, there were some special factors. Investments in British Leyland were political decisions, and the government supported Chrysler/Talbot. General Motors could override consideration of short-term demand and profitability when deciding Vauxhall's investment programme, while Ford UK has been very profitable and could finance investment. Also, the motor industry may have had realistic hopes of recovery,

[5] See Appendix 8.2.

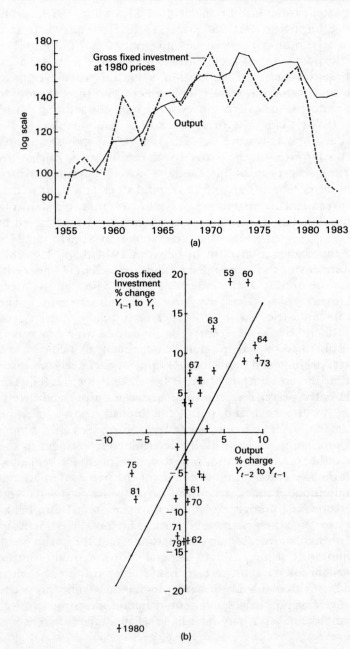

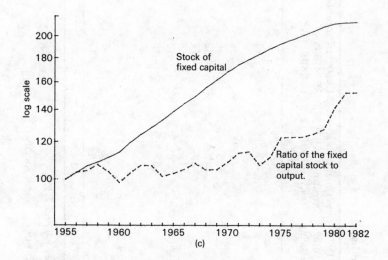

DIAGRAM 8.5   Manufacturing industry gross fixed investment
and output

(a) Indices 1955/7 = 100.
(b) Scatter diagram of year to year percentage changes.[a]
     $Y = -2.4 + 1.87X; R^2 = 0.59.$
(c) The stock of fixed capital (gross) at 1980 prices. Indices 1955 = 100.

Sources: (a) *ETAS* 1984, and *Economic Trends* March 1984; (b) *National Income and Expenditure* 1983, and earlier issues.

[a] Labelled years correspond to output; investment figures relate to the following year.

unlike sections of the textile industries which compete with low wage countries.

On a more general level, the competitive market pressure to raise quality and reduce costs may to some extent explain the surprising buoyancy of UK investment in the 1970s; investment expenditure was not so much 'pulled' by demand as 'pushed' by intense market pressure to introduce the latest technology.

Another factor stimulating investment has been world trade. British firms which are internationally competitive go on investing and increase output, while other firms contract. Britain's membership of the EEC may be an important factor here, creating prosperity for some firms and damaging others.

TABLE 8.2 *Manufacturing industries, investments, and output*

	Gross Investment in 1975 £m.	Gross Investment as % of total for manufacturing	Output in 1975 as a % of total for manufacturing	% Change in gross investment 1974/6 (av.) to 1980/82 (av.)	% Change in output 1974/6 (av.) to 1980/2 (av.)
Food	285	8.1	7.7	+3	+4
Drink and Tobacco	181	5.1	3.3	−25	+2
Coal and Petroleum Products	111	3.2	1.3	+78	−18
Chemicals	546	15.5	8.2	+16	+1
Iron and Steel	513	14.6	5.0	−77	−33
Non-ferrous metals	78	2.2	1.7	−25	−17
All Engineering	760	21.6	26.4	−17	−16
(Electrical)	(258)	(7.3)	(9.5)	(−6)	(+7)
Vehicles	270	7.7	9.8	+38	−15
Textiles, Leather, and Clothing	233	6.6	9.6	−55	−25
Paper, Printing, and Publishing	211	6.0	8.3	+9	−5
Other Manufacturing[a]	334	9.5	18.7	−16	−17
Total	3,522	100	100	−14	−11

Source: *Monthly Digest of Statistics*, June 1983, and earlier issues, tables 1.8 and 7.1.

[a] Includes timber, furniture, bricks, pottery, and glass, and metal goods not elsewhere specified.

A possible explanation of the buoyancy of manufacturing investment could be an increase in the price of labour relative to the price of machinery. If the cost of machinery cheapened relative to labour, substitution would occur. The relationship between the two prices is tracked in Diagram 8.6. Earnings increased by two-thirds, relative to prices of plant and machinery, between 1963 and 1983, though there was a brief period in the mid-1970s when earnings increased more slowly than prices of plant and machinery. Moreover, it is quite possible that improvements in the quality of machinery are not fully allowed for in the price indices for machinery.[6] Thus a part of the explanation of buoyant investment in manufacturing which was concentrated on plant and machinery, may be the rising cost of labour relative to the price of machinery.

Other changes influencing the cost of labour relative to capital were changes in employers' national insurance contributions and tax allowances for capital investment. The latter were remodelled and effectively increased by the introduction of free depreciation in 1974. This was a change which cheapened capital relative to labour and encouraged investment to replace employees.

Profitability and Interest Rates

There are many problems with the accelerator model. Some of the difficulties have already been suggested. The other main problem is that the accelerator ignores financial factors which are not linked closely to the *expected* volume of sales and output. In practice investment is related to past levels of profitability from which the finance for much investment is found, and to the prevailing interest rates which represent the opportunity cost of investment.

Actual profitability for manufacturing was on average exceptionally low during the 1970s. The fall in the share of profits in GDP in the 1970s was reported in Chapter 5. Profitability on existing capital is one indicator of the profitability of new investment, though not a conclusive one, as new technology, larger scale, and new markets could make

[6] See Appendix 8.3.

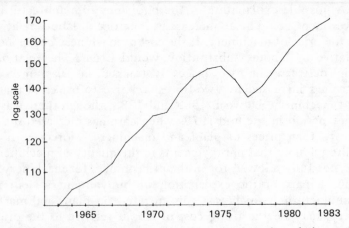

DIAGRAM 8.6   Index of earnings in manufacturing relative to
the prices of plant and machinery

investment profitable even where the return on existing
capital is low. Profits are also a source of finance for new
investment.

Industrial and Commerical Companies

The financial data published in *ETAS* does not include
separate figures for manufacturing. They do distinguish
data for industrial and commercial companies, which include
North Sea oil and some service sector activities as well as
production. Financial companies are excluded. In this section
the data for industrial and commercial companies are used to
examine the relationship between corporate saving and
investment.

Industrial and commercial companies accounted for 57
per cent of private sector fixed investment in 1979. Diagram
8.7 shows the relationship between their savings and gross
fixed investment between 1963 and 1982. Savings by
companies is defined for this purpose as retained profits,
profits before deducting depreciation, but after deducting
stock appreciation, taxes, and dividends.[7]

The clear message of Diagram 8.7(a) is that corporate

[7] See Appendix 8.4.

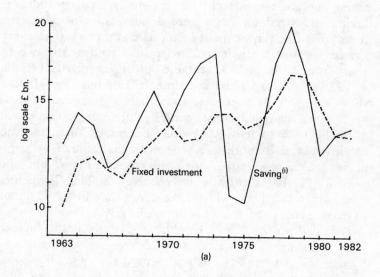

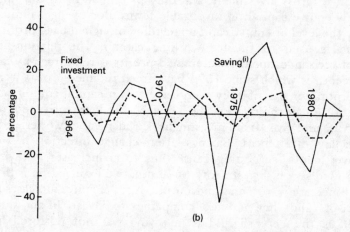

DIAGRAM 8.7   Industrial and commercial companies savings[i] and investment at 1980 prices

(a) Time series.
(b) Year to year percentage changes.

Source: *ETAS* 1984.

[i] Saving by companies is defined in the text and the Statistical Appendix, 8.4.

saving and gross investment are very similar in magnitude, i.e. taking industrial and commercial companies in aggregate, their gross fixed investment in the UK averages out at a very similar amount to their retained profits. During the twenty years from 1963 to 1982, retained profits averaged £14.3 bn at 1980 prices, and fixed investment £13.3 bn. This relationship is unlikely to be a curiosity. Much of the retained gross profits are depreciation provisions which companies would normally wish to reinvest. It may be argued that the ratio of distributed to undistributed profits is tailored by companies to accommodate their investment plans, but the evidence is that dividends are relatively stable. Companies like to increase their dividends year by year and are reluctant to make a cut, so retained profits are largely a residual.

Retained profits affect the ability of companies to finance their investment internally and by borrowing. Capital raised by new issues of equity has represented a very small proportion of gross investment, and only profitable firms can raise new equity capital on favourable terms. Borrowing is limited by the level of equity capital including ploughed-back profits, and is used to finance working capital. The relationship between investment and retained profits is reinforced by tax incentives which since 1974 have freed retained profits from corporation tax if they were invested in capital equipment.

Although the relationship between the levels of corporate saving and gross fixed investment is evident, the two series do display differences. Savings often change direction before investments, suggesting cause runs from increases in saving to increases in investment. An alternative explanation is that an increase in demand and output first generates increases in profits and then induces companies to invest. In the mid-1970s the very sharp fall in saving was not mirrored by investment. Diagram 8.7(b) shows the year to year percentage changes for savings and investment.

The relationship between investment and corporate saving can be likened to that between consumption and personal disposable income. The close tie between saving by companies and gross fixed investment is important because of its implications for the financing of investment. It is also significant for another reason. The Keynesian scheme laid stress on the

divorce between *ex ante* saving and investment. In fact the
profits and retained profits of companies are important
determinants of their investment, and the same probably
applies to many unincorporated enterprises which are
grouped in the personal sector.

Interest Rates

The relationship between gross fixed investment and short-
term interest rates is shown in Diagram 8.8. This is the
interest rate which may influence the extent to which firms
borrow and use short-term funds. In fact industrialists must
have been unsure about the real rates of interest they were
paying during the 1970s, because of the difficulty of forecasting the rate of inflation and short-term money rates of
interest very far ahead. Earlier it was shown that manufacturing investment was buoyant in relation to output
during the 1970s, and diagram 8.8 shows real short-term
interest rates were low during the 1970s. The relationship is
the one which would be expected; low or negative interest
rates encourage investment. The year to year changes in
investment and interest rates do not seem to have a close
relationship. This is not surprising, and can be explained by
the lags between decisions to invest and investment expenditure, the effect of taxation to distort the return on investments, and the effects of the recession on investment.

Diagram 8.8 shows borrowing by industrial and commercial
companies. There was an explosion of borrowing from 1972;
this reflected the demand for working capital to finance the
increased value of stocks caused by rapid inflation. The
definition of corporate savings used for Diagram 8.7 excludes
stock appreciation—stock appreciation was deducted from
profits. Companies borrow to finance part of their stocks
and pay interest on the loans, so some stock appreciation
is available for fixed investment. This could explain why
gross fixed investment held up in the mid-1970s, in spite of
the fall in saving excluding stock appreciation.

Conclusions on Investment in Manufacturing Industries

Investment in manufacturing industries did not collapse

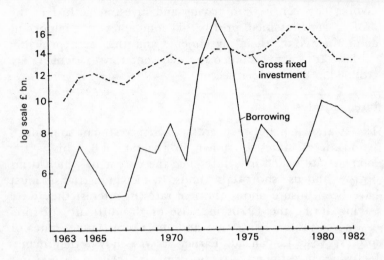

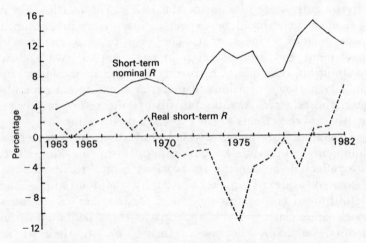

DIAGRAM 8.8   Industrial and commercial companies fixed
investment, borrowing, and interest rates at 1980 prices.

Sources: *ETAS* 1984, and *Economic Trends* March 1984.

during the 1970s as the accelerator theory predicts. Explanations of this resilience are the pressure to invest to maintain
competitiveness, the differing experience between and within
industries, with some companies profitable and expanding

output, and the relationship between retained profits and investment which was reinforced by tax concessions. Other (possible) contributory factors were negative real interest rates and the rising cost of labour relative to the price of plant and machinery.

Housing

Housing investment is another important element in total fixed investment. The supply of housing is determined by the existing stock of housing because of the slow rate of change of the stock. For example, in 1979 construction of new houses and structural improvements to existing houses accounted for 16 per cent of total gross fixed investment, but represented only 2½ per cent of the value of the housing stock. The inelastic supply means that increases in demand are largely reflected in increases in prices which encourage the construction of more new houses.

It is useful to distinguish between long-run and short-run factors in the demand for housing. The former include demographic and social factors such as an increase in the married proportion of the population, and a reduction in the multiple occupation of houses, which increase the demand for houses. Tax concessions to owner occupiers have also contributed to increasing demand. Capital gains on owner occupied houses are tax free, while interest on mortgages can, within limits, be deducted from taxable income. Since the price of houses increased faster than retail prices in the 1970s, investment in housing was a good protection against inflation and was seen to be so. For explaining the cyclical behaviour of demand, changes in real income, prices of houses, interest rates and the availability of loans predominate.

Concentrating on the interest-sensitivity of housing demand, a close relationship between private investment in housing and interest rates might be expected. Lower interest rates make mortgages cheaper and borrowing more attractive, and building societies limit mortgages so that repayments do not exceed some multiple of income; thus reductions in nominal interest rates increase the size of loans borrowers can take. Simultaneously, low interest rates facilitate borrowing by builders and encourage construction of new houses.

Housing investment and short-term interest rates are compared in Diagram 8.9; it can be seen that the relationship is not very close. None the less, from 1963 to 1972 the trend of private housing investment was for an increase, while nominal short-term interest rates were broadly stable. From 1972 nominal interest rates increased and private investment in housing fell away; the low real interest rates about 1975 did not bring about an increase in investment, their effect may have been offset by other changes. On a shorter time scale, year to year changes in private investment in housing and nominal interest rates during the 1970s tend to move in opposite directions as would be expected. Investment in housing usually falls in the year interest rates rise and in the following year, and rises in the year interest rates fall and the following year.

Factors dampening the relationship between interest rates and the demand for housing are the taxation system, mentioned above, and controls on mortgages. Credit squeezes at times curtailed the availability of funds both for mortgages and loans for builders.

Public sector investment in housing is influenced by longer-term factors, prevailing government policy and pressures on public spending, which are considered in Chapter 9, rather than by interest rates.

The Service Sector

Table 8.3 shows that the service industries are an important and growing sector of the economy. They include transport, communications, the distributive trades, insurance, banking, other financial services, professional and scientific services, social and other miscellaneous services. These industries accounted for 52 per cent of output in 1979, and their output grew by 18 per cent between 1972 and 1982. Gross investment in the services sector was more than twice that in manufacturing throughout the 1970s, and increased by 2 per cent between 1972 and 1982.

The growth in service sector investment can be analysed

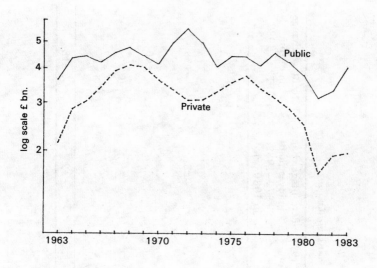

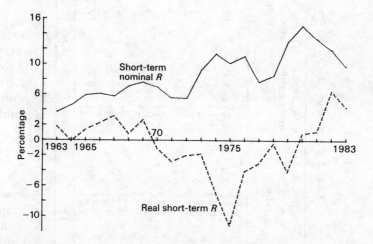

DIAGRAM 8.9   Gross investment in housing at 1980 prices and
interest rates

Sources: *ETAS* 1984: and *Economic Trends* March 1984.

by type of asset. For investment in vehicles, ships and aircraft, and plant and machinery an important factor providing growth has been the rise in purchases of assets by the insurance, banking, finance, and business services industries for leasing to other industries, from £395m. in 1975 to £1,105m.

TABLE 8.3 Service Industries Investment and Output

	Gross investment in 1979 £bn.		As % of total investment		Output in 1979 as % of total output	Percentage change in investment 1972–1982 in 1980 prices	Percentage change in output 1972 to 1982
Wholesale distribution	0.9		2.6				
Retailing and repairing	1.5	3.0	4.4	8.7	13.5	+5	−3
Hotels and catering	0.6		1.7				
Transport	2.2		6.4		4.6	−46	+3
Communication	1.1		3.2		2.5	−28	+38
Banking, finance etc.							
Leased assets	1.7		5.0				
Other assets	1.4	4.4	4.0	12.7	10.9	+149	+45
Business services	1.3		3.7				
Education	0.7		2.0				
Health services	0.6	1.3	1.6	3.6	8.3	−27	+17
Roads	0.8		2.4				
Other	2.2	3.0	6.3	8.7	12.2		
Total	15.0		43.0		52.0	+2	+18

Source: *National Income and Expenditure*, 1983.

by 1979. Tax incentives have played a major part in this development, since by owning and leasing assets the financial institutions obtain the capital allowances for tax. If this investment were to be attributed to manufacturing and other sectors, it would have a significant effect on the total rate of investment in these sectors.

Investment in new buildings and works is the largest element of service sector investment. The important components here are the financial services sector (their own buildings), education and health services, roads and miscellaneous public services. An additional influence on investment in distribution is the relative yield on investment in shops which is shown in Diagram 6.3. Part of the explanation for the low yield on shops is that the return was inflation-proofed. The low yield on, and correspondingly high capital values of, shops encouraged construction of new retail outlets, but the importance of this factor should not be exaggerated, since construction accounted for only a third of retail investment in 1980.

Investment in Stocks

In addition to fixed investment, firms invest in stocks of raw materials, work in progress, and finished goods. Investment in stocks, or stockbuilding, is the change in the volume of stocks held between the beginning and end of a period. Although stockbuilding between 1971 and 1982 was a small component of GDP—stockbuilding averaged 0.3 per cent of GDP—changes in stockbuilding were significant. It was the most erratic component of demand; stockbuilding in 1973 was equivalent to 2.4 per cent of GDP, whilst the change from stockbuilding in 1974 to destocking in 1975 represented 2.7 per cent of GDP. The impact of changes in stockbuilding on demand are examined in Chapter 12.

Firms hold stocks because of the inability to synchronize the receipt and use or sale of goods for technological and commercial reasons. Production takes time and there are indivisibilities, and economies of scale associated with production, storage, transportation, and large transactions. Also, stocks are held as a precaution against unexpected flucuations

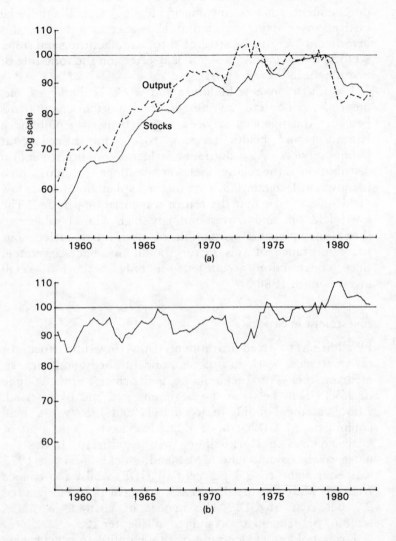

DIAGRAM 8.10   Manufacturing stocks to manufacturing output
(4th Q 1979 = 100)

(a) Indices of stocks at 1980 prices and production.
(b) Index of the stocks to output ratio.

Sources: *ETAS* 1984, and *Economic Trends* December 1983.

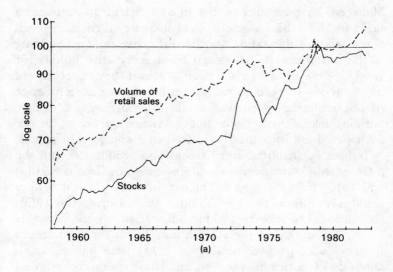

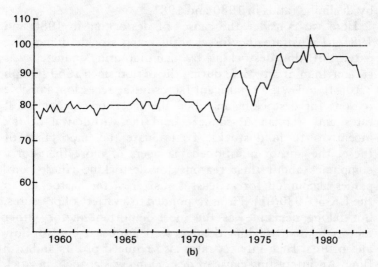

DIAGRAM 8.11   Index of retail stocks to retail sales
(4th Q 1979 = 100)

(a) Indices of stocks at 1980 prices and volume of retail sales.
(b) Index of stocks to sales ratio.

Sources: *ETAS* 1984, and *Economic Trends*, December 1983.

in demand, and to help smooth changes in production. Managers have an idea of the most efficient stock to sales ratio for their businesses; if sales increase, then stocks will rise to restore this ratio. Another influence on stockbuilding is the advantage to be gained from speculative holding of stocks. Some firms increase their stocks if they expect prices of the goods stocked to rise, but other firms make a practice of not acquiring speculative stocks. Stocks may also change without management intending a change to occur; an unanticipated fall in demand will lead to a piling up of stocks.

Indices of manufacturers' stocks and production, and the ratio of stocks to production, are shown in Graphs 8.10(a) and (b). The data suggest changes in stocks lagged behind changes in production by about a year. During the 1960s the ratio of stocks to production cycled around a stable trend. For retailers, the fluctuations in the ratio of stocks to retail sales (shown in Diagram 8.11) were milder. From about 1973 both ratios moved up. These rises were followed by declining ratios in 1980 and 1981.

Here we consider the causes of destocking in 1980 and 1981 to illustrate the forces influencing stockbuilding. The extent of this destocking by manufacturing industry was greater than at any time during the period since 1959 (Graph 8.10(a)) and was a significant factor in the recession. Possible reasons for destocking included the recession, high interest rates and a financial squeeze, and the withdrawal of tax incentives to hold stocks. To evaluate the importance of these, the author questioned managers of more than forty companies about their reasons for destocking (these companies accounted for at least a quarter of the destocking in the UK in 1980/81). Firms responded to a variety of pressures, but falling demand was the most important factor. Other factors related to falling demand were a squeeze on cash flow and profits. High interest rates also reduced profits and cash flow. An interesting cause of destocking was changes in stock relief for taxation. Stock relief contributed to the rise in stocks from the mid-1970s. After 1974 companies were permitted to deduct the increase in the *value* of their stocks between the beginning and end of their accounting year from their profits assessable to tax, so profitable companies had an incentive to increase the *volume* of their stocks, to reduce their tax liabilities. From 1980 this incentive to increase stocks was removed and this led to some destocking. The slowing of inflation which had encouraged some stock-building in the 1970s, was another factor contributing to destocking.

Some Conclusions

In this chapter the movements in the level of investment, changes in its composition, and possible explanations for these changes have been described. Private fixed investment has been more stable than envisaged by Keynes. The impact of pessimistic expectations and a sour economic climate on investment in the 1970s were less dramatic than might have been expected. Moreover, investment changes followed changes in output, rather than leading changes in aggregate demand. Nevertheless, the *failure* of investment to increase substantially during the 1970s was serious, and to some extent confirmed Keynes's uneasiness about leaving investment solely to market forces, a point taken up in later chapters.

9

Government

Introduction

In this chapter the increasing importance of the state in the economy is examined. The endogenous and exogenous elements of government expenditure are distinguished, and the political and demographic influences on the components of expenditure are discussed. In particular, the extent to which Keynesian fiscal remedies for unemployment were implemented during the 1970s is considered.

Government Expenditure

Some Statistics

The public sector includes central government, local authorities, and the public corporations. The latter are usually considered separately, and the category 'general government' consolidates central and local authorities only. Government expenditure can be grouped into three broad categories: capital expenditure on infrastructure items such as roads, hospitals, etc., current expenditure on goods and services, and transfer payments to individuals within the economy. Wage and salary payments to public employees are an important component of current expenditure. Transfer payments which include social security payments, unemployment benefit, pensions and debt interest are not a part of the government component of aggregate demand, as this would involve double-counting. These expenditures are income of the recipients. Some proportion of this income is spent on the purchase of goods and services for consumption (and some saved), and it is at this point that it makes its contribution to aggregate demand. The relative importance of these categories of expenditure can be seen from Table 9.1 and Diagram 9.1.

TABLE 9.1 Share of government expenditure in GDP at current market prices[a]

| | Total government expenditure[b] | | Government consumption as % of GDP | Government investment as % of GDP | Current grants and subsidies as % of GDP | Debt interest as % of GDP |
| | £ bn | as % of GDP | | | | |
	(1)	(2)	(3)	(4)	(5)	(6)
1970	20.9	40.7	17.5	4.8	10.5	3.9
1971	23.5	40.8	17.8	4.5	10.3	3.6
1972	26.4	41.4	18.3	4.4	11.3	3.6
1973	30.5	41.5	18.2	5.0	11.2	3.7
1974	39.2	46.9	19.9	5.3	13.4	4.3
1975	51.5	48.9	21.8	4.8	13.6	4.0
1976	58.5	46.6	21.3	4.4	13.6	4.3
1977	61.9	42.7	20.2	3.4	13.5	4.4
1978	71.9	43.2	19.9	2.8	14.0	4.3
1979	85.2	43.8	19.7	2.7	14.1	4.6
1980	103.8	45.6	21.3	2.5	14.3	5.0
1981	116.3	46.2	21.7	1.8	15.3	5.3
1982	128.2	46.5	21.7	1.7	15.8	5.3
1983	138.7	46.1	21.9	1.9	16.0	4.9

Source: *ETAS* (1984), and *Economic Trends*, March 1984.

[a] Excludes Public Corporations.

[b] Columns (3) to (6) do not sum to col. (2). Capital transfers and net lending by government, which are included in cols. (1) and (2), are not included in cols. (3) to (6).

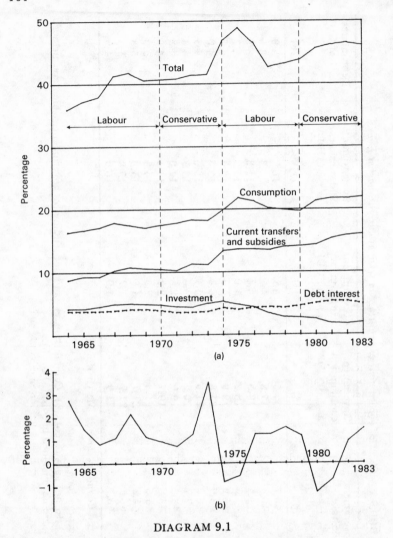

DIAGRAM 9.1

(a) Government expenditure as a percentage of GDP.
(b) Year to year percentage changes in GDP at 1980 prices.

Sources: *ETAS* 1984, and *Economic Trends*, March 1984.

Total government expenditure is of enormous significance
for the economy. In 1979 it amounted to over £85 bn, 44
per cent of GDP. Column (2) of Table 9.1 shows government
expenditure as a percentage of GDP, both at current prices.

TABLE 9.2   *Employment*

	Private sector		Public sector		Unemployed		Working population
			(millions)				
		(figures in brackets percentages of the working population)					
1970	18.3	(72.2)	6.5	(25.7)	0.5	(2.2)	25.3
1975	17.7	(68.7)	7.3	(28.1)	0.8	(3.2)	25.9
1980	17.8	(66.7)	7.4	(27.7)	1.5	(5.7)	26.7
1982	16.5	(63.0)	7.0[a]	(26.5)	2.8	(10.4)	26.5

Source: *ETAS* 1984, p. 99 and 198.

[a] Public sector employment in 1982 included (in thousands): central government employment 2,346, of which HM forces 324, and the national health service 1,287; local authority employment 2, 931, of which education 1, 483; and public corporations 1, 759.

TABLE 9.3   *Components of government consumption of goods and services in 1979*

	£ bn	% of total
Defence	8.9	24
Education	7.3	20
National Health Service	8.3	22
Other[a]	12.5	34
Total	37.0	100

Source: *National Income and Expenditure*, 1983.

[a] Other includes expenditure on the maintenance and lighting of roads, housing, police, personal social services, etc.

Changes in GDP at current prices are made up of volume and price changes, and this percentage shows whether government expenditure is keeping pace with these volume and price changes. Between 1964 and 1975 general government expenditure as a percentage of GDP increased from 36 to 48.9 per cent, and since 1970 it has always been above 40 per cent. The sharpest increases occurred when real GDP was falling in 1974, 1975, and 1980. Within the total expenditure the most important element is government consumption, at around 20 per cent of GDP. Public investment, which was discussed in Chapter 8, fell by 60 per cent as a percentage of GDP between 1970 and 1983. The increasing importance of transfer payments, current grants, and subsidies is in part caused by the high unemployment in the 1970s.

The importance of the state in the economy is again illustrated by the employment data shown in Table 9.2. Public sector employment represented more than a quarter of total employment (including self-employment). During the 1970s private sector employment fell, while public sector employment and unemployment increased. Between 1980 and 1982 both private and public sector employment declined.

General Government Consumption of Goods and Services

Table 9.3 shows the main components of government current expenditure on goods and services. Expenditure on defence, education, and the National Health Service are similar.

There are, however, some problems in assessing changes in government consumption. Diagram 9.2 shows the movement of the deflator for general government consumption of goods and services relative to the GDP deflator. It was obtained by taking government consumption at the prices then current for each year as a percentage of government consumption revalued at 1980 prices for the same year. The deflator for government consumption rose faster, by 32 per cent, than the GDP deflator between 1964 and 1983. However, owing to the manner in which the *quality* of services bought by the government is measured (or in most cases not measured), there is little scope for productivity improvements to show up in the record, and this affects the deflator. For example, the *output* of teachers is measured by the numbers of teachers and pupils! Changes in productivity are not measured and are largely unmeasurable. A substantial proportion of government consumption is expenditure on labour-intensive services for which productivity changes are not measured (education, health, and social services), and where wages keep pace with those in the rest of the economy. As a part of the apparently faster increase of prices of goods and services

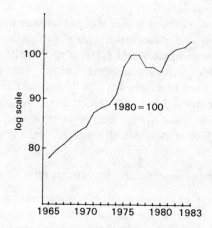

DIAGRAM 9.2   The deflator for government consumption
relative to the GDP deflator

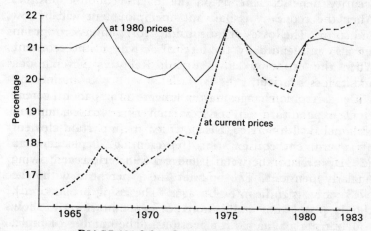

DIAGRAM 9.3   Government consumption
as percentage of GDP at current prices and at 1980 prices

Sources: *ETAS* 1984, and *Economic Trends*, March, 1984.

bought by the government is not price increases at all, but
increases in productivity, the change in government consumption at 1980 prices under-estimates the growth of real
government consumption. Diagram 9.3 shows government
consumption as a percentage of GDP at both current and

and 1980 prices. In 1980 price terms the trend is constant, while in terms of current prices the percentage has risen.

The differential between movements of prices for general governmnet consumption and GDP is not explicable in terms of errors in productivity measurement alone. True productivity improvements may be faster for goods and services bought by the private sector. Also, movements of wages affect the differential. At times when public sector wages are rising relatively rapidly, as in 1980, the differential increases.

What Determines Government Expenditure?

In elementary Keynesian analysis, government expenditure is considered to be autonomous, determined without reference to the rest of the economy. In practice much of government expenditure is far from autonomous. For example, the number of people claiming uenmployment and social security benefits depends on the macro-economic position. When the economy is buoyant unemployment will be low, and so on. The losses of, or subsidies for, public corporations are also influenced by the level of activity in the economy. When the economy slows British Railways' revenue falls and its losses mount.

Demographic changes have a longer-run impact on government expenditure on services such as education and the National Health Service (NHS), which are important elements of government consumption (representing 20 per cent and 22 per cent of the total), and on transfer payments, particularly pensions. The amount spent per head within the NHS varies significantly by age.[1] The rising proportion of elderly people has implications for expenditure on the NHS and transfer payments for pensions. (The number of people

[1] *Health and personal social services*
Estimated gross current expenditure per head in 1981/2.

Age	£	Age	£
0–4	260	65–74	455
5–15	175	75+	1,160
16–64	145		

Source: The Government's Expenditure Plans 1984/5 to 1986/7. Cmnd. 9143-II. HMSO, Feb. 1984.

over 75 is expected to increase by 24 per cent between 1978
and 1986.) In contrast, the sharp fall in children of school age
is a factor now reducing government expenditure on education and transfer payments for child benefits. (The total
school population is expected to fall by 17 per cent between
1978/9 and 1986/7.)

The level of, and changes in, government expenditure are
also determined by political decisions and commitments.
Labour governments have an inclination to increase government expenditure. They have a general preference for the
public rather than the private sector, a desire to spend more
on public programmes, and choose reflation to combat unemployment rather than retrenchment to fight inflation.
Conservative governments aim for a lower ratio of public to
private expenditure, and Mrs Thatcher's government has
given priority to reducing inflation. Behind the political
decisions there is a wide spectrum of views about public
expenditure and taxes which are intimately linked with
views concerning the distribution of income and equality. At
one extreme is the view that, in spite of the immense differences in ability and earning power within the community,
any move to redistribute the incomes determined by the
market towards the less able, is charity, and that it should
be left for people to make gifts privately. At the other
extreme, equality, to be achieved through highly progressive
taxation and government expenditure, is advocated.

Equality and redistribution are not the only issues. Another
is the efficiency with which the state can provide services,
though state, or collective, payment for services does not
preclude private production of the services. It is claimed by
Conservatives that public provision is inherently less efficient
than production by competitive private firms.

Diagram 9.4 shows the growth of government expenditure
in 1980 prices on the National Health Service and education,
two of the main components of government consumption,
and compares them with consumers' expenditure on other
services.[2] The rapid growth of the health and education

---

[2] The comparisons are made in constant (1980) price terms. This is less un-
satisfactory when comparing different services than when comparing expenditure
on services and goods.

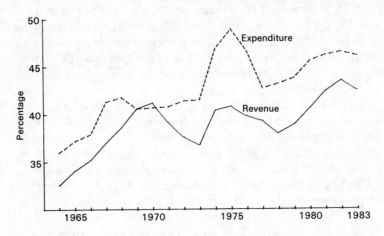

DIAGRAM 9.4   Indices of expenditure on services (at 1980 prices)
(1970 = 100)

Sources: *ETAS* 1984, and *Economic Trends*, March 1984.

services has contributed to the rise in government expenditure. Apart from the demographic forces and policy preferences already mentioned, the growth reflects increasing demand for these services which would emerge if they were paid for directly by consumers; they seem the equivalent of superior goods. In part, the increases may also reflect the demand-generating effects of free goods.

Taxation and Government Revenue

Diagram 9.5 shows the growth of general government revenue as a percentage of GDP since 1964. Here again the important point is the rapid increase; revenue has been increased to pay for the increased expenditure. General government revenue as a percentage of GDP increased by 30 per cent between 1964 and 1983. North Sea oil contributed to this increase, and by the fiscal year 1982/3 taxes on North Sea oil represented 2.8 per cent of GDP, and 6.5 per cent of general government revenue.

The main sources of general government revenue in 1979 are related to GDP in Table 9.4. Taxes on income include corporation tax, and taxes on expenditure include taxes on

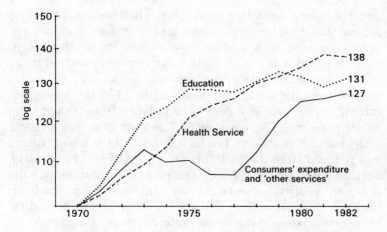

DIAGRAM 9.5   General government revenue and expenditure
(as % of GDP both at current prices)

Sources: *ETAS* 1984, and *Economic Trends*, March 1984.

TABLE 9.4   *General government revenue in 1979*

	£ bn.	As % of total revenue	As % of GDP
Taxes on income	25.0	33.1	12.9
Taxes on expenditure	29.8	39.4	15.3
National Insurance contributions	11.5	15.2	5.9
Rent etc.	3.2	4.2	1.6
Interest and dividends	3.4	4.5	1.7
Other	2.6	3.4	1.3
Total	75.6	100.0	38.9

Source: *National Income and Expenditure,* 1983.

other components of expenditure besides consumers' expenditure. Taxes on expenditure exceeded taxes on income in 1979.

So far total tax revenue has been outlined; now taxes on personal income are considered. In 1979 income taxes represented 13 per cent of personal income, and national insurance contributions a further 7 per cent. These calculations show the average rates of taxes on personal income. Marginal rates of tax are more relevant for many economic decisions, and they vary according to income. High marginal rates of income tax have applied to incomes in Britain, but this has been combined with a wide range of provisions which have made it possible for many with large incomes to avoid these rates. (Pension contributions and mortgage interest could, within limits, be set against income.) In 1979 the maximum rate of tax on earned income was reduced from 83 per cent to 60 per cent. The basic rate of income tax, which is the marginal rate of income tax for the bulk of the labour force, was reduced from 33 to 30 per cent. (In 1975/6 the rate had been as high as 35 per cent.) The rate of corporation tax on company profits has been 52 per cent, but companies have been allowed substantial deductions from profits, including 'free depreciation' which was referred to in Chapter 8. In the 1984 Budget the rate of corporation tax was reduced to 35 per cent, and the provisions for free depreciation and stock relief were removed. The high marginal rates of tax mean that changes in income have had a large impact on taxes and government revenue. A rise in GDP results in a proportionately larger increase in tax revenue.

Conservative governments prefer lower and less progressive taxes. The reductions in income tax rates in 1979 were offset by increases in VAT, which raised the percentage of taxes on expenditure in the total tax revenue. Between 1978 and 1982 taxes on expenditure, as a percentage of total general government receipts, rose from 36.3 to 39.3. Earlier, between 1970 and 1975, taxes on income had increased relative to taxes on expenditure, since taxes on expenditure were held down to check price increases.

An International Comparison

Table 9.5 compares the level and changes in government expenditure and taxation during the 1970s for the UK, the USA, Japan, and some European countries. In 1981 government outlays for the UK were a smaller proportion of GDP than for the other European countries, though the USA and Japan had lower levels both of expenditure and taxation.

TABLE 9.5   *International comparisons of total government outlays and current receipts as percentages of GDP*

	Outlays			Current revenue		
	1970	1981	1981 as % of 1970	1970	1981	1981 as % of 1970
Sweden	43.7	65.3	149	47.0	59.0	126
Italy	34.2	50.8	149	30.4	38.7	127
Germany	38.7	49.3	127	38.5	44.6	116
France	38.9	48.9	126	39.0	46.1	118
UK	39.3	47.3	120	40.7	43.4	107
USA	32.3	35.4	110	30.4	33.7	111
Japan	19.4	34.0	175	20.7	29.3	142

Source: OECD. *Historical Statistics 1960–81*, p. 64.

The rather similar levels of government expenditure in relation to GDP, and the simultaneous increases, suggest that there are common forces propelling public expenditure. These include the world recession, which increased expenditure and reduced the growth of GDP, and may include common pressures for increases in expenditure on health, education, and, in the 1980s, defence.

The fact that the proportion of GDP taken in taxes is similar in Britain and the other countries listed, is noteworthy. The tax burden in Britain is not exceptional. It is possible that the slow growth of the economy makes taxes particularly unpopular here.

The PSBR

So far government expenditure and revenue have been examined separately. Now we consider the net financial injection into the economy—the PSBR— the balance between the government's expenditure and net lending and its revenue. The PSBR is a financial concept; it is not a measure of the physical resources taken by the government. (Many of the payments made by the government, and most of its revenue, are not payments for goods and services.) Capital as well as current revenue items are included before the PSBR balance is struck. For example, investment expenditure and the proceeds of privatization are included. As companies like

British Leyland and British Telecom are inside the public sector, the PSBR is an artificial balance.

The Keynesian scheme of fiscal demand management rests on increases in government expenditure and reductions in taxes generating demand. It follows that a government should consider the impact of its fiscal decisions on demand. For example, tax reductions for high income earners would be expected to have less direct effect on consumers' demand than an increase in pensions, because the former would save a higher proportion of their increase in post-tax income. Nevertheless, during the 1970s the financial balance, the PSBR, has become the focus of attention for assessing the expansionary or deflationary nature of fiscal policy—the fiscal stance. Table 9.6 shows the PSBR during the 1970s. From a zero balance in 1970, it shot up to 10 per cent of GDP by 1975, and halved by 1977. The large PSBR suggests that the government was providing substantial injections into the economy in 1975 when unemployment was rising.

Some of the effects of changes in economic activity on government expenditure and revenue have been noted earlier in this chapter. The effects on the PSBR, the balance between the two, are proportionately much greater. The action of some taxes and benefits to partially offset movements in demand has led to the use of the term 'automatic stabilizers'. They damp down, or stabilize, changes in aggregate demand.

The Cyclically-adjusted PSBR

Estimates have been made of a hypothetical 'cyclically-adjusted' PSBR. This shows what the PSBR would have been if the economy had operated at a steady level of unemployment. Estimates of the hypothetical cyclically-adjusted PSBR from 1972 to 1976 are shown in Table 9.7, based on an assumed high level of employment. The estimates demonstrate what the PSBR would have been if the government had maintained tax rates and benefits at the actual rates, but the economy had continued to operate at the level of unemployment in 1973. In 1975 the PSBR would have been 5.1 per cent compared to the actual 10.0 per cent of

TABLE 9.6   *The PSBR*[a]

	Total £ bn.	As % of GDP at market prices
	(1)	(2)
1970	0.0	0.0
1971	− 1.4	− 2.4
1972	− 2.1	− 3.2
1973	− 4.2	− 5.8
1974	− 6.4	− 7.7
1975	− 10.5	− 10.0
1976	− 9.2	− 7.4
1977	− 6.0	− 4.2
1978	− 8.4	− 5.0
1979	− 12.6	− 6.5
1980	− 12.2	− 5.4
1981	− 10.7	− 4.3
1982	− 5.4	− 2.0
1983	− 11.7	− 3.9

Source: *ETAS* 1984, and *Economic Trends*, March 1984.

[a] Negatives indicate a borrowing requirement, positive signs indicate surpluses.

GDP. These calculations indicate that nearly half of the PSBR in 1975 was attributable to the economy operating at a lower pressure of demand than in 1973 and the operation of the automatic stabilizers, rather than to a deliberate budget deficit to combat the recession. Similar calculations for 1984, based on 1973 employment levels, would show the cyclically-adjusted PSBR in massive surplus. Although such estimates make an important point about the PSBR, that the government's fiscal stance measured by the cyclically-adjusted PSBR is deflationary in 1984, the precise calculations would be based on such hypothetical assumptions about GDP that they would provide only a general guide for policy. By 1984 the economy had diverged far from the 1973 level of unemployment, and a rapid return to it is unlikely.

So far two definitions of the PSBR—in money terms and cyclically-adjusted—have been considered. Next the real PSBR, the money PSBR reduced by the fall in the real value of public authorities' monetary liabilities caused by inflation (referred to in Chapter 7), is described. The figures in Table

TABLE 9.7   *Cyclically-adjusted PSBR*

| | Actual PSBR | | Cyclically adjusted PSBR[a] | |
	£ bn.	As % of GDP	£ bn.	As % of GDP
1972	− 2.1	− 3.3	− 1.1	− 1.7
1973	− 4.2	− 5.8	− 4.2	− 5.8
1974	− 6.4	− 7.7	− 5.7	− 6.9
1975	− 10.5	− 10.0	− 7.3	− 5.1
1976	− 9.1	− 7.3	− 3.5	− 2.8

Source: Based on estimates given in *National Institute Economic Review*, May 1977, p. 17.

[a] The cyclically-adjusted PSBR is estimated by taking the mid-1973 level of unemployment as the 'high employment' base, and assuming an underlying rate of growth of productive potential of 2½ per cent per annum. The adjustment can only be approximate because it depends upon assumptions about which components of demand would have increased to get the higher hypothetical GDP.

9.8 show that the real PSBR was often positive and deflationary in the 1970s.

The monetary adjustment reflects the fact that, during a period of inflation, part of the interest payments by the public sector represents a repayment of capital rather than an income payment. If agents base their decisions upon their income after monetary adjustment for inflation, then there is a strong case for the government to focus on the real PSBR rather than the money PSBR as a guide to its fiscal stance. But there are practical problems to this approach: governments would have to adopt an expansive fiscal policy of cutting taxes, or increasing expenditure, when they expected inflation to accelerate, which could lead to further inflation. And, though the effects of inflation eroding the real value of private sector monetary assets does help to explain the rise in personal saving during the 1970s, it is unlikely that the public reacts predictably to changes in the rate of inflation when deciding the proportion of income to save.

The cyclical adjustment and the monetary adjustment are not mutually exclusive. The two adjustments shown in the final two columns of Table 9.8 indicate that the cyclically-adjusted fiscal stance was in surplus in real terms in the mid-

TABLE 9.8   *The 'Real' PSBR*

	Money PSBR		Gain on monetary assets £ bn.	Real PSBR		Real Cyclically-adjusted PSBR[a]	
	Total £ bn.	as % of GDP		Total £ bn.	as % of GDP	£ bn.	as % of GDP
1970	0.0	0.0	+ 2.7	+ 2.7	+ 5.3		
1971	− 1.4	− 2.4	+ 3.2	+ 1.8	+ 3.1		
1972	− 2.1	− 3.2	+ 3.1	+ 1.0	+ 1.6	− 2.0	− 3.1
1973	− 4.2	− 5.4	+ 4.0	− 0.2	− 0.3	+ 0.2	+ 0.3
1974	− 6.4	− 7.7	+ 9.3	+ 2.9	+ 3.5	− 3.6	− 4.3
1975	− 10.5	− 10.0	+ 11.9	+ 1.4	+ 1.3	− 4.6	− 4.4
1976	− 9.2	− 7.4	+ 7.5	− 1.7	− 1.4	− 4.1	− 3.3
1977	− 6.0	− 4.2	+ 9.4	+ 3.4	+ 2.4		
1978	− 8.4	− 5.0	+ 6.7	− 1.7	− 1.0		
1979	− 12.6	− 6.5	+ 14.5	+ 1.9	+ 1.0		
1980	− 12.2	− 5.4	+ 12.2	0	0		
1981	− 10.7	− 4.3	+ 11.0	+ 0.3	+ 0.2		
1982	− 5.4	− 2.0	+ 7.3	+ 1.9	+ 0.7		

Source: *Bank of England Quarterly Bulletin,* June 1982 and June 1983; and *NIER,* May 1977.

[a] The cyclical and real adjustments were summed to calculate the real cyclically-adjusted PSBR.

1970s, the reverse of the fiscal stance portrayed by the figures for the raw PSBR.

Conclusions

We have seen that government expenditure is very far from the autonomous and easily controllable factor implied by the *G* of macroeconomic equations. Demographic changes, pressures for increased expenditure on the health service and education, and the level of activity in the economy, all affect government expenditure.

We are now in a position to consider the question posed in the introduction—were expansionary Keynesian fiscal policies followed in the 1970s? It is necessary to examine the real cyclically-adjusted PSBR. In the early 1970s fiscal policies were used to stimulate the economy. By 1974 this stimulus, as measured by the cyclically-adjusted PSBR, reached 6.9 per cent of GDP, but then declined to 2.8 per cent by 1976. Simultaneously the acceleration in inflation eroded the real stimulus to the economy; in 1974 the real cyclically-adjusted PSBR was −4.3 per cent of GDP (Table 9.8). The government sector had a surplus in real cyclically adjusted terms: the real fiscal stance was deflationary. Other pressures on governments (fear of inflation, and balance of payments difficulties) precluded vigorous use of Keynesian fiscal policies to combat unemployment. Table 9.8 shows that from 1979 to 1982 the real fiscal stance was neutral, or mildly deflationary—there was a positive real PSBR. But from 1980 the level of economic activity was very low, so the cyclically adjusted real PSBR was very deflationary. The constraints and limitations on the use of fiscal policy to regulate the economy are the subject of the next three chapters.

10

Imports, Exports, and the Balance of Payments

The final elements of aggregate demand, exports and imports, are the subject of this chapter. Exports of goods and services are a positive component of aggregate demand, and imports are a negative component, or leakage, from aggregate demand. Table 10.1 summarizes the balance of payments in 1979. The *current account balance*—£0.6 bn—is the difference between exports and imports of goods and the credits and debits for invisible transactions. In addition to these income flows, there are short and long-term capital flows. In 1979 there was a net inflow of £1.8 bn on the capital account, and Britain was allocated £0.2 bn of SDRs.[1] In theory the sum of the current account balance, SDRs allocated, and the balance of the capital flows, which was £1.4 bn, should equal the change in the reserves—*the balance for official financing*. Each component of the balance of payments is estimated independently, the balance for official financing from recorded changes in reserves, and exports and imports from data on UK trade, etc. The account does not balance because of errors and omissions, and the balancing item, which was £0.4 bn, restores the balance.

The balance of payments has been a constant source of concern for Britain's post-war governments. While it is true that the balance of payments must balance, in the sense that all the revenue and capital transactions are offset by official financing, the balance may be struck after drawing down reserves at an unsustainable rate. Pressure on the reserves may originate from a deficit on the current account and/or investment and capital account flows. Moreover, a perfectly acceptable balance of payments position can co-exist with a high level of unemployment as in 1981 and 1982. For a satisfactory equilibrium there must be no tendency towards

[1] SDRs are special drawing rights; a paper, international reserve asset allocated by the IMF.

TABLE 10.1   *The balance of payments in 1979*

The current account

	£ bn.		£ bn.
Imports of goods	44.1	Exports of goods	40.7
		Deficit on visible trade	3.4
	44.1		44.1
Invisible debits	20.9	Invisible credits	23.8
Invisible surplus	2.9		
	23.8		23.8

The capital account

Investment and other capital transactions (net inflows)	1.8	Current account deficit	0.6
Allocation of SDRs	0.2	Balance for official financing	1.9
Balancing item	0.4		
	2.5		2.5

Source: *Economic Trends*, March 1984.

a persistent reduction in the reserves when the economy is operating at an acceptable level of output and employment. However, it is important to recognize at the outset that the balance of payments has not been the fundamental problem of the British economy. The balance of payments can be likened to a scoreboard which records the state of Britain's relative competitiveness. This is determined by the exchange rate, the terms on which we trade with other countries, and most importantly, the competitiveness of industry and its ability to adapt. This chapter starts with a review of the post-war development of UK trade. Then the forces determining competiveness are considered.

Balance of Payments Statistics

The balance of payments through the 1970s is summarized in Table 10.2, and a longer view is shown in Diagrams 10.1(a), (b), and (c). The statistics are shown as percentages of GDP at current market prices; this adjustment means that the figures are related to the changing price level and to the changing volume of output of the economy which affects its ability to adjust to reduce balance of payments deficits. (Over long periods, changes in actual output are a fair indicator of potential output.)

Historically, the main features have been a visible trade deficit (for goods) roughly balanced by an invisible surplus (for services). The current account balance shown in Diagram 10.1(a) fluctuated between surplus and deficit throughout the 'stop-go' years from 1950 to 1967; a deficit was often the signal for a 'stop'. Diagram 10.1(b) shows the components of the current account, and unemployment. Years of lowest unemployment coincide with the largest deficits, as in 1951, 1955, 1974, and 1979, or followed them one year later, as in 1961, 1965, and 1969. The explanation of the link is that when unemployment is low output is high relative to capacity, and imports are sucked in by the high demand and the visible deficit is increased. The reason unemployment follows the maximum deficit in some years is that unemployment lages behind changes in output; firms may not change employment simultaneously with changes in output, but after a lag.

TABLE 10.2 *U.K. Balance of Payments as Percentages of GDP*[a]

	Exports of goods (1)	Imports of goods (2)	Visible balance (3)	Invisible balance (4)	Current account balance (5)	Capital transfers and allocation of SDRs (6)	Capital flows (net) (7)	Total for official financing (8)	Balancing item (9)
1971	15.7	15.4	+ 0.3	+ 1.6	+ 2.0	+ 0.2	+ 3.1	− 5.7	+ 0.4
1972	14.8	16.0	− 1.2	+ 1.5	+ 0.4	+ 0.2	− 1.1	+ 1.8	− 1.3
1973	16.2	19.8	− 3.5	+ 2.2	− 1.3	− 0.1	+ 0.2	+ 1.1	+ 0.1
1974	19.6	26.0	− 6.4	+ 2.5	− 3.9	− 0.1	+ 1.9	+ 2.0	+ 0.1
1975	18.3	21.5	− 3.2	+ 1.7	− 1.4	0	+ 0.1	+ 1.4	− 0.1
1976	20.1	23.2	− 3.1	+ 2.5	− 0.7	0	− 2.4	+ 2.9	+ 0.2
1977	21.9	23.5	− 1.6	+ 1.6	0.0	0	− 2.9	− 5.1	+ 2.2
1978	21.1	22.0	− 0.9	+ 1.6	+ 0.7	0	− 2.6	+ 0.7	+ 1.2
1979	20.9	22.7	− 1.8	+ 1.5	− 0.3	+ 0.1	+ 0.9	− 1.0	+ 0.2
1980	20.8	20.2	+ 0.6	+ 0.9	+ 1.6	+ 0.1	− 0.6	− 0.6	− 0.4
1981	20.3	18.8	+ 1.5	+ 1.4	+ 2.9	+ 0.1	− 2.9	+ 0.3	− 0.3
1982	20.2	19.3	+ 0.9	+ 1.2	+ 2.0	0	− 1.2	+ 0.5	− 1.3
1983	20.2	20.3	− 0.2	+ 0.8	+ 0.7	0	− 0.7	+ 0.3	− 0.3

Scources: *ETAS* 1984, and *Economic Trends*, March 1984.

[a] Columns (1) − (2) = (3)
  Columns (3) + (4) = (5)
  Columns (5) + (6) + (7) + (9) = − (8)

Following the 1967 devaluation of sterling, the visible trade balance improved until 1971, although the extent to which this improvement may be attributed to devaluation is uncertain (for the reasons given in Chapter 12).

From 1971 the balance rapidly deteriorated, so that by 1974 the visible trade deficit amounted to £5.35 bn—more than 6 per cent of GDP. From this low level it improved, though with a set-back in 1979, to stand at a surplus of 1.5 per cent of GDP in 1981, before falling back to a small deficit in 1983. Several factors were involved in this pattern of events—increases in the prices of imports, particularly oil imports, changes in exchange rates, the level of activity in the domestic economy and abroad, and the UK oil production. The visible balance excluding oil is also shown in Diagram 10.1(b). In spite of the low level of activity in the economy in 1983, the non-oil visible deficit represented 3 per cent of GDP, similar to the non-oil deficit in 1974. In 1983 the non-oil visible deficit was offset by a surplus for oil, in contrast to 1974 when the oil deficit increased the visible deficit.

Diagram 10.1(c) shows that trade has become increasingly important for the UK during the 1970s; as oil and other commodity prices rose, imports formed a higher proportion of GDP. In addition, the volume of imports and exports increased faster than GDP during the 1970s. The increasing relative importance of trade during the 1970s contrasts with developments before the mid-1960s when trade was falling in relation to GDP.

In 1979 imports and exports of goods were a little over 20 per cent of GDP, and trade in goods and services combined represented a third of GDP. An index of the terms of trade for goods is also shown in Diagram 10.1(c); when the prices of our exports increase relative to import prices, the terms of trade 'improve', and the index rises.[2] In 1973 and 1974 the terms of trade fell as oil and other commodity prices increased.

Diagram 10.1(a) provides a comparison of the current

---

[2] If Britain's export prices rise relative to its import prices it may not 'improve' the economy. If the rise in export prices reflects increases in UK costs and leads to a loss of markets it will be harmful.

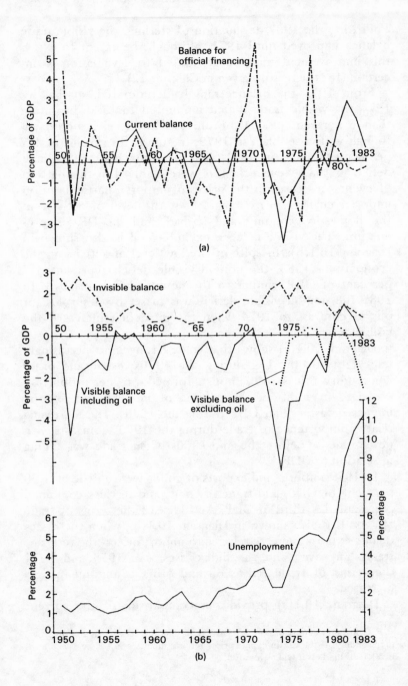

(a)

(b)

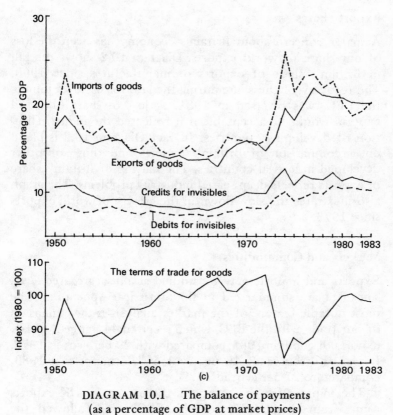

DIAGRAM 10.1   The balance of payments
(as a percentage of GDP at market prices)

(a) The current balance and the balance for official financing.
(b) The visible and invisible balances.
(c) Exports and imports as % of GDP.

Sources: *ETAS* 1984, and *Economic Trends*, 1984.

account balance and the balance for official financing. The
current balance is a large component of the balance for
official financing, so it is not surprising that they move
together. There is another link between the two balances. A
feature of the balance for official financing is that it was
heavily in surplus in 1971 and 1977: the inflow of reserves
represented more than 5 per cent of GDP in both years. The
current account was favourable in 1971, and in 1977 the
current account was improving. The strength of the trading
account encouraged capital inflows.

Export Shares

A major concern about Britain's economy has been the loss of our share of world exports. Diagram 10.2 shows the fall in Britain's share of exports of manufactures since 1960. The recovery of the share during the late 1970s, after joining the EEC, was reversed in 1981. A loss of share of world exports would be acceptable if it reflected the industrialization of developing countries. In fact Diagram 10.2 is based on a comparison of Britain's exports and those of other developed industrial countries. The halving of Britain's share of exports reflects deep-seated industrial problems. The graph also illustrates the slow-down in the growth of world exports since 1973.

Markets and Commodities

Exports and imports may be studied at a disaggregated level. The data are summarized in the Statistical Appendix.[3] The most notable feature of the market analysis is the expansion of our trade with the EEC, which received 44 per cent of UK exports of goods in 1983, compared with 29 per cent in 1970. It was the source of 46 per cent of UK imports in 1983, compared to 27 per cent in 1970.

The impetus for the change in the pattern of UK exports came from membership of the EEC. This followed the progressive loss of the trading privileges Britain held in colonial and Commonwealth markets. These changes were of great importance: in 1950 British industry was oriented towards the home, colonial, and Commonwealth markets. In 1984 Europe is the home market for many British firms. A key to understanding movements of the balance of payments is appreciation of the lags between these changes and their full consequences. It takes time to take advantage of new markets for exports; marketing organizations have to be built up, and special designs of products may be required.

The main change in the commodity pattern of Britain's trade is the increase in fuel exports and the reduction in the volume of fuel imports. The share of manufactures in Britain's

[3] See Appendix 10.1 and 10.2.

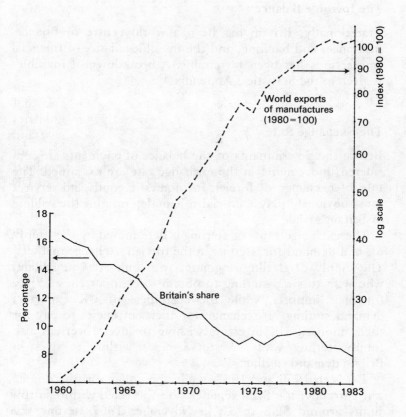

DIAGRAM 10.2   Britain's share of world trade in manufactures[a]

Source: *NIER*, May 1984 and earlier issues.

[a] World Trade includes exports of manufactures by eleven advanced
industrial countries.

exports has inevitably declined as North Sea oil exports have
increased. Between 1970 and 1983 overseas manufacturers
increased their share of Britain's imports from 50.5 to 68 per
cent. The share of food and basic materials halved. Increasing imports of manufactures is a long-standing trend. In 1950
imports of manufactures represented only 18 per cent of
total imports, and a quarter of Britain's exports of manufactures; by 1983 imports of manufactures exceeded exports
of manufactures by 16 per cent.

The Invisible Balance

Traditionally, Britain has been a world centre of finance, insurance, and banking; and the invisible balance of financial transactions has been favourable. A breakdown of invisibles is given in the Statistical Appendix.[4]

The Exchange Rate

Before the determinants of the balance of payments are considered, movements in the exchange rate are examined. The rate of exchange of foreign for domestic goods and services must obviously play a crucial role in determining the volume of Britain's trade.

The exchange rate for sterling is determined by the supply of, and demand for, sterling in the foreign exchange markets. The supply of sterling originates with importers in Britain, who wish to swap sterling to obtain foreign currency to pay for their imports, while the customers of UK exporters demand sterling in exchange for their currencies to pay for their imports. UK investors wishing to invest overseas also supply sterling, while investors overseas wishing to invest in Britain demand sterling.

Between 1950 and 1967, while the dollar was the dominant currency, the $:£ exchange rate was fixed within narrow limits around $2.8 to £1; in November 1967 sterling was devalued to $2.4 to £1. There were some adjustments to other exchange rates; the franc was devalued in 1958, and the DM revalued by small amounts on several occasions. Apart from these changes, exchange rates were fixed—pegged to the dollar—during the period from 1950 to 1970. Governments of countries other than the USA, maintained their exchange rates by regulating and balancing the supply and demand for their currencies by adding to, or reducing, their currency reserves. It was shown in Chapter 2 that UK and World inflation rates were similar during this period. Fixed exchange rates are said to have imposed discipline for a common inflation rate set by America. The contrary argument is that

[4] See Appendix 10.3.

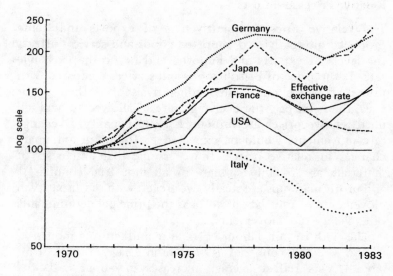

DIAGRAM 10.3   Indices of exchange rates relative to sterling
(1970 =100)

Sources: *ETAS* 1984, and *Economic Trends*, March 1984.

the fixed exchange rate system could be maintained only so
long as inflation rates were similar.

Diagram 10.3 shows the movements of relative exchange
rates since 1970, which was taken as the base for comparative
purposes because it preceded the floating of exchange rates.
This does not mean that exchange rates were in stable equilibrium in 1970; in fact the fixed exchange rate system
collapsed because of disequilibrium. The diagram shows the
movement of selected currencies and a composite index,
the effective exchange rate,[5] relative to sterling. The yen,
DM, and franc rose against sterling between 1970 and 1975.
In 1975 and 1976 these currencies and the dollar rose relative
to sterling. The trend was reversed from 1977 to 1980,
when sterling appreciated against all the other currencies,
but the change-round for the dollar occurred before that
for the DM and yen.

[5] The effective exchange rate is a weighted average of exchange rates, with the
weights depending upon trade flows.

Relative Prices and Costs

The relative price competitiveness of exports and home produced alternatives to imported goods and services affects the levels of exports and imports, and hence the exchange rate. If the price of British goods and services compared with prices at which our main trading rivals offer their goods rises, then *cet. par.* the exchange rate, if allowed to, will fall until relative prices are brought back to equality. Exchange rate movements would be expected to follow or anticipate changes in relative prices. If we assume that unit costs of materials are roughly similar for all industrial countries,[6] and profit mark-ups are steady, we are left with the disparity in movements of unit labour costs as the principal determinants of exchange rate movements.

The path of unit labour costs in manufacturing industry[7] in the selected countries is shown in Diagram 10.4. Unit labour costs reflect average increases in labour costs per hour, of which wages are the largest item; other labour costs include social security charges. Increases in the volume of output per person-hour—improvements in productivity—reduce unit labour costs. Wages in Britain have increased more rapidly than those in the other countries, apart from Italy, and during the 1970s productivity increased more slowly in Britain than in other countries, apart from the USA. Italian unit labour costs increased at about the same rate as those in the UK throughout the 1970s. Unit labour costs in all the other countries fell relative to those in the UK. To what extent do these differences explain movements of exchange rates? Diagram 10.5 shows movements in exchange rates adjusted for movements in unit labour costs—these indices show the changes in real exchange rates. Plainly, movements in unit labour costs can explain a substantial part of the changes in exchange rates. Real exchange rates move in much closer harmony than actual exchange rates. The adjusted

---

[6] The USA has indigenous supplies of many raw materials which other countries import, and its prices have diverged from those ruling in countries which rely on imports.

[7] Manufacturing is the main sector affected by international trade, and the statistics for it are more comprehensive and reliable. None the less, it is a qualification to this analysis that it is restricted to manufacturing.

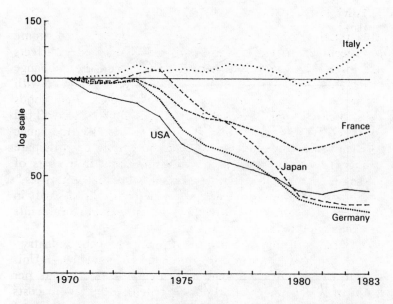

DIAGRAM 10.4   Indices of unit labour costs relative to UK unit labour costs (1970 = 100)

Sources: OECD, *Historical Statistics 1960–81*, p. 94, and *Economic Outlook*, December 1983, p. 52.

yen, DM, franc, and lira all rose relative to sterling in 1973, and they stayed above the 1970 real parities until 1978. Rapid wage inflation in Britain, and the rise in sterling, then increased Britain's real exchange rate. By 1980, in real terms, all five currencies were below their 1970 level relative to sterling. The dollar followed a separate path; from 1970 it declined relative to the other currencies. By 1980, in real terms, the dollar had fallen by a half relative to sterling. After 1980 the dollar recovered, and in 1983 stood at 71 per cent of its 1970 real parity.

The relationship between costs and exchange rates runs in both directions. If Britain's costs increase, the exchange rate falls, and it may move before the changes in costs in anticipation of them. If the exchange rate changes this will lead to changes in costs. Import prices are a component of costs, and they will rise more or less in proportion to a fall in sterling. An increase in consumer prices caused by an increase

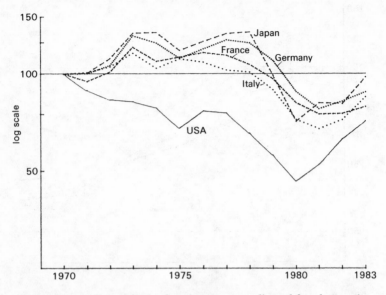

DIAGRAM 10.5   Indices of exchange rates adjusted for changes in
unit labour costs relative to the UK index[a]

Sources: Data for Diagrams 10.3 and 10.4.

[a] For manufacturing industries.

in import prices may lead to increases in wages which will
feed into costs.

If changes in earnings and productivity were the only cause
of exchange rate movements, the indices in Diagram 10.5
should remain at 100. Divergences from this base show the
extent to which other factors, including intervention by the
central authorities, influence exchange rates. The UK exchange rate fluctuated for a number of reasons besides our
relatively rapid increase in wages and slow growth of productivity. An obviously important factor causing the recovery
between 1976 and 1980 was the influence of oil, described
in Chapter 2. Since 1976 the UK has become increasingly
self-sufficient in oil, and sterling, as a result, appreciated
considerably. The US, in contrast, became increasingly
dependent on oil imports during the 1970s (see Diagram 2.7),
and the dollar fell. The real depreciation of the yen in 1979
and 1980 shown in Diagram 10.5, was in part due to the

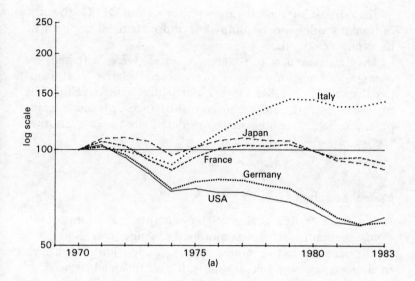

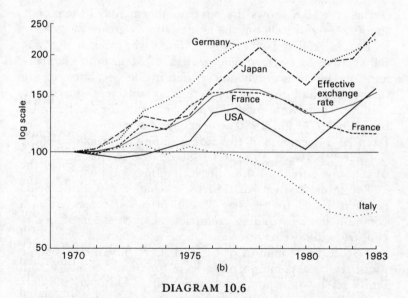

DIAGRAM 10.6

(a) Indices of M$_1$ and quasi money relative to the UK; (1970 = 100).

(b) Indices of exchange rates relative to sterling.

Source for M$_1$ and quasi money: *International Financial Statistics*, various issues.

increased cost of the oil Japan imports from OPEC—the cost of Japan's oil imports jumped to more than 50 per cent of its exports of goods.

The movements of exchange rates were affected by domestic conditions which determined relative cost competitiveness, but other factors, particularly the development of North Sea oil and oil price disturbances, played a major part. Monetary conditions, considered next, were another factor.

Money Supply

It has been argued that monetary factors are an important, even dominant, factor determining exchange rates. Relatively rapid increases in the money supply in one country will suck in imports, cause a net capital outflow, and lead to a fall in the exchange rate.

Diagram 10.6 shows the relative movements of the money supply. Only in Italy has the money supply grown faster than in Britain, and it is the only country whose exchange rate fell relative to sterling. The growth of M in both Germany and the USA was much slower than in the UK, but the path of the DM and the dollar were very different relative to sterling. There were some sharp movements of exchange rates between 1975 and 1980 which have no counterpart in differential movements of the money supply. For example, the dollar fell between 1977 and 1980 relative to sterling in spite of the slow growth of the American money supply.

The monetary explanation for exchange rate movements is often linked to 'the law of one price'. If prices are at a common level in trading countries, an increase in M in one country will raise its price level, and its exchange rate will fall to restore the common price level. Certainly there is some pressure for a common price level for *traded* goods, within limits set by transport costs and tariffs. Although the data analysed so far relate to costs, not prices of exports or consumer prices, they do suggest that there is some flexibility. Diagram 10.5 witnesses an effective devaluation of sterling during the period 1971 to 1976. Our costs and prices fell relative to those of Germany, France, Japan, and Italy, though they increased relative to costs and prices in the USA.

Competitiveness

Diagram 10.5, which showed the movement of the inverse of unit labour costs adjusted for exchange rate changes relative to the UK, is the best measure available of Britain's competitiveness. Diagram 10.7 gives two additional measures of competitiveness, relative export prices and relative wholesale prices. As would be expected, export prices move less than unit labour costs because the costs of UK firms include material as well as labour costs, and these are set in world commodity markets and are not reduced by devaluation. Also, UK firms have to set prices in competitive markets. When our costs fall relative to those of our competitors firms may not pass on all the reductions in lower prices, and they may be unable to fully pass on increases in relative costs. In fact the extent to which relative export prices moved—by 9 per cent between 1971 and 1976—repudiates the strict application of the so called 'law of one price'. The movement of relative wholesale prices, which is for home sales not export sales, is closer to that for labour costs.

So far the discussion has focused on *movements* of relative prices and costs. Throughout the 1970s the *level* of wages was lower in Britain than in Germany, our principal competitor, and the same applies to the USA. A new enterprise which could match productivity in Germany had lower labour costs in Britain.

The Effects of Changes in Exchange Rates

Britain's competitiveness, measured by relative unit labour costs, did improve following the 1967 devaluation, and improved again when sterling floated down in 1973 and 1974. Some of the first improvement was lost between 1969 and 1971, but not all of it. In 1971 relative unit labour costs were still 9 per cent below their 1966 level. Only in 1980, when sterling rose like a phoenix, were the effects of earlier devaluations on relative unit labour costs wiped out.

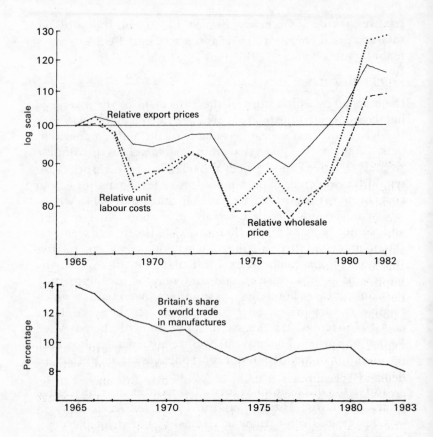

DIAGRAM 10.7   Measures of UK trade competitiveness[a]
(1965 = 100)

Sources: *ETAS* 1984, *Economic Trends*, March 1984, and *NIER*, May 1984 and earlier issues.

[a] The indices show movements of UK prices and costs relative to weighted averages for competitors. Downward movements indicate increased competitiveness.

Devaluation of sterling was a deliberate policy, though the extent of devaluation got out of hand in 1976. Was it effective? The results of devaluation depend upon the effects of increased competitiveness not relative export prices alone, as firms may simply increase profit margins on exports and overseas market-ing expenditure in response to a devaluation. Here the relationship between relative costs and market share is considered. From the mid-1970s Britain's share of world trade in manufactures (shown in Diagram 10.7) did stabilize. Allowing for lags between changes in costs and performance, the devaluations may have been a factor in this improvement. Since the revaluation of sterling in 1980 the slide in Britain's share has recommenced.

Factors Affecting Exports and Imports

The forces which determine exports and imports can be divided into three groups—income movements, relative price movements, and a rag-bag category of other factors. Since the 1950s Britain's imports and exports have grown more slowly than those of our competitors. The main causes of this are included in the other factors, in particular the slower improvement in the specifications and quality (broadly defined) of our goods and services.

Some economists emphazise the link between income and trade, that the income elasticity of world demand for British exports is low. Our exports grow slowly relative to the growth of world income, while the income elasticity of Britain's demand for imports is high. Consequently Britain has to increase aggregate demand more slowly than the world average to avoid an excess of imports over exports. Changing relative prices—reducing the relative price of British goods and services—is seen as one way of offsetting any unfavourable income or other factors. However, the price elasticities of demand for our exports and our demand for imports are reckoned to be moderate, and so substantial changes in relative prices are required to move the balance of payments.

(a) The 'Other' Factors

The 'other' factors which determine our trading performance are difficult to specify and measure; none the less, as we attach the greatest importance to them, they are considered first. They exclude factors which enter into measured unit costs—changes in costs including wages, in measured productivity,

and in exchange rates. They include the development of new
and better products, and the improvement of financial and
marketing packages which accompany many transactions.
They have to be considered relative to the improvements made
by German, Japanese, and other competitors.

Included in the other factors is the emergence of some
developing countries as significant exporters of manufactures.
This intensified competition in world markets, and made the
retention of existing market shares by the established
countries far more difficult. They had to adapt and produce
new exports. Table 10.3(a) shows the changing shares of
world exports of manufactures. Over the twenty-year period
the share of the developing countries in world trade has
more than doubled, but still remains quite small at 9 per
cent. In the 1970s the exports of some Asian developing
countries grew rapidly, but the data do not suggest that it is
developing countries which are the source of Britain's economic difficulties. Developed countries still account for four-
fifths of world trade, and Britain has a surplus with developing
countries. Also, many developing countries have an insatiable
demand for imports only limited by their ability to export.

(b) Income

In modern macroeconomic models the level of aggregate
demand in world markets is the prime factor determining
Britain's exports.

TABLE 10.3   *World exports*

(a) *Shares in world exports of manufactures*

	Developing countries	Centrally planned economies	Developed market economies
1960	3.9	12.4	83.8
1970	5.0	10.1	84.9
1980	9.0	8.1	82.9

(b) *Destination of developed countries exports*
(Percentages)

1963	25.7	3.3	71.0
1960	20.5	3.9	75.6
1978	26.0	5.0	69.0

Source: UNIDO *World Industry in 1980.*

Diagram 10.8 shows the relationship between the growth of exports for the UK, West Germany, and Japan, and OECD exports, which are used as a proxy for the growth of world demand. Plainly, the growth of world exports is a significant factor explaining variations in the growth of British exports, which include exports of oil. The constant, −2.9, generated by the regression test shows that in the absence of any growth in OECD exports UK exports would fall by 2.9 per cent; there is a trend for UK exports to fall by 2.9 per cent a year. The coefficient of X indicates that for every one per cent increase in OECD exports, UK exports increase by 1.07 per cent. The constant term for Japan suggests its trend change in exports is much more favourable, +7.6 per cent a year. Germany's is negative, −1.1 per cent. The low R^2 for Japan also suggests that Japan's export growth is not closely dependent on the rate of growth of total OECD exports.

The pressure of demand in Britain is also a significant factor. When domestic demand is slack British firms push sales elsewhere, particularly in Europe. The recession in Britain in 1981, which was deeper than in competitor countries, may have been a cause of our good export performance in relation to our costs at that time.

In the Keynesian system the principal determinant of imports is aggregate demand in the UK. Diagram 10.9 shows the relationship between imports of *goods* and the growth of GDP; changes in the volume of imports are plotted against changes in real GDP for the period since 1965. This period includes the development of North Sea oil, which directly kept down the growth of imports. There emerges a positive relationship between the two, although not a particularly close one. The equation indicates that imports of goods increase at twice the rate of increase of GDP, and that there is a very small trend increase in the growth of imports, but the equation may exaggerate the effects of income on imports, and underestimate the trend increase in imports for reasons given below. The equation indicates a high marginal propensity to import (MPM). With imports of goods representing 20 per cent of GDP, the MPM (for *goods*) would be about 0.4.

One factor which determines the effect of a change in home demand on imports is the source of the change. A rise

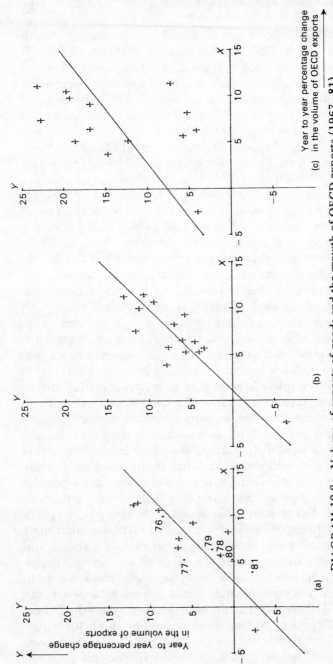

DIAGRAM 10.8   Volume of exports of goods and the growth of OECD exports

(a) UK; $Y = -2.9 + 1.07X$, $R^2 = 0.67$.   (b) West Germany; $Y = -1.1 + 1.13X$, $R^2 = 0.74$.
(c) Japan; $Y = 7.6 + 0.85X$, $R^2 = 0.19$.

Source: OECD *Historical Statistics 1960–81*.

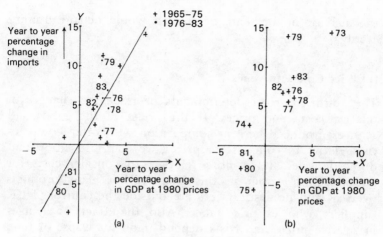

DIAGRAM 10.9   Growth of imports and GDP.

(a) Imports of all goods 1965–83.
(b) Non-oil imports of goods 1973–83.

Source: *ETAS* 1984, and *Economic Trends*, March 1984.

in government expenditure on defence, or the education or
health services, will result in a smaller increase in imports
than will a rise in personal consumption or stockbuilding. A
substantial fraction of the year to year changes in income are
made up of stock changes (see Chapter 12) and, as stocks are
import intensive, this gives a high short-run income elasticity.

Following an expansion of demand, imports of consumer
and other goods will rise; if expansion is rapid, domestic
industries are unlikely to be able to increase output fast
enough to maintain their share of the market, and so imports
will increase rapidly to fill the gap. The increase in imports
may be exacerbated by UK firms stockbuilding to get ahead
of price rises and shortages of supply. When demand falls
again, import penetration does not decline. This is the
'ratchet' effect; the proportion of imports rises in a boom
but does not fall in a recession. Overseas firms which increase their market share during a boom will try to hold
on to their increased share of the market. A disproportion-
ate part of import growth may occur in periods of expansion, and this bunching may inflate the apparent income
elasticity of imports. In the absence of booms much of

the increase in the share of imports would be spread more evenly.

(c) Price Competitiveness

The third group of determinants of trade are changes in relative costs and prices. If the prices of the goods and services produced here in competition with other countries rise relative to competitors' prices, we shall lose export and domestic sales. It is more relevant to consider costs for reasons given earlier in this chapter. For many products overseas and domestic prices are outside the control of UK suppliers, who are price takers. Also, the effects of changes in relative prices and costs depend upon the elapse of time from the change, and the responsiveness of suppliers in Britain and overseas to changes in prices. For many imports of materials and categories of food there is no British supply; the effects of changes in price work through the substitution of other products, and for materials this is usually a slow process requiring technical development.

(d) The Elasticities

The first point to be made about the income and price elasticities for both exports and imports is that they are shrouded in a mist of conflicting estimates. Estimating elasticities is complex. They vary according to the coverage (for example, goods or goods and services) and the extent of spare capacity in the economy, and they are likely to change through time. Perhaps the most serious problem is to disentangle the effects of the 'other' factors. Movements of income and prices have trend components—our income grew less rapidly than incomes in other countries, and for quite long periods our prices moved in one direction against some other countries though at varying rates, so the trend change may include some income and price effects as well as the effects of other factors. Also the effects of price changes are lagged, so they merge into trend effects.

The uncertainty about the magnitude of the elasticities is illustrated by the survey of estimates made by Thirwall and

TABLE 10.4   *Thirwall's survey of estimates of elasticities for the UK*

	Imports	Exports
	(The range of estimates surveyed)	
Income		
U.K. income	1.6 to > 3	
World income		0.86 to ≃ 1
Prices	− 0.2 to ≃ 1	0.44 to 2.8

Source: A. P. Thirwall, *Balance of Payment Theory and the United Kingdom Experience,* London 1980, pp. 204, 210–11, 230–1, 237–8.

summarized in Table 10.4. This uncertainty is important when considering prescriptions for Britain's balance of payments.

The Capital Account

So far in this chapter the flows of exports and imports of goods and services have been considered. Britain's external assets and liabilities are also important; they are summarized in Table 10.5. The accuracy of the estimates is uncertain; the Bank of England admits that 'considerable margins of error are unavoidable'. A serious qualification to the estimates is the inclusion of direct investment overseas—that is the net assets of businesses overseas owned by UK companies and individuals—at book values, which are likely to greatly understate their current value. The same applies to direct investment in the UK by owners based overseas.

For what they are worth the figures show that at the end of 1981, Britain's external assets exceeded her liabilities by £26.6 bn. (compared to a surplus of £8.6 bn. at the end of 1978). The increase in net external assets has resulted from the current balance of payments surpluses, £13 bn. during the three years 1979 to 1981, and changes in the value of assets and liabilities.

A notable feature of the external assets and liabilities is the size of the official reserves relative to the total assets and liabilities—only 4 per cent. Even if all banking and other commercial claims and liabilities are excluded, they are only 16 per cent. The exchange reserves are also modest in relation to trade flows, equivalent to about ten weeks'

TABLE 10.5   *UK external assets and liabilities, 31 December 1981*

Assets	£ bn.	
Private Sector		
Direct investment overseas[a]	41.6	
Portfolio investment overseas	22.0	
Other investment overseas	0.6	64.1
Total banking and other commercial claims		233.5
of which UK banks advances in foreign currencies		(210.0)
Public Sector		
Inter-government loans by the UK	1.2	
Subscriptions to international financial organizations	1.8	
Other	0.6	3.6
Official reserves		12.0
Total external assets		313.1
Liabilities		
Private Sector		
Direct investment in the UK[a]	26.8	
Portfolio investment in the UK	5.8	
Other investment in the UK	4.7	37.3
Total banking and other commercial liabilities		234.6
of which UK bank's deposit liabilities in foreign currencies		(215.5)
Public Sector		
Inter-government loans to the UK	1.6	
Foreign currency borrowing	4.3	
Other	8.6	14.5
Total external liabilities		286.4
Surplus		26.8

Source: Bank of England Quarterly Bulletin, June 1982.

[a] Estimated book value of net assets.

exports and imports of goods. Another comparison is with the total wealth of the community; the reserves represent only 1 per cent of total wealth, though people could not take all of this out of the UK *en masse*.

The reserves are directly controlled by the Bank of England, but if they were allowed to fall substantially, or rapidly, this would cause speculation against sterling. Until 1979 capital outflows were controlled, but since then private overseas investment from the UK has increased and was £11.2 bn. in 1981.

Even before the 1979 release of exchange controls the government had only limited control over capital transfers. Many commercial companies were in a position to speculate on expected movements in the exchange rate, and move cash into or out of Britain. With the freeing of capital movements the scope for speculative movements has been increased. Since 1979, North Sea oil and the depth of recession in Britain has buoyed up the balance of payments, and the outflow of capital has had the useful effect of keeping down the exchange rate. However, if events took a turn for the worse due to a slump in the price of oil or an increase in political uncertainty in Britain, the slim reserves could evaporate; the government has little control over the other components of the balance of payments or the components of the external balance sheet. It can raise UK interest rates to attract deposits, but that policy may clash with policies designed for the domestic economy. Much of this loss of control was probably an inevitable consequence of the growth of international trade.

The Balance of Payments Constraint

In theory and practice the volume of Britain's imports is tied to the growth of output and income of the economy. If the government operates policies which lead to a rapid growth of output and income, imports are sucked in and the balance of payments deteriorates. If the growth of Britain's exports had been buoyant, the growth of imports would not have been a cause for concern, but in practice our exports have increased relatively slowly. The sources of Britain's problem, slow product improvement and slow improvement in productivity (which is discussed in Chapter 13), are the causes of the slow growth of exports.

Solutions for problems do not necessarily have to attack their roots. One policy advocated for dealing with the balance of payments constraint is to impose import controls. This and other policies for tackling the constraint are reviewed in Chapter 12.

11

The Multiplier and Crowding-Out

Introduction

The subject of this chapter is the impact of fiscal policy on the level of activity in the economy. Firstly, using a number of restrictive assumptions including a constant rate of interest and an accommodating money supply, we estimate the size of the multiplier, which measures the increase in output following an injection of demand, whether it originates from a change in fiscal policy or from elsewhere. We then examine the implications of relaxing the assumptions, and the extent of crowding-out. Do supply restrictions prevent the multiplier from expanding output? Are injections of demand dissipated in the form of price increases? The multiplier and crowding-out, although often considered separately, are two facets of the same issue.

The Multiplier

Suppose the Government decides to build a new road network. The construction companies contracted by the Government to build the roads will hire or retain additional workers and buy materials; the workers will spend their wages on consumer goods, other firms will produce more such goods, and so on. The impact on output is greater than the initial injection. The lags in this multiplier process reflect the elapse of time between the Government deciding to increase expenditure and placing the contracts, between the placing of contracts and the work being carried out, and between the payment of wages and the purchase of consumer goods.

The process can be stated with more precision. If the marginal propensity of the community to buy domestically produced goods out of an increase in income is C, and the injection is A, the total increase in output where the elapse of time caused by the lags between each round of expenditure is $1,2,3 \ldots n$ can be expressed as:

$$\sum_{t=1}^{t=n} \Delta Y_t = A + CA + C(CA) + C(C^2A) \ldots C(C^nA)$$
$$0 < C < 1$$

This is the sum to infinity of a geometric progression which may be written:

$$\sum_{t=1}^{\infty} \Delta Y_t = A\left(\frac{1}{1-C}\right)$$

The bracketed term is the multiplier. The greater the value of C (and the lower the leakages $(1-C)$), the larger is the multiplier, and the greater the impact on the economy of a fiscal injection.

The multiplier process entails the following assumptions:
(a) Prices and wages are fixed.
(b) The supply of goods is infinitely elastic.
(c) Interest rates are fixed.
(d) Monetary policy is accommodating.
(e) There is no increase in taxation.
(f) Investment is fixed.
(g) The exchange rate is fixed.
Assumptions a to e tend to exaggerate the multiplier process, whilst f and g tend to minimize it for reasons described below. It is also assumed that there are no effects on expectations or wealth. In practice these effects could influence the size of the multiplier in either direction.

To estimate the multiplier the leakages through which the initial increase in the flow of income is dissipated must be estimated. (If there were none, the increase in income at each round would be spent in full and the multiplier would be infinite.) The leaks are direct taxation (on personal income and profits), indirect taxation, saving (by the personal and corporate sectors), spending on imports, and the diversion of exports to the home market. The greater the leaks, the weaker the multiplier.

Estimates of the Multiplier

Estimates of the *marginal* propensities to save, tax, and import should be used to calculate the multiplier, but to gain a first crude estimate of the size of the leakages the average propensities for 1979 were used. These can be readily calculated from published data. The estimates are shown in Table 11.1.

Firstly, input–output data for 1974 were used to estimate the approximate distribution of a £100m. injection into the economy for a road-building programme. Imports would increase by £15m. and indirect taxes by £2m.; the remainder of the initial expenditure of £100m. would increase income from employment by £54m. and gross profits by £29m. The results of the first round would be an increase in output and income of £83m. The second stage of the analysis was to divide this increase in domestic income between leakages and the increase in personal disposable income. Then the use made of the increase in personal disposable income was estimated. The estimated second round increase in domestic output and income was £26m. The lags in the multiplier process vary—the effects of an injection on dividends and spending out of dividends may follow a year or more after the effects on wages—so the successive rounds of the multiplier process do not fall into tidy periods of time.

The ratio of the second round increase in output and income to the first round is 26 to 83. Applying this ratio to subsequent rounds gives a final increase in output of £121m. resulting from the initial injection of £100m. Even this low multiplier is an exaggeration because *average* propensities were used to estimate the leakages. The *marginal* propensities to save, tax, and import are higher than the average propensities.[1]

The low estimate of the multiplier implies that fiscal changes have little impact on demand beyond the direct effects. This was not the view of Keynes or of policy makers in the 1950s. In his original 1931 article, Kahn specified the multiplier not in terms of income, but of employment.[2]

---

[1] See Appendix 11.1.
[2] R. F. Kahn, 'The Relation of Home Investment to Unemployment', *Economic Journal*, 1930.

TABLE 11.1   *The multiplier*

Injections £m.		Leakages £m.	
Round 1			
1. Initial injection for a road building programme	100		
2.		Imports	15
3.		Indirect taxes	2
4. Income from employment	54		
5. Gross profits	29		
6. First round increase in domestic output and income	83	First round leakages	17
Round 2			
7. Income from employment	54		
8.		Direct Taxes and NI contributions	11
9. Increase in PDI	43		
10. Gross trading profits	29		
11.	83	Taxes and employer's NI contributions	10
12.		Undistributed company profits	10
13. Increase in dividends	9		
14.		Taxes on dividends	3
15. Increase in PDI	6		
16. Total increase in PDI	49		
17.		Savings	6
18.		Indirect taxes	5
19.		Imports	12
20. Second round increase in domestic output and income	26	Second round leakages	57
21. Sum of the first and second round increase in domestic output and income £109m.			

His data translate into a multiplier of 1.75, which he suggested was a conservative estimate. Since 1931 all the leaks have increased.

Modifications to the Multiplier

It has been assumed that investment is fixed, that it is independent of output changes. In contrast, the accelerator theory described in Chapter 8 has investment as a function of changes in output. The version of the multiplier which incorporates an accelerator-type investment function has been termed the 'super-multiplier'. If a simple accelerator model were applicable, its effects in boosting the multiplier would be substantial. Alternatively, and more plausibly, it could be assumed that the extra retained profits of companies, 10 per cent of the initial injection alone (shown in row 12 of Table 11.1), are invested.[3]

A further modification of the multiplier would place more stress on permanent income and less on current income. This change would alter the structure of the multiplier response. Suppose there is an increase in government expenditure on a road-building programme leading to a rise in wage and profit incomes. It is argued that initially people regard the increase in income as temporary and spend little of it, giving a lower value for the multiplier.[4] Provided income continues at its higher level, people begin to adjust their estimates of permanent income upwards, and increase their consumption. The main multiplier effects are then lagged after the initial injection while permanent income adjusts, and the 'impact' multiplier is reduced. It follows that the opposite case, a fall in income believed to be temporary, should lead people to dis-save or borrow to maintain permanent consumption, though in practice not everyone can borrow.

---

[3] See Appendix 11.2.
[4] This is not plausible for the additional wage earners in the case of a road-building programme. The effect could be more serious if the injection took the form of a reduction in direct taxes.

The Multiplier and Fiscal Policy

The direct impact of a fiscal change to which the multiplier is applied depends on the form of the initial injection. Employment of extra teachers will mean a direct increase in domestic output and income to the value of the injection. A road-building programme would have less direct impact on personal income because of the leakages into imports and indirect taxes. A reduction in direct taxes would involve proportionately larger direct leakages for saving as well as larger leaks into imports and indirect taxes.

The impact of a fiscal injection has been considered. The leakages into taxation are revenue for the government, and any reduction in unemployment pay cuts government expenditure. The estimates show 31 per cent of the initial expenditure of £100m. recovered as increases in taxes and national insurance contributions by the end of the second round. Unemployment pay would be reduced because of the extra employment created by the injection, so a half or even more of an initial injection for a road-building programme could be offset by increases in tax revenue and reductions in expenditure. There would be lags before the outflows were recouped. These relationships have important implications, apart from their impact on the multiplier. If a government gets into a position of substantial deficit and has to cut the deficit, a vicious circle of cuts in expenditure, declining income, and falling tax revenues can occur.

Crowding-Out

The modern multiplier is quite small. Even so, our estimates were based on a number of very restrictive assumptions, which are now relaxed. Traditionally, the crowding-out debate centred around the proposition that if the Government finances a budget deficit by issuing bonds, this would raise the rate of interest and thereby crowd-out private investment expenditure. Here crowding-out is considered in a slightly different sense; to what extent is *private* expenditure affected by Government expenditure?

The traditional debate on crowding-out was very much

alive in Keynes's own day. For forty years it seemed that the Keynesian view had triumphed over the 'Treasury View' that there is complete crowding-out. The waters are far muddier now. Monetarists and Conservatives have latched onto Mr Callaghan's speech to the Labour Party Conference in 1976 in which he declared that:

We used to think that you could just spend your way out of recession, and increase employment, by cutting taxes and boosting government spending. I tell you in all candour that that option no longer exists, and that in so far as it ever did exist, it worked by injecting inflation into the economy. And each time that happened, the average level of unemployment has risen. Higher inflation, followed by higher unemployment. That is the history of the last twenty years.

It is the circumstances in which crowding-out may occur that are now examined.

(a) Financing the Deficit

The crude 'Treasury' view related to a shortage of real resources, and in particular, of real savings; it assumed there existed a fixed supply of savings (loanable funds) and that sales of government debt would displace private debt. An increase in Government expenditure would raise the rate of interest because income was fixed and the supply of savings was inelastic, thus crowding-out private investment by the same amount as the initial injection.

For Keynes, this analysis was untenable; total savings should not be regarded as fixed in an economy in which there existed unemployed resources. In Keynes's model saving is a positive function of income. From a situation below full employment, and with an accommodating money supply, an injection into the economy would raise income, and income would rise until leakages equalled the injection. The deficit would be self-financing in the longer-term in the sense that it generated extra savings and taxation, once the multiplier effects of the injection worked through.

(b) Monetary Crowding-out

The central authorities may not pursue an accommodating

monetary policy, as has been assumed so far. One alternative is to finance all the extra expenditure by the sale of bonds; this would put upward pressure on interest rates. In this case monetary crowding-out occurs, due not to a shortage of savings but a shortage of money. Kahn was aware of the importance of his assumptions about the money supply for assessing the multiplier effects of injections.

If ... the increased demand for working capital that may result from increased employment [is] made the occasion for a restriction of credit, then any attempt to increase employment—whether it is by way of road building or by any other means, or indeed, by awaiting the return of world prosperity—may be rendered nugatory.[5]

Kahn's argument was that the money supply should be allowed to increase initially to provide 'bridging finance', since the savings generated by the expansion only accrue after the initial deficit, so finance must be sought from the banks in the short term. This expansion of the money supply helps to keep interest rates stable in the face of fiscal expansion. As higher savings are generated the debt can be funded, i.e. long-term debt would be exchanged for short-term debt. Nevertheless, if fiscal expansion is maintained and output increases, this will increase the transactions demand for money and put some pressure on interest rates which will crowd-out investment and consumption expenditure. The outcome depends on the responsiveness of the demand for money, investment, and consumption to changes in interest rates. Keynesians stress the flexibility of the monetary relationships[6] and advocate an accommodating expansion of the money supply.

British governments have funded a large part of their deficits by borrowing in the long-term bond market. Although an injection may increase saving, it may not lead to an equivalent expansion of funds available for the purchase of

[5] Ibid., p. 175.
[6] Keynesians would expect the extra bonds to be bought without much pressure on interest rates during a period of recession, and that funds would be reallocated within the capital market so that money balances are used without much change in yields. The money balances do not have to be invested in the extra bonds. Borrowers who are displaced by the sale of bonds will raise funds from other sources, and there may be several links in the chain between money balances and investment in the extra bonds.

bonds, so an expansionary fiscal policy could lead to an increase in the interest rate on long-term bonds relative to yields on other assets. Also, the government dominates the borrowing side of the long-term bond market. If the market is aware that the government has a substantial extra borrowing requirement, buyers may hold back from buying bonds and force up interest rates, because they expect a fall in the price.

(c) Prices and Supply

Two of the assumptions made earlier to estimate the multiplier concern the impact of an increase in demand on prices and supply. It was assumed that the increase in demand did not lead to increases in prices and that supply was completely flexible. Monetarists and new classical economists claim that the effect of a government injection, which is paid for by increasing M, would be to increase prices which would crowd-out the effects of the injection on output. Mr Callaghan referred to a link between injections and prices.

The effects of injections on prices depend on the state of the economy into which demand is injected. Historically there have been periods of 'intense depression', as in the early 1930s when there was excess capacity and supply was elastic. At such times changes in unemployment have little impact on wages and hence prices. The Phillips relationship implied that for any reduction in unemployment from below 5 per cent there would be some trade off; an increase in demand, output, and employment would result in faster wage increases and inflation.[7] The effects of fiscal expansion on prices, since the collapse of the Phillips relationship, are obscure. It is unlikely that the impact of falling unemployment on wage and prices has diminished, but the position in 1984 is closer to that of the 1930s: mass unemployment would dampen the response of wages to falling unemployment with a moderate expansion of demand.[8]

[7] The increase in demand and output may also increase productivity, and so offset some of the increase in wages.

[8] The response of prices to fiscal expansion also depends upon the form of the fiscal stimulus. A reduction in indirect taxes would initially moderate wage and price rises.

Monetarists believe the PSBR, and particularly the unfunded PSBR (that part of the PSBR not funded by sales of
bonds, or other securities, to the non-bank public), to be
important for inflation. Looked at from the supply of funds
side, changes in £M$_3$ consist of the unfunded PSBR plus
changes in sterling-lending by UK banks to the UK private
sector, plus net lending by banks based overseas to the UK
private sector. The unfunded PSBR increases the money
supply directly and indirectly by providing the banks with
reserve assets to act as a base for increased lending. Monetarists argue that if the PSBR is not funded it leads to increases
in the money stock. This, given their other beliefs, is
inflationary.

If prices do rise then this would cause crowding-out by
reducing the increase in the real money supply.[9] Other
short-term mechanisms which lead to crowding-out if prices
rise are an increase in saving by the personal sector, fiscal
drag,[10] and reductions in the share of home and export
markets held by domestic producers unless there is a
compensating devaluation.[11]

There is a distinction between this sort of crowding-out
from the one described earlier. In the first, increased government spending drives up the interest rate since total savings
are considered fixed. In the second, aggregate demand *does*
increase, but only temporarily. The increase in aggregate
demand itself causes prices to rise which cause a reduction
in aggregate demand.

(d) Exchange Rate

So far it has been assumed that the exchange rate is fixed. It
is quite unrealistic to assume a fixed exchange rate in present
circumstances. A net injection into the economy would
increase imports, reduce exports and put pressure on sterling. *Ceteris paribus*, sterling would fall in value and this

---

[9] This assumes the money supply is not expanded to accommodate higher
prices as well as the fiscal expansion, and that a contraction of the real money
supply reduces demand for the reasons given in Chapter 3.

[10] Money tax revenue rises faster than money income because of progressive
tax rates.

[11] See Appendix 11.3.

would increase international demand for domestic production; crowding-in, by reducing imports and increasing exports. The fall in sterling would create pressure for higher wages and prices. Again, in 1984 the high level of unemployment may smother this pressure.

(e) Wealth Effects

An injection will create a number of conflicting wealth effects. We start with the wealth creating effects.

(i) The issue of extra cash, bills, or bonds will create extra financial assets, cash, or claims to future interest payments and repayments of loans.

(ii) A net injection could generate a future flow of income and hence wealth. For example, a road-building programme will result in an income flow and hence an increase in present wealth by cutting future transport costs.[12]

(iii) If the injection increases the output of the economy that will raise profits, equity prices, and wealth.

The wealth reducing effects of an injection are:

(i) If investment is crowded-out that will reduce the future flow of income and wealth.

(ii) If the injection is financed by borrowing, the implicit liability for increased taxes to pay the interest on the borrowing is a liability, reducing the wealth of the private sector.

(iii) If the injection leads to an increase in interest rates that reflects a fall in bond prices and, through portfolio effects, falls in other asset prices and so less wealth.

(iv) If an injection leads to an increase in prices that will reduce the real value of financial assets and financial liabilities.

On an a priori basis, it is not possible to say whether the wealth effects of injections will be positive or negative. But if an injection is made at a time of substantial spare capacity and is effective in increasing output without inflating prices, then the wealth effects are likely to be positive.

(f) Expectations

An effect of relaxing the assumption that expectations will

---

[12] See Appendix 11.4.

not be affected by an injection is that the process of adjustment, including changes in the exchange rate, will be accelerated. An injection would generate an expectation of a falling
exchange rate, and movements of deposits out of sterling
would bring forward the change. Also changes in the money
supply to accommodate an injection could lead to outflows
of currency and to speculative movements in the same
direction. If investors expect an injection to lead to faster
inflation, that may cause them to try to increase liquidity.

If agents already expected the government to inject demand
into the economy, that would reduce the boost to the
economy created by an injection because some of its effects,
for example on asset values and expected future income, would
have been discounted. In practice, not all the effects will have
been discounted,[13] and if an expected injection is not made,
agents will make adjustments which lead to a fall in demand.

Crowding-in

If a government injection does succeed in sustaining a higher
level of activity in the short term, there may be some long-
term crowding-in. Government injections in the form of
investment, or investment incentives, may increase the
capacity and hence output of the economy, while a higher
level of capacity utilization may generate more investment
and increase the capacity of the economy. There could be a
similar effect on employment. Maintenance of a higher level
of employment may increase the pool of skills and experience.

Summing Up

A number of effects which will multiply, crowd-out, or
crowd-in, a government injection of demand into the economy
have been listed. The final result depends upon the initial
expenditure and the method of financing the expenditure.
But starting from a position of substantial unemployment
and unused industrial capacity, and with an accommodating
increase in the money supply, there is no a priori reason to

[13] An injection of demand which takes the form of employing more people
in the public sector is unlikely to have been fully discounted by the employees.
Many of them would be unable to borrow to anticipate their expectations.

conclude that an injection will be crowded-out. If the injection is financed by bond sales without an accommodating money supply, then some crowding-out may occur. But if government-bond financed injections are completely crowded-out, this must apply to private loan-financed injections as well.

The Evidence on Crowding-out

Evidence of the relationship between government injections to the economy and the level of economic activity, the money supply, and interest rates are now examined. The qualifications to using the PSBR as a measure of the injection of demand into the economy by the government, because of the varying impact of different categories of government expenditure and taxes on demand, and the effects of cyclical changes in the economy and inflation on the PSBR, were described in Chapter 9. Nevertheless, Mrs Thatcher's government has attached great importance to the size of the PSBR measured in *money* terms, so the relationships between the crude PSBR and other economic variables are analysed in Table 11.2 and Diagram 11.1.

The relationship between the PSBR and the level of economic activity measured by unemployment is not close. Unemployment in 1970 was 2.6 per cent of the labour force, and the PSBR as a percentage of GDP was zero. By 1975 the PSBR was 10 per cent of GDP and unemployment averaged 3.4 per cent. The explanations for this perverse relationship are that other forces were depressing demand, offsetting the effects of the increase in government injections on demand, output, and employment, and the increase in unemployment and the recession increased the PSBR. The other forces included the increase in personal savings partly caused by rapid inflation. In this period the effects of injections were not crowded-out by a tight monetary policy. The rapid growth of the real money supply in 1972 and 1973 is shown in Table 3.4.

The PSBR fell to 4.2 per cent of GDP in 1977, while unemployment increased to 5.5 per cent. Then the PSBR increased to 6.5 per cent of GDP in 1979 as unemployment fell to 5.1 per cent. The increase in unemployment from

TABLE 11.2   The PSBR

	PSBR £ bn.	PSBR as % of GDP	Un-employ-ment %	Funded PSBR as % of GDP	Unfunded PSBR as % of GDP	Sterling lending to the UK private sector as % of GDP	Change in £M$_3$ as % of GDP	Col 2 as a ratio of col 7	Col 5 as a ratio of col 7	Interest Rates Short-term	Interest Rates Long-term
	(1)	(2)	(3)	(4)	(5)	(6)	(7)	(8)	(9)	(10)	(11)
1970	0.0	0.0	2.2	− 0.2	+ 0.2	+ 1.6	2.9	0.0	− 0.1	7.0	9.3
1971	1.4	2.4	2.9	− 3.7	+ 1.3	+ 2.6	3.9	0.6	− 0.3	5.6	8.9
1972	2.1	3.2	3.2	− 1.6	− 1.7	+ 8.7	7.5	0.4	0.2	5.5	9.0
1973	4.2	5.8	2.3	− 3.1	− 2.6	+ 8.2	9.1	0.6	0.3	9.3	10.8
1974	6.4	7.7	2.1	− 3.8	− 3.9	+ 4.1	3.9	2.0	1.0	11.4	14.8
1975	10.5	10.0	3.4	− 5.3	− 4.7	− 0.4	2.2	4.5	2.1	10.2	14.4
1976	9.2	7.4	5.1	− 4.6	− 2.8	+ 2.7	2.8	2.6	1.0	11.1	14.4
1977	6.0	4.2	5.5	− 5.9	+ 1.7	+ 2.2	2.9	1.4	− 0.6	7.7	12.7
1978	8.4	5.0	5.5	− 3.6	− 1.4	+ 2.8	4.0	1.3	0.4	8.5	12.5
1979	12.6	6.5	5.1	− 5.6	− 0.9	+ 4.4	3.3	2.0	0.3	13.0	13.0
1980	12.2	5.4	6.3	− 4.1	− 1.3	+ 4.4	4.8	1.1	0.3	15.1	13.8
1981	10.7	4.3	9.0	− 4.5	+ 0.2	+ 4.5	3.6	1.2	− 0.1	13.4	14.8
1982	5.4	2.0	10.4	− 3.8	+ 1.8	+ 6.4	2.7	0.7	− 0.7	12.0	12.9
1983	11.7	3.9	11.2	− 3.6	− 0.3	+ 4.3	2.9	1.3	0.1	9.8	10.8
Average		4.8	5.3	− 3.8	− 1.0	+ 4.0	4.0	1.4	0.3	10.0	12.3

Sources: *ETAS* 1984, and *Economic Trends*, March 1984.

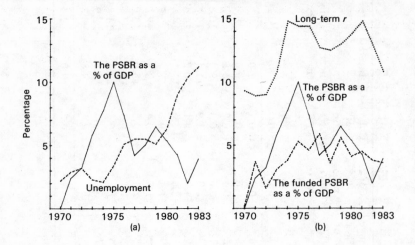

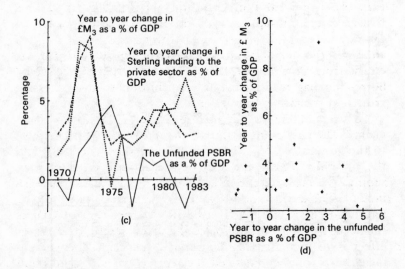

DIAGRAM 11.1   The PSBR, unemployment, interest rates, and £M₃

(a) The PSBR and unemployment.
(b) The PSBR and interest rates.
(c) The PSBR and £M₃.
(d) The PSBR and £M₃.

1979 coincided with a falling PSBR in spite of the recession increasing some types of government expenditure, as the new government cut the expenditure plans it inherited and raised taxes. Experience during this period is compatible with a negative (Keynesian) relationship between changes in the PSBR and unemployment. However such perusal of the PSBR and unemployment cannot determine the extent of crowding-out, as the effects of other changes which affect output and unemployment cannot be isolated.

Financing the PSBR

Some links in the chain of relationships between changes in the PSBR and unemployment are now examined. The method of financing the PSBR is significant for the impact of the PSBR on the economy. Table 11.2 shows the break-down of the PSBR into 'funded' and 'unfunded' elements.

In 1980 the government was confident that a relationship existed between the PSBR and the money supply. It claimed that 'the relationship between the PSBR and the growth of the money supply is important but not a simple one . . . But although the relationship between the PSBR and £M$_3$ is erratic from year to year, there is no doubt that public sector borrowing has made a major contribution to the excessive growth of the money supply in recent years.'[14]

To what extent do the data in Table 11.2 bear out these claims? The first point to note is the size of the PSBR relative to the growth of £M$_3$. Columns 8 and 9 show the PSBR and the unfunded PSBR as ratios of the growth of the money supply. On average, the PSBR was greater than the increase in £M$_3$. The average ratio was 1.4. The average ratio for the unfunded PSBR was 0.3. If a PSBR of 1 per cent of GDP is financed by short-term borrowing from banks, the direct effect is to increase £M$_3$ by about 3 per cent. This govern-ment borrowing would swell the reserve assets of banks and enable them to increase their lending. Plainly a large PSBR cannot be wholly funded by increasing notes and coin in circulation, or short-term borrowing from banks, without a large impact on the money supply.

[14] *Financial Statement and Budget Report 1980/81*, HMSO, 1980, p. 16.

The unfunded PSBR, and the year to year growth of £M$_3$, and sterling-lending to the private sector are shown in Diagram 11.1(c), and 11.1(d) is a scatter diagram of the unfunded PSBR and the growth of £M$_3$. The table and diagram certainly confirm the Treasury comment that the relationship between the PSBR and £M$_3$ is 'not a simple one' and is 'erratic from year to year'. It is not the case that the unfunded PSBR is the main source of changes in £M$_3$; bank lending to the private sector averaged four times the unfunded PSBR. Private sector lending and £M$_3$ move in close harmony, which is not surprising since lending to the private sector is the main source of an increase in £M$_3$. It is true that the increases in bank reserve assets attributable to a government deficit do facilitate an increase in lending by banks, and hence the money stock. Nevertheless over the period 1977 to 1982 the unfunded PSBR was negative, yet £M$_3$ continued to increase rapidly.

The government claims that an increase in sales of government debt depresses bond prices and thus raises the rate of interest. Table 11.2 and Diagram 11.1(b) provide a comparison of the PSBR, the funded PSBR, and the behaviour of interest rates.[15] The three variables increased between 1970 and 1975, reflecting the effects of expansionary policies and the recession on the PSBR and higher inflation on interest rates, rather than direct causal relationships. Between 1979 and 1982, Mrs Thatcher's government reduced the PSBR by 57 per cent in spite of the upward pressures on the PSBR created by the recession, and inflation fell during 1982, yet interest rates remained very high. The theoretical proposition that extra bond sales lower the price of bonds and raise interest rates is not at fault, but there are many other factors which affect interest rates.

The inter-relationships between fiscal policy, the PSBR, monetary policy, and prices and output in the economy are complex, and the observations presented cannot resolve the arguments about them. An alternative approach for assessing the effects of fiscal policy and other injections is to simulate changes on elaborate econometric models of the

[15] Long-term interest rates are shown in Diagram 11.1(b), as much of the funding by the authorities is in the long-term bond market.

economy, but in practice this has not resolved uncertainty about the effects of injections either. One version of the Treasury forecasting model estimates that 42 per cent of a bond-financed injection will be crowded-out after four years. But the National Institute's model estimates a large crowding-in effect equal to 82 per cent of the initial injection. The overtly monetarist London Business School model estimates slight (5 per cent) crowding-out, while the CEPG sees very substantial crowding-in.[16] The differences reflect different estimates of the effects on the exchange rate, prices, etc., but despite the differences there is no indication of complete crowding-out after four years. These estimates were made on models based on analyses of data for periods when unemployment was much lower than in 1984, and so crowding-out was greater than it would be now.

Conclusions

Analysis and estimation of the effects of a fiscal stimulus or other injection of demand into the economy are complex. One response to this complexity is to adopt sweeping assumptions and claim that crowding-out is complete. This conclusion is not supported by a priori arguments or the evidence.

The extent of crowding-out depends on the circumstances and the character and extent of the injection. Our conclusion is that, at times of widespread recession, crowding-out would not occur if the money supply was increased to accommodate an injection. If the money supply was not accommodating, partial crowding-out would occur, but at least initially there would be some increase in demand and output.

[16] R. C. Bladen-Hovell, 'Crowding-Out in U.K. Macro-models', in Artis *et al.*, *Demand-Management, Supply Constraints and Inflation*, Manchester, 1982.

12

Keynesian Policies

The Use of Keynesian Policies

The 1950s and 1960s

A popular view of the post-war economy is that Keynesian policies were operated during the 1950s and 1960s, and resulted in a low level of unemployment; during the 1970s they failed and were abandoned by Mrs Thatcher from 1979. Matthews has long since undermined this interpretation.[1] His argument is that the governments of the 1950s and 1960s maintained surpluses of current revenue over current expenditure. He claims that prosperity during this period can be attributed to buoyant private investment demand. Matthews catalogues possible ways in which Keynesian governments contributed to prosperity. For example, the belief that governments would boost demand if evidence of a recession emerged maintained industrialists' confidence and hence investment expenditures; but his argument is that Keynesian policies of fiscal management were not the main cause of prosperity compared to the inter-war and pre-1914 periods. They were simply not required.

Matthews used the balance of current revenue and expenditure to measure the fiscal stance. The measure used in Chapter 9 is the PSBR which includes capital expenditures and revenue. Using a similar measure to the PSBR, Ward and Neild have shown that the fiscal balance averaged −3.8 per cent of GNP during the 1950s, and −2.9 per cent during the 1960s.[2] According to this measure, the government was providing a significant stimulus. Nevertheless, there was buoyant world demand in the 1950s and 1960s. If governments had

[1] R. C. O. Matthews, 'Why Has Britain had Full Employment Since the War?', *Economic Journal*, September 1968.
[2] T. S. Ward and R. R. Neild, *The Measurement and Reform of Budgetary Policy*, London, 1978.

operated a more restrictive fiscal policy and devalued, employment may well have remained at a high level.

Summary of the Record during the 1970s

Table 12.1 summarizes the economic record for the 1970s. At first glance the record of the 1970s is damning for Keynesian policies. While nominal aggregate demand—GDP at current prices—rose by 342 per cent between 1970 and 1980, £M$_3$ rose by 276 per cent, and the PSBR rose from zero to 10 per cent of GDP in 1975, and was 5.4 per cent of GDP in 1980, the real output of the economy rose by only 17 per cent. It is claimed by monetarists that these figures show that boosting monetary demand does not increase output. In fact this is a naïve interpretation of the events of the 1970s.

Table 12.1 shows the violent stimulus given to demand in 1972 and 1973 at a time when the world economy was booming. In 1972 and 1973 £M$_3$ increased by 50 per cent. The PSBR as a percentage of GDP increased from 2.4 per cent in 1971 to 5.8 per cent in 1973. In cyclically-adjusted terms, the PSBR increased from 1.7 per cent of GDP in 1972 to 5.8 per cent in 1973 (Table 9.7). The panicky burst of expansionism was followed by a rapid rise in the general price level and contractionary policies. Nevertheless, the episode is of interest. It shows that there are potential dangers when politicians use Keynesian policies.

From 1974 monetary policy was not expansionary, and the real money supply fell in four of the five years between 1975 and 1979. Between 1975 and 1977 the PSBR was reduced from 10.0 to 4.2 per cent of GDP. Though the PSBR increased again in 1978 and 1979, the real PSBR shown in Table 9.8 was on average positive (deflationary) between 1975 and 1979. Keynesian policies of expansion were not used after 1975. Keynesian policies did not fail; they were not used.

A Comparison with Three Per Cent Per Annum Growth

To gain a true impression of the sources of the slow-down of the economy it is useful to compare the actual movements of

TABLE 12.1 *The economic record 1970–83*

	(1) GDP at 1980 prices	(2) Retail prices	(3) PSBR as % of GDP change	(4) £M₃ year to year % change	(5) Real £M₃ year to year % change	(6) Real Treasury bill rate
1970	+1.9	6.3	0.0	5.3	−0.9	−1.1
1971	+1.5	9.4	−2.4	11.4	+1.8	−2.8
1972	+2.5	7.3	−3.2	20.1	+11.9	−2.0
1973	+7.0	9.1	−5.8	25.2	+14.8	−1.8
1974	−1.6	16.0	−7.7	17.7	+1.5	−6.8
1975	−1.1	24.2	−10.0	8.9	−12.3	−11.2
1976	+2.5	16.5	−7.4	8.2	−7.1	−4.1
1977	+2.5	15.9	−4.2	7.8	−7.0	−3.0
1978	+3.1	8.3	−5.0	14.6	+5.8	−0.4
1979	+2.4	13.4	−6.5	12.7	−0.6	−4.1
Average 1970s	+2.1	+12.6	−5.2	13.2	+0.8	−3.7
1980	−2.6	18.0	−5.4	15.7	+2.0	+0.9
1981	−1.4	11.9	−4.3	16.7	+4.3	+1.2
1982	+1.9	8.6	−2.0	11.5	+2.7	+6.5
1983	+3.0	4.6	−3.9	10.8	+5.9	+4.4

Sources: *ETAS* 1984, and *Economic Trends*, March 1984.

the economy with the hypothetical movements in the same economy with an annual rate of growth of 3 per cent. Growth of at least this rate was required to prevent unemployment rising during the 1970s.

To establish a base from which to estimate the counterfactual position of the growing economy, the growth of the economy between 1959 and 1969, which averaged 3.1 per cent per annum, was extrapolated to 1979. In brief, the growth was spread between the components of aggregate demand in proportion to their relative rates of growth between 1959 and 1969. The results of the exercise are summarized in Table 12.2.

If the output of the economy had grown at 3.1 per cent compound from 1969, aggregate demand in 1979 would have been £251.2 bn. at 1980 prices. In the event it was £232.9 bn. The shortfall for fixed investment, £22.9 bn., was in fact *greater* than the shortfall of GDP of £18.3 bn. While actual consumption in 1979 was 101 per cent of the projected figure, and government consumption was 104 per cent of its projected level, fixed investment was only 64 per cent of its hypothetical level. In fact, fixed investment grew rapidly between 1959 and 1969, and a continuation of this trend may not have been necessary to provide the productive capacity to achieve 3 per cent growth in the 1970s. However, if investment had been stepped up, the potential output of the economy would have increased faster. The comparisons lend support to Keynes's concern about lagging investment, though ironically it was not private investment but public investment (as was shown in Chapter 8) which accounted for much of the shortfall. Private fixed investment also grew more slowly during the 1970s, but the slower growth of public sector fixed investment accounted for about two-thirds of the shortfall.

Returning to Table 12.2, in spite of GDP increasing at less than the 3.1 per cent growth trend, actual exports were above, and imports were near to, the projected levels in 1979. If GDP

TABLE 12.2   *A comparison of hypothetical growth of 3.1 per cent between 1969 and 1979 and actual growth*

	Actual growth rate 1959–69 at 1980 prices	Hypothetical GDP in 1979 with 3.1% p.a. growth at 1980 prices	Actual GDP in 1979 at 1980 prices	Difference actual– hypothetical
	%	£bn.	£bn.	£bn.
Consumption (C)	2.5	136.9	137.9	+1.0
Government Consumption (G)	2.1	45.7	47.6	+1.9
Fixed Investment (I_S)	5.6	64.5	41.6	−22.9
Stockbuilding (I_S)	(3.1)[a]	2.1	2.5	+0.4
Exports (E)	5.1	63.1	63.3	+0.2
Imports (M)	4.8	61.1	59.9	−1.2
Gross Domestic Product (GDP)	3.1	251.2	232.9	−18.3

Source: *ETAS* 1984.

[a] Stocks are assumed to change in proportion to changes in output.

had in fact grown at 3.1 per cent a year, then imports would
have grown much faster than they actually increased, unless
counteraction—devaluation or the introduction of import
controls—had been taken. This was the balance of payments
constraint on growth described in Chapter 10.

A detailed Look at the 1970s

A similar comparison of the actual movements of the components of aggregate demand and the projected movements
on the basis of 3.1 per cent growth was made year by year
for the 1970s, and the results are illustrated in Diagram 12.1.
In 1970 and 1971 the economy was below, but close to,
trend. In 1972 it was further below trend. Growth in 1973,
however, made up for the shortfall in the previous three
years. Thereafter the economy performed below the hypothetical 3.1 per cent growth rate in eight out of ten years.
The only component of demand which was close to the
projected growth in most years was government consumption.
Consumption, stockbuilding, exports, and imports were well
above projected growth in some years, and well below it in
some others. Fixed investment was below its projected
growth in all years.

Looking at years of recession, in 1974 and 1975 the shortfall of consumption was an important cause of the recession.
The savings ratio rose in 1974 and 1975 in spite of a fall in
real personal disposable income. Destocking in 1975 and
1980 represented a large part of the fall in GDP below
projected growth, though a substantial part, perhaps 50 per
cent, of the destocking was matched by imports being below
trend. Consumption growth was below projected growth
throughout the period 1974–7.

Turning to the periods of expansion, in 1973 stockbuilding was the single largest source of faster than projected
expansion, but again allowance must be made for the impact
of stockbuilding on imports; it is the most import-intensive
component of aggregate demand. In 1976, when growth of
GDP was slightly above the projected 3.1 per cent rate, the
largest deviation was for stockbuilding, but this did not apply

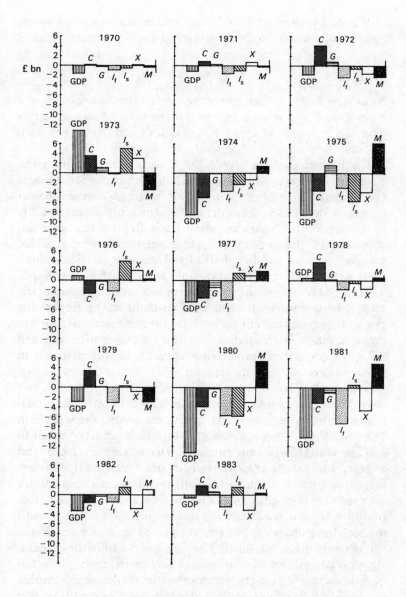

DIAGRAM 12.1   Deviations from hypothetical 3.1 per cent
growth trend £bn.

Source: The methods of estimation are described in the text.

in 1978. In 1978 and 1979 the expansion was led by consumption, which was above projected growth in both years.

Prediction

Next we examine whether the actual movements of the economy were foreseen by the Treasury.The purpose of this exercise is to see whether Keynesian policies were not used because they were not deemed to be required.

On Budget day each year the Government publishes the *Financial Statement and Budget Report*. Each Report records the Treasury's forecasts for output and the components of aggregate demand for the first half of the budget year and the first half of the following year. Each Report also contains estimates of the growth of GDP from the first half of the previous year to the first half of the budget year. These forecasts and estimates have been used to construct Table 12.3. The 'A' rows show the forecast percentage changes to the components of demand and total demand in the Report for the year shown; the 'B' rows show the estimated percentage changes made in the Report for the following year; and the 'C' rows are estimates of what actually happened made in 1981.

The projections are for only a year ahead at a time, but over these successive short time spans Governments did foresee what was happening to the economy. From 1975/6 onwards they expected and got only slow growth. Between 1975/6 and 1979/80 expected growth averaged 1.7 per cent a year, and actual growth was 1.6 per cent a year. Governments did not budget to take up the slack in the economy and reduce unemployment. Keynesian policies during this period were not tried, though they were needed. The reasons are not far to seek: Governments placed increasing emphasis on cutting inflation, until Mrs Thatcher explicitly made it the prime objective of economic policy in 1979.

A principal difficulty for short-term forecasting, revealed by Table 12.3, is forecasting consumption. During the period 1972/3 to 1976/7 it increased more slowly than expected, then for two years faster than expected. There are relationships between the savings ratio, income, and inflation but the relationships were not predictable in the mid-1970s. This made for difficulty in regulating aggregate demand. Stock-building too is generally reckoned difficult to forecast. In practice the direction of stockbuilding (or destocking) was foreseen in all years except one, 1974/5. The extent of the changes were not always foreseen, particularly the destocking in 1980/1. As described in Chapter 8, reactions to inflation, this time by firms, and the adjustment of the tax system to allow for inflation, contributed to the sharp movements of stocks.

Limitations on the Use of Keynesian Policies

The balance of payments constraint was the main obstacle to the use of expansionary policies during the 1950s and 1960s. As world trade was freed the balance of payments constraint on expansionist policies tightened. The second obstacle was the threat of inflation. Policies designed to weaken these obstacles to expansionary policies are now examined.

The Balance of Payments Constraint

The degree of expansion necessary to create full employment in 1984 would result in a balance of payments imbalance, since a large percentage of the increased demand would go to overseas producers. The relationship between output and employment is considered in Chapter 14; here it is assumed that if GDP were increased by an extra 10 per cent, unemployment would fall by 6 per cent. If imports and the reduction in exports attributable to an increase in domestic demand represent half the increase in demand, then the rise in net imports attributable to the rise in demand necessary to increase output by 10 per cent, would be 10 per cent of GDP, over £20 bn., ten times Britain's current account balance of payments surplus in 1983, and more than the reserves. The 50 per cent figure does not exaggerate the propensity to import and reduce exports if rapid expansion occurred.

The principal policies to alleviate the balance of payments constraint are devaluation and import controls.

TABLE 12.3   Forecast and actual changes in aggregate demand[a]

		C	Public investment	Private investment	Percentages[b] (Stocks)	G	E	M	GDP	GDP deflator
1969/70	A	+0.5	+2.1	+6.0	+1.3	+1.5	+5.5	+1.6	+2.4	
	B	+2.1	−2.3	−2.3	+0.8	+0.9	+8.3	+2.2	+2.5	
	C	+1.7	−0.5	+3.5	+0.8	−0.2	+8.8	+3.0	+1.9	6.1
1970/1	A	+4.0	+3.8	+4.1	+1.3	+2.0	+3.9	+5.8	+3.5	
	B	+3.3	+2.8	+2.1	−0.9	+1.7	+1.3	+6.6	+1.5	
	C	+3.1	+3.2	+2.7	+0.7	+2.2	+5.2	+7.6	+2.2	9.7
1971/2	A	+4.6	+2.7	+0.3	+0.5	+1.5	+3.1	+5.8	+2.1	
	B	+3.9	+3.4	+2.8	+0.3	+3.0	+5.3	+5.6	+2.6	
	C	+4.8	−5.8	+5.1	+0.1	+3.7	+5.3	+5.9	+2.3	11.4
1972/3	A	+5.6	+3.6	+8.8	+1.7	+2.9	+5.2	+9.2	+5.7	
	B	+6.4	−2.7	+4.1	+1.0	+4.6	+3.3	+10.0	+5.3	
	C	+6.1	+0.5	+7.3	+1.6	+4.9	+4.2	+11.8	+5.0	9.9
1973/4	A	+4.3	+5.2	+6.7	+1.7	+4.0	+6.8	+6.6	+5.2	
	B	+1.2	+3.9	+0.8	+0.3	+3.0	+7.8	+6.8	+1.4	
	C	+0.4	+5.5	−2.1	+1.8	+2.4	+11.4	+6.5	+2.1	12.2
1974/5	A	+2.4	−2.1	−5.0	+0.4	+2.5	+4.7	+1.1	+2.4	
	B	+2.1	−1.2	−5.7	−0.3	+3.4	+2.2	−3.2	+2.1	
	C	0	+1.2	−5.0	−0.2	+4.4	+1.1	+4.1	+0.3	29.9
1975/6	A	+1.4	+1.3	+3.4	−0.4	+4.3	+3.5	+2.2	+0.8	
	B	−1.4	+3.8	−3.5	−1.6	+3.3	−0.7	−0.7	−1.3	
	C	−1.7	+1.5	+1.1	−0.7	+3.2	+2.7	−2.0	+0.9	15.9

1976/7	A	+1.8	+1.2	+1.8	+0.4	+0.4	+9.5	−7.9	+3.9	
	B	+1.1	−10.6	0	+0.1	+1.8	+9.1	+7.4	+1.5	
	C	+0.3	−10.5	+5.1	+1.8	−0.7	+8.6	+4.9	+2.8	12.7
1977/8	A	−0.1	−6.6	+3.6	+0.6	0	+5.3	+2.0	+1.6	
	B	+2.1	−5.9	+2.0	0	+0.5	+4.4	+2.4	+0.6	
	C	+2.7	−9.9	+11.0	+0.8	+0.4	+4.4	+0.1	+2.2	11.9
1978/9	A	+4.6	+3.1	+3.3	+0.4	+2.3	+4.8	+8.9	+2.8	
	B	—	—	—	—	—	—	—	—	
	C	+5.8	+7.4	+2.1	+1.2	+2.2	+1.1	+7.8	+1.5	11.4
1979/80	A	+1.5	−6.1	−0.9	0	+0.2	+3.0	+2.5	−0.7	
	B	+1.4	−5.9	+1.2	+0.1	+0.6	+3.6	+8.6	−0.5	
	C	+1.8	−1.0	+5.8	+0.2	+1.8	+4.4	+7.5	+0.4	17.9
1980/1	A	+0.4	−17.2	−2.7	−0.4	−0.2	−2.1	−0.4	−2.2	
	B	−0.1	−24.6	−4.0	−3.5	+1.8	−4.9	−8.7	−3.8	
	C	+0.2	−11.1	−3.5	−3.1	+1.5	−4.7	−10.6	−3.0	13.5

Sources: *Financial Statement and Budget Report* for each year, and *ETAS* 1982.

[a] 'A' for 1969/70 is the forecast growth of *C* etc., between the first half of 1969 and the first half of 1970 made for the 1969 budget. 'B' is the estimated growth over the same period made for the 1970 budget, and 'C' is the estimate of what actually happened made in 1981.

[b] Apart from stocks, changes are year to year percentage changes. For stocks the figures are changes in stocks as a percentage of GDP.

Devaluation

Devaluation of the sterling exchange rate is designed to shift the relative prices of imports and exports to boost demand for the latter and dampen demand for the former. The main problem of devaluation as a remedy is that it has an inflationary impact on the domestic price level; directly, through the effect of more expensive imports on retail prices, and indirectly, as higher import prices squeeze real incomes and contribute to wage-push inflation.

The initial effects of a devaluation worsen the balance of payments as import prices in sterling rise faster than export prices in sterling, and this precedes the effects on the volume of imports and exports. Provided there is surplus capacity in the economy, and wages do not rise during this initial stage to offset the beneficial effect of lower costs, the balance of payments should improve and the output of the economy should in time rise above its pre-devaluation level.

In practice, it is very difficult to measure the impact of devaluation on an economy. Apart from uncertainty about the size of the price elasticities described in Chapter 10, other events occur simultaneously and obscure the effects of exchange rate changes. The 1967 devaluation in which sterling was devalued from \$2.80 to \$2.40 to £1 is used as an example. From 1969 to 1971 the current account showed distinct improvement (Graph 10.1(b)). However, the devaluation was accompanied by a substantial deflationary package in which government spending was curtailed, a ceiling was placed on bank lending, and there was an increase in the bank rate from 6½ to 8 per cent. Unemployment continued to climb. The balance of payments surpluses were as much a result of deflationary policies and the increased unemployment, which restricted demand for imports, as the devaluation itself.

There are other reasons why the effects of devaluation are difficult to assess. Any improvements in the growth of exports will be lagged, and the duration of the lag is uncertain. Expectations about further exchange rate movements play a part; business men consider the expected future exchange rate when planning their investment and production programmes. In 1977, when the DM had risen relative to the dollar, many German business men believed the rate would have to fall again soon and so they held on to their export markets.

Another frequently overlooked characteristic of devaluation policies is that they act mainly as a stimulus to the older, more labour-intensive industries, with low productivity, because the main effect of devaluation is to reduce Britain's relative labour costs. New industries wishing to invest in modern capital equipment must pay world prices for much of their capital equipment and increasingly for their technically qualified manpower; devaluation provides less incentive here.

Some evidence that devaluation leads to improvements in Britain's cost competitiveness, and tentative evidence that improvements in relative costs resulted in Britain maintaining its share of world exports of manufactures, were reported in Chapter 10. Treasury economists have estimated the effects of devaluation. Their estimates of the effects of a 5 per cent devaluation are summarized in Table 12.4. The estimates are for a substantial effect on the current balance of payments after two years; it would improve by the equivalent of 1 per cent of GDP. If a devaluation had the effects estimated then after two years unemployment would be reduced by about ½ per cent of the labour force. The improvement in the current balance of payments would allow further reflation of demand and output of about 1 per cent

TABLE 12.4   *Effects of a five per cent devaluation*[a]

	GDP at factor prices %	Retail prices %	Current balance of payments as percentage of GDP	Real take-home pay %	Unemployment '000s
After 2 years	+1.2	+1.5	+1.0	−0.5	−85

Source: J. Odling-Smee and N. Hartley, *Some Effects of Exchange Rate Changes*, Treasury Working Paper No. 2, 1978.

[a] The changes shown are relative to no change in the exchange rate.

of GDP, without worsening the balance of payments from its initial position. The reduction in unemployment would be about ½ per cent of the labour force, to give a total reduction in unemployment of 1 per cent. Extrapolating, a 20 per cent devaluation would reduce unemployment by 4 per cent. All this assumes other countries do not follow the devaluation. However, the principal argument of the Treasury paper was that the effects of devaluation would in time be eaten away by a faster increase in prices. It is not possible to assess, on the basis of past evidence, how much of the devaluation would be offset by wage and price increases in present conditions of high unemployment.

During 1984, sterling was an over-valued currency (in the sense that we could not balance imports and exports at a satisfactory level of employment at the prevailing exchange rate). Devaluation could provide a stimulus to the export sector. Nevertheless UK wages are still below the levels in many parts of Europe, and the high pound has forced productivity improvements. The dangers of devaluation are the complacency it might restore to British industry, calling to a halt the drive for, and acquiescence by unions in, greater efficiency since 1979, and the impetus it would give to faster inflation.

Import Controls

An alternative means of removing the balance of payments constraint would be the implementation of protectionist policies. Import controls would restrict either the price or the quantity of imported goods and services through a system of tariffs or quotas.

The Cambridge Economic Policy Group advocate uniform tariffs for different products but with some selectiveness to maintain shares of different sources of supply at constant levels. Like devaluation, the effect is to alter the structure of relative prices to stimulate demand for domestically produced goods. It is claimed that, unlike devaluation, real income is not squeezed and so the boost to inflation is not as acute. With import controls there will be general inflation as a result of increased prices of imported goods, but import controls can be accompanied by tax cuts financed out of tariff revenue. The advocates of import controls claim that the growth of demand for home-produced goods would break the grip of the cumulative relative decline of the British economy.

The projections of the CEPG suggest that import controls could raise employment by 4–8 per cent by 1990, and aggregate output by 6–16 per cent, compared with the alternative 'base projection' of deflationary monetary and fiscal policy. In the 1979 *Review* they stated that, 'None of this implies that inflation will necessarily fall under the import control strategy, but only that growth made possible by import restrictions is likely to make inflation less of a problem than it otherwise would have been.'

The arguments against import controls are that they would provide protection for industries, and they would have to rise indefinitely as imports became increasingly competitive. Mr M. Fg Scott has estimated that a uniform tariff of 50 per cent would have been necessary in 1985, and that a 100 per cent tariff would be required in 1990.[3] There is also the danger of retaliation by the countries from whom the UK currently imports; the UK would face explusion from the EEC and would be subject to tariffs on her own exports into the Common Market countries. Consumer choice of available goods and services would be restricted. It is likely that controls would cause an increase in the inflation rate. Firms would take advantage of protection to reverse the reduction in profit margins which occurred during the 1970s, and workers in some industries favoured by protection (the motor industry is an example) would try to restore or improve their relative pay.

There is no denying the need for expansion, but that alone does not make the case for import controls. Nor do the arguments that the models used to support free trade are invalid, because they assume full employment, the absence of economies of scale, etc., clinch the debate, because the advocates of controls do not have a tested theory of the operation of controls. Controls may allow some increase in

[3] M. Fg. Scott, W. M. Corden and I. M. D. Little *The Case Against General Import Restrictions*, London, 1980, p. 45. Mr Scott's estimates were based on the CEPG's own projections.

output in the short-term, but it is their long-term impact which is crucial and which is difficult to assess. One cause of this difficulty is that we cannot be sure what the alternative without controls will be; the future buoyancy of world trade is uncertain. The effects of controls would also depend on their composition and the terms negotiated with other countries. There is no reason to suppose that any model can forecast the effects of import controls, because of the uncertainty about the position without them, reactions to them, and because of the absence of experience of controls.

Extensive controls and withdrawal from the EEC would result in a diversion of exports to the home market. This would involve substantial resource losses. When Britain debated entry to the EEC the direct resource gain was reckoned to be about 10 per cent of the extra trade generated. If trade were cut we would expect the resource loss to be proportionately greater now. Production of many items which are now imported would require the creation of new capacity and designs for which scarce research and development resources would be required. However *if* the resource loss through loss of economies of scale, learning effects, and reduced efficiency were 25 per cent of the reduction in trade, and *if* trade was cut by 10 per cent of GDP—a third of total trade—the loss would be only 2½ per cent of GDP, small compared to the idle capacity of at least 10 per cent of GDP. If trade were cut to this extent there would be severe short-term problems of changing production capacity and of ever rejoining the EEC or the world free-trading system, because scarce research and development resources would be dissipated on producing import substitutes. Other EEC countries, however, may not react in a self-destructive manner by excluding British exports, in the event of Britain introducing controls. In practice import controls may not lead to a large cut in trade; the negotiations might end in limited controls, which would not be a panacea for the balance of payments constraint either.

Limited import controls, designed to slow the need for adaptation to a more manageable rate, and to provide some temporary protection for the development of new products and production capacity in industries where Britain lags, may have advantages. Controls would be concentrated against imports from countries such as Japan which have not allowed access to their markets. The problem here could be that many of the imports shut out would be replaced by imports from other countries at higher prices.

Industrial Policy

Can a government significantly improve the balance of payments by industrial policy? It is doubtful whether British governments have done so in the past. It is sometimes claimed that governments in France and Japan have had an important influence on industrial development, and that industrial banks have had a similar impact in Germany and Sweden. The key areas for government intervention are the provision of finance for projects and the education and training of the labour force.

   In large measure a government has to depend on industrialists to formulate projects, but it can finance projects which would not be financed by the private sector. Justifications for such intervention are that the government can include the extra tax revenue and unemployment benefits which will be saved as part of the return on the investments. If the investments ease the balance of payments constraint, there may be large effects on the output of the economy through a release of the balance of payments constraint on the growth of demand. The other justification is that the private sector has failed to invest at a rate to fully utilize the resources of the economy.

Incomes Policies

The second and related barrier to expansionist policies is the threat of inflation. The Keynesian remedy is an incomes policy. The Phillips curve implied that the level of unemployment and rate of inflation depended upon the level of effective demand: unemployment if demand was low, inflation if it was high. During the 1950s and 1960s attempts were made to improve the trade-off with incomes policies. When the Phillips curve collapsed in the 1970s incomes policies were again tried to stem wage increases. In fact, there were only short periods during the 1970s with no incomes policy in operation—the first year of the Heath government 1970–72, 1974–75, and 1979 when the Conservatives were again in power. The persistence of inflation at high levels throughout the decade shows that these policies did not achieve their objective.

It is difficult to assess the effects of individual incomes policies, and even more difficult to assess the effects of all the incomes policies operated in the 1960s and 1970s. We cannot estimate what would have happened in their absence, and how far they undermined acceptance of existing and market-determined differentials. Since the policies were directly affecting decisions so much of the time, and creating anomalies which affected wage claims after the policies were abandoned, there is no period available to assess the alternative position without the policies.

Table 12.5 lists the incomes policies operated during the 1970s, and the pay restrictions or 'norms' which were set. The compulsory periods of Mr Heath's incomes policy may have stabilized wage inflation in the short-term. With hindsight, the introduction of threshold agreements was a mistake, given the decision to reflate the economy in 1972/3 and the oil price disturbance. It has been estimated that wages increased by an extra 10 per cent in 1974 because of threshold agreements.[4] Labour governments can claim some success with incomes policies, particularly the reduction in wage inflation in 1977. But Diagram 12.2 points to any success of incomes policies being short-term; in 1973/4 there was a marked increase in earnings, and in 1978 the rise became steeper as Labour's incomes guidelines disintegrated. Maybe circumstances were particularly unpropitious for operating incomes policies during the 1970s, because the oil-price shock was forcing up prices, and the incomes policies may have been badly conceived and managed. However, there are other fundamental factors—both economic and political—that must be considered when examining the failures of incomes policies.

[4] M. V. Posner, 'Problems of the British Economy', in *Public Policies in Open Economies*, edited by K. Brunner and A. H. Meltzer, North Holland Publishing Co., 1978, p. 6.

TABLE 12.5 *Incomes policies in the 1970s*

		Pay restrictions (1)	Implementation (2)	Results: year to year percentage changes	
				Wage rates (3)	Earnings (4)
LABOUR	1969–70	2½–4½%	Voluntary but with powers of delay	9.9	12.1
	1971–2	(n−1) policy	Voluntary, government example in public sector	12.9	11.2
CONSERVATIVE	1972–3	Freeze	Compulsory	13.8	12.9
	1973	£1 plus 4% (12 month rule)	Compulsory	13.7	13.5
	1973–4	7% or £2.25 plus threshold payments	Compulsory	19.8	17.8
Labour's Social Contract	1974–5	Maintenance of real wage only (12 month rule)	Voluntary	29.5	26.5
	1975–6	£6 maximum (12 month rule)	Voluntary	19.3	15.5
	1976–7	5% with £2.50 minimum, £4 maximum	Voluntary	6.6	10.2
	1977–8	10% average earnings guideline	Voluntary	14.1	14.5
	1978–9	5% average earnings guideline	Voluntary	15.0	15.6

Sources: (1) and (2), Dornbusch and Fischer in Caves and Krause (eds.), *Britain's Economic Performance*, Washington 1980; (3 and 4), Table 5.1.

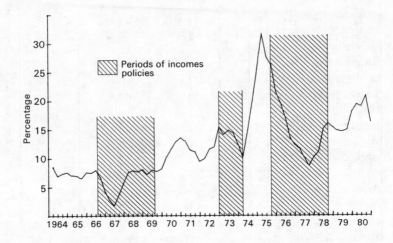

DIAGRAM 12.2   Earnings and income policies
(percentage change compared to the same quarter a year earlier)

Source: *ETAS* 1984.

The reasons for the failure of incomes policies to control wage inflation were growing irritation with restrictions and anomalies, real-wage aspirations, failure to achieve acceptable agreement on wage and income distribution, and the advantages for some groups of not having an incomes policy.

Since many groups managed to claim special circumstances or 'productivity' deals, any set 'norm' was regarded as a minimum by all groups and drifted upwards or was avoided. Secondly, as illustrated in Diagram 12.2, the policies tended to be followed by 'catching-up' settlements, both to restore previously existing differentials and to re-establish target real wages.

Throughout the period, there was a lack of consistent principles for determing wage and income differentials—market forces, fairness, and union power were all at different times involved in settlements. Furthermore, the 1970s saw a marked shrinkage of differentials, at least between those with, and those without, educational qualifications.[5] There have been difficulties, too, in setting differentials between public and private sector workers.

[5] *NIER*, August 1982, p. 54.

Political forces have been involved in the breakdown of incomes policies. Under the Heath government opposition to the incomes policy took the form of big strikes backed by union leaders and union–government confrontations. The problems were of a different nature under the 1974–9 Labour government. The Social Contract was a voluntary restraint on wage claims in return for social and industrial legislation which the unions favoured. However, the bargain was struck with the union leaders, and as opposition to the policy grew, the rank and file union members began to fight wage restraint and thus official union policy. This eventually forced the leaders to go along with the wishes of their members. The contrary argument is that the Social Contract collapsed because the government gave in to financial pressures and did not boost demand and create increases in real incomes.

It might be conceded that an income policy is the extra weapon needed in the battle against inflation and unemployment, and that such a policy is a better way of reducing wage inflation than mass unemployment. The puzzle for Britain remains that of finding a feasible, acceptable, and effective formula which provides for wage and income differentials without freezing them.

Conclusions

The 1970s started with high hopes of improved economic performance. They ended with the rejection of Keynesian policies, their substitution by monetarism, and control of inflation being given precedence over the promotion of a low level of unemployment.

In Britain, unlike some other European countries with strong labour movements, powerful labour groups have not accepted the operation of a highly devolved capitalist system. They have been unaware of the flexibility and efficiency required to operate a capitalist economy well. In spite of the lack of experience with centralized planning in Britain, they were confident of its efficacy. The failure of managers in Britain to create competitive products and achieve co-operation with their labour force may have contributed to these attitudes. The political friction made for acute difficulties in tackling the external shocks to the economy during the 1970s.

In 1972 and 1973 caution in the use of Keynesian policies was swept aside in an attempt to boost output by 'super-expansionism.' Output did expand but prices rose and were spurred on by commodity and oil price rises. Thereafter, uncertainty about inflation, and in the mid-1970s the balance of payments constraint, forestalled any real attempt to use Keynesian policies. Since 1979 Mrs Thatcher has spurned the use of Keynesian policies, apparently believing in Keynes's words that 'there [is] no means open to a government whereby to mitigate economic distress at home except through the competitive struggle for markets.'[6]

[6] *General Theory*, p. 382.

13

Labour Productivity

Caves and Krause, in their survey, *Britain's Economic Performance* concluded that: 'Britain's economic malaise stems largely from its productivity problem, whose origins lie deep in the social system.[1] The slow growth of labour productivity in Britain, compared to that in other advanced industrial countries, and its causes have been at the root of Britain's relative economic decline.

The two paradigms which were outlined in earlier chapters do not provide general theories for explaining international differences in productivity growth. Monetarists, harking back to the dicta of Adam Smith, stress the advantages of competition and market forces. They consider supply-side forces as of primary importance. Keynesians focus on the importance of the growth of demand for generating greater output, and the causal link between the growth of output and improving labour productivity. Keynesians, too, can quote Adam Smith. He explained the importance of the division of labour for achieving efficiency, brought about through learning-by-doing and inventing new machinery, and wrote that the division of labour is 'limited ... by the extent of the market'.[2]

The modern theory of growth originated with the Harrod–Domar model, which analysed the problem of maintaining stable growth of demand to match the growth of the potential output of an economy in a dynamic framework. This problem became the focus of much theoretical debate. Neoclassical economists claimed that if prices, and particularly interest rates, were flexible the economy would gravitate to equilibrium growth at a high level of employment. In practice, during the 1950s and 1960s western economies did grow with low and stable levels of unemployment. For Britain the

[1] R. E. Caves and L. B. Krause, *Britain's Economic Performance*, Washington, 1980, p. 19.
[2] Adam Smith, *Wealth of Nations*, London, 1890, p. 13.

problem was not maintaining employment; it was the slow growth of labour productivity and hence potential output.

Theory alone cannot explain economic development; theories have to be tested to assess their explanatory power. However, the limitations of growth theory go deeper. Sen concluded that 'much of modern growth theory is concerned with rather esoteric issues. Its link with public policy is often very remote'.[3] In their *Theory of Economic Growth*, Hahn and Matthews concluded that 'it would be difficult to claim that any of the models [of growth] we have discussed goes far towards explaining ... differences [in rates of growth between countries].'[4] This conclusion was published in 1964, but in 1982 Hahn reiterated it; 'Nor ... has economic theory much helped in accounting for the ... relative British decline'.[5]

The theory of growth does provide a list of the factors and forces which contribute to growth—the rate of accumulation of human and physical capital, economies of scale, learning, technical progress, and the reallocation of resources. Attempts have been made to quantify the contribution of each influence on growth—growth accounting—but they have not been very successful, due to conceptual and measurement problems. In any case this approach does not answer many interesting questions, such as why Britain's investment is low by international standards, though estimates of the contribution of low investment to slow growth have been made.

Measurement

The usual measure of labour productivity is output per person or per person-hour. The output of an economy, sector, trade, or firm is related to the inputs of one factor of production, labour. Labour productivity measured in this way is affected by the quantity and quality of the other factors of production, particularly the capital equipment

[3] A Sen, *Growth Economics*, London, 1970, p. 9.
[4] F. H. Hahn and R. C. O. Matthews, 'The Theory of Economic Growth a Survey', *Economic Journal*, 1964.
[5] 'Reflections on the Invisible Hand', by F. Hahn, *Lloyds Bank Review*, April 1982.

employed with labour. There are severe problems for measuring output and the input of labour. Differences in products, including quality differences, are persistent sources of difficulty for measuring output. Another source of qualification to most estimates of labour productivity is the measurement of labour inputs; allowing for differences in the skills and experience of employees presents problems which are often just ignored. When output is divided by the number of employees, the most gifted managers and highly trained technicians count for no more than unskilled recruits.

The problems of measuring changes in output and productivity are less acute for manufacturing than for most other sectors, so we concentrate on manufacturing. In the increasingly important service sector the problems of measuring and comparing the quality of service impede productivity comparisons. The manufacturing sector is the most important sector for trade, generating exports and competing against imports, but it may exaggerate the weakness of Britain's productivity performance. Agriculture is an example of a sector where Britain has relatively high output per person compared with most European countries and Japan. The service sector, although its relative output per person is higher than that of manufacturing, compares unfavourably with Britain's competitors. So too does output per person in the fuel and power, and construction, sectors, although the fuel and power sector improved its performance sharply during the 1970s and is coming more into line with other countries.[6] The manufacturing sector may exaggerate Britain's poor relative performance, but it is not atypical.

Diagram 13.1 shows the growth of labour productivity for the UK economy as a whole; it increased by 52 per cent between 1960 and 1982. There was a marked slowing in the growth of productivity from 1973. Diagram 13.1 also shows the growth of output per person and per person-hour for manufacturing industry. Output per person for manufacturing increased more rapidly than output per person for the economy as a whole until 1973, and output per person-hour grew still more rapidly. By 1983 output per person-hour in manufacturing was more than double its 1960 level. The

[6] *National Institute Economic Review*, August 1982.

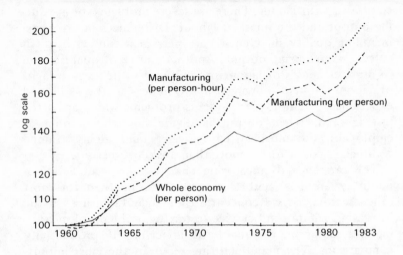

DIAGRAM 13.1   Indices of output per person and per person-hour
(1960 = 100)

Source: *ETAS* 1984, p. 97, and *Economic Trends*, March 1984.

slow-down in productivity growth from 1973 for the economy
as a whole was mirrored by manufacturing. All three indicators show an improvement in productivity in 1981 and
1982.

Diagram 13.2(a) shows the movement of output per
person for manufacturing since 1950. Between 1950 and
1973 the trend growth of output per person was 2.9 pr cent
per year. The same data with free-hand trend lines, shown in
Diagram 13.2(b), indicate some speeding up of growth
between the 1950s and the 1960s, before the relapse after
1973. Table 13.1 shows that the 1970s slow-down in productivity improvement was general across all manufacturing
industries.

International Comparisons

International comparisons of labour productivity between
two countries can be made in terms of the growth of productivity through time and in absolute terms. Both types of
comparison have been dismal for Britain's manufacturing

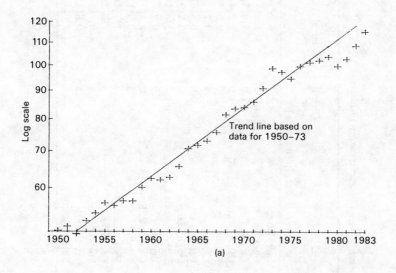

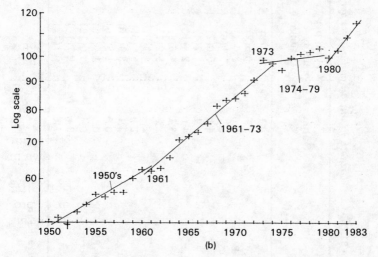

DIAGRAM 13.2   Index of output per person for manufacturing
(1980 = 100)

(a) Trend 1950–73; Log $Y = 3.83 + 0.029t$.
(b) Free-hand trend lines.

Sources: *ETAS* 1984, and *Economic Trends*, March 1984.

TABLE 13.1 *Growth of output and output per employee in manufacturing industries*

1968–73	Output %	Output per employee (per annum)	1973–79	Output %	Output per employee %
			(Rank, in order of size, in brackets)		
1 Chemicals	6.1	5.8(3)	Inst. Eng.	2.7	4.2(1)
2 Electrical Eng.	5.9	6.6(2)	Chemicals	2.0	1.7(5)
3 Coal and Pet. Prods.	5.6	8.0(1)	Electr. Eng.	1.9	3.0(3)
4 Instrument Eng.	5.1	5.1(6)	Other Manuf.	1.0	2.7(4)
5 Timber	4.5	5.0(7)	Food	0.7	2.0(5)
6 Bricks	4.1	5.7(4)	Clothing	0.7	3.7(2)
7 Other manufact.	4.0	2.8(13)	Paper	−0.5	0.6(8)
8 Paper	3.1	4.6(8)	Mech. Eng.	−1.0	0.2(9)
9 Food	2.8	3.2(11)	Metal Goods NES	−1.7	−1.6(16)
10 Clothing	2.4	4.3(9)	Bricks	−1.9	0.9(7)
11 Textiles	2.3	5.6(5)	Coal & P. Prods.	−2.2	−0.1(11)
12 Mechanical Eng.	2.1	3.9(10)	Timber	−2.3	−0.5(12)
13 Vehicles	0.9	1.3(16)	Vehicles	−2.5	−1.5(15)
14 Metal Goods NES	0.9	1.4(15)	Leather	−2.6	0 (10)
15 Metal Manufacture	0.4	3.0(12)	Metal Manuf.	−3.1	−0.7(14)
16 Leather	−0.6	2.7(14)	Textiles	−3.2	−0.6(13)
17 Shipbuilding	−1.0	0.1(17)	Shipbuilding	−3.3	−2.0(17)

Source: *NIER*, August 1981.

sector. A careful comparison, based on Census of Production data made by Mr S. J. Prais, implies that in 1979 labour productivity, measured by output per person, was 40 per cent higher in Germany, and 205 per cent higher in America, than in Britain.[7] Although Mr Prais's estimates are comprehensive (they are for the whole of the manufacturing sector), there are qualifications to comparisons of productivity based on the adjustment of the value of output for differences in price levels, which is the main method he uses, because of the difficulty of comparing prices.[8] A comparison made by the author of differences in labour productivity at the operations of a small sample of international companies in 1979 suggests that the differences in productivity between America and Britain might be smaller than estimated by Mr Prais, and that America is less far ahead of Germany. These estimates suggest Britain has a special productivity problem. The estimates are summarized in Table 13.2

Table 13.3 compares the *growth* of output per person in manufacturing for the UK and other industrial countries. Although America has higher labour productivity than Britain, her labour productivity has, like Britain's, improved slowly. The comparisons also show that the productivity slow-down after 1973 was not confined to the UK.

What Determines the Level of Productivity

In 1973, and again in 1980, the author studied differences in labour productivity within *international* companies.[9] The managers of these companies are in a good position to know the reasons for any differences in productivity. Chart 13.1 shows these forces, starting with output per person. In the short-run the potential output of products, production runs, and output per person are set by the mix of skills,

[7] S. J. Prais, *Productivity and Industrial Structure*, Cambridge University Press, 1981.

[8] Comparisons of prices of goods may not allow accurately for differences in quality. Also, some of the differences in prices are attributable to differences in prices of inputs of raw materials, not the value added in manufacture. During the 1970s the prices of oil and some other raw materials were lower in the USA than in Europe.

[9] The results of the first study were published in *Labour Productivity Differentials within International Companies*, Cambridge University Press, 1976.

TABLE 13.2   *International comparisons of productivity differentials for manufacturing industries and within international companies*

	Compared to UK			Compared to Germany
	Germany	France	USA	USA
All manufacturing industry				
Prais[a] (1978)	+34	–	+202	+125
National Institute[b]	+52 to +62	+80	+176 to +202	+74 to +100
A small sample of international companies				
Unweighted average[c]	+26	+22	+37	+4
Weighted average	+42	+21	+54	0
More reliable estimates[d]	+38	+26	+62	

[a] S. J. Prais, *Productivity and Industrial Structure*, Cambridge 1981, p. 279.

[b] *National Institute Economic Review*, August 1982, p. 11 (these comparisons are given as indicative of the central findings).

[c] The comparison between the UK and Germany was for operations of 25 companies, the comparison with France 18, and with the USA 22.

[d] The sample was divided into two groups, the more and the less convincing estimates. The two groups were of approximately equal numbers.

capital equipment, products, and demand for products of each business. Within these parameters output per person is determined by the performance of employees, which is influenced by the controls, incentives, and attitudes listed in the chart.

Behind the short-run determinants of productivity lies a history of entrepreneurial opportunities and decisions. Present opportunities are set by the past history of the businesses in assembling a combination of employees, assets, and positions in markets. The scope for assembling a productive combination is affected by the stock of skills in the labour force, the engineering, scientific, and management resources in the economy, and other factors grouped in Row B. Finally, some of the influences on these factors, such as the flows of

TABLE 13.3   *Real valued added per person employed in*
manufacturing
(average annual growth rates)

	1960–73	1973–79	1979–81	(1979–83)[a]
Japan	9.7	6.5	6.6	(4.1)
France	6.7	4.1	0.9	(1.4)
Italy	6.4	3.1	2.6	(0.5)
Germany	4.7	3.2	0.7	(1.8)
UK	3.6	0.8	0.6	(3.2)
USA	3.4	0.9	0.5	(1.8)

Source: OECD, *Historical Statistics 1960–81*, p. 48.

[a] Movements in real value-added in 1982 and 1983 were estimated
from output and employment data.

trained employees from the educational system in each
country, are shown in Row C.

In the very long term the development and introduction
of new products and techniques, and the introduction of new
machines and processes, are the crucial determinants of
labour productivity, and changes in effort are relatively insignificant. The relationships can be illustrated by the manufacture of pins, a significant industry when Adam Smith
wrote *An Enquiry into Nature and Causes of the Wealth of
Nations* in 1776. During the following 200 years there was a
hundred-and-seventyfold increase in labour productivity in
the manufacture of pins attributable to technical progress
involving the substitution of new types of machinery for
hand operations. Differences in effort rarely account for
more than a twofold difference in labour productivity.[10]
There are feedback relationships. If new equipment, processes,
etc., are set up or operated less efficiently at one location
than others, this will slow the rate of investment and
productivity growth at that location.

So far the forces determining labour productivity within
international companies have been considered. One noteworthy distinction between a comparison of performance of
the businesses of these companies in different countries, and

[10] C. F. Pratten, 'On Pin Manufacture', *Journal of Economic Literature*,
March 1980.

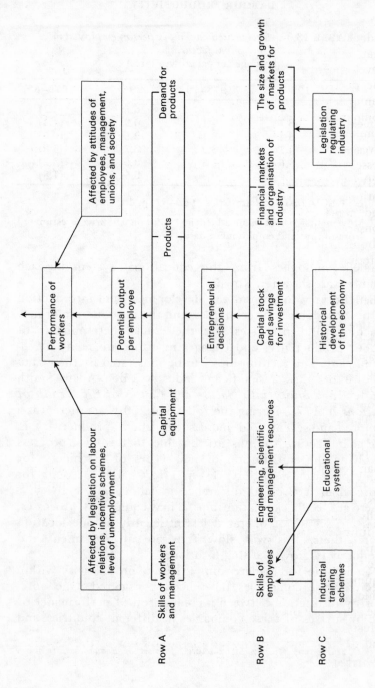

CHART 13.1 *The forces determining labour productivity differentials between countries*

Row A　Skills of workers and management

Affected by attitudes of employees, management, unions, and society

Affected by legislation on labour relations, incentive schemes, level of unemployment

Performance of workers

Potential output per employee

Entrepreneurial decisions

Demand for products

Products

Capital equipment

Row B　Skills of employees

Engineering, scientific and management resources

Capital stock and savings for investment

Financial markets and organisation of industry

The size and growth of markets for products

Historical development of the economy

Legislation regulating industry

Row C

Industrial training schemes

Educational system

independent companies operating in different countries, is that many international companies organize research and development on a world basis. So the relative importance of the development of new products for the success of companies and labour productivity is unlikely to emerge from a comparison of performance *within* international companies. Similarly, the availability of finance and the assessment of investment projects are more standardized between the businesses of international companies in different countries than between independent companies. The effects of any international differences for the assessment, selection, financing, and management of investment projects could be of more consequence when assessing the causes of differences in labour productivity for countries than for the businesses of international companies.

The Relationship between Demand and Growth

Is the reason for Britain's slow growth of labour productivity the slow growth of demand, and hence output—the Keynesian diagnosis? Or is the slow growth of labour productivity, and the supply-side factors which cause it, the reason for the slow growth of demand and output in Britain—broadly the monetarist view?

The Keynesians' focus on the growth of demand as the key to productivity improvement reinforced their advocacy of demand management policies. Their reasoning goes deeper than reliance on the familiar maxim, 'success breeds success'. If output increases, labour productivity should improve; first as firms take up spare capacity and any scope for more fully utilizing labour already employed. Once existing capacity is fully utilized, further increases in productivity emerge as capacity is increased; expansion enables firms to take advantage of the economies of scale and install machinery and equipment which incorporate the latest techniques, and which they might not buy to replace existing machinery in the absence of expansion. Important examples of scale effects are the spreading of fixed (labour intensive) design and development costs over a larger output of the products to which these fixed costs relate—this assumes that the increase in output is achieved without increasing the product range—and the use of more mechanized or automated methods of production at higher scales of output which are not economic for lower volumes. Some economists push the chain of cause and effect further; they hypothesize that the increase in productivity, attributable to an increase in output, will increase competitiveness and so stimulate further increases in demand and output—they label this sequence 'cumulative causation'. They claim Britain's economy is caught in a downward spiral of cumulative causation—falling output leading to declining productivity and profitability, relative to competitors, and further loss of markets.

Entry to a vicious circle by declining relative efficiency and slow innovation is equally plausible. Declining efficiency raises costs and leads to a slow growth of demand and output.

The fact that there is a relationship between output growth and productivity is well established. One of the first studies which quantified the relationship was by W. E. G. Salter.[11] Using data for the period 1924 to 1950, Salter showed that there were large differences in the growth of labour productivity between industries, and that 69 per cent of the variance in the growth of output per head could be accounted for by the differential growth of output between industries. Salter recognized that causation ran in both directions, but he was unable to allocate the extent of causation. Salter concluded that the primary explanations for differences in growth of productivity were improved techniques of production and economies of scale. For assessing Salter's work it is worth noting that his selection of industries was inevitably biased towards those with a relatively unchanging product mix, for which changes in output and productivity can be measured. The engineering industries, which are important exporters, were omitted because it is difficult to measure changes in their output of constantly evolving and improving products. Later work on the output–productivity relationship for industries within a country, and between countries, have not quantified the relative importance of the channels of causation.

[11] W. E. G. Salter, *Productivity and Technical Change*, Cambridge University Press, 1966.

The data for output per employee for manufacturing industries in Table 13.1 indicate that the relationship persists. The ranking of industries for output and output per employee are similar; industries with good growth of output during the 1970s, chemicals and electrical engineering, had relatively rapid growth of productivity. The clothing industry is a notable exception: it managed a big improvement in output per employee between 1973 and 1979 despite very little growth. However, firms in this industry can install more productive machinery without rebuilding factories, and reap additional economies of scale in spite of slow growth of the total output of the industry. The industry has a fragmented structure with many factories; as some factories close others can increase their output and scale. Also, product rationalization and the introduction of longer production runs can occur at factories with a static total output.

The relationship between output and productivity growth also applies to the manufacturing sector as a whole. Rapid growth of output and productivity go together, and this relationship is shown in Diagram 13.3. There was a rapid growth of output per person-hour between 1963 and 1964, 1967 and 1968, and 1972 and 1973 when output grew rapidly. Between 1974 and 1975, and 1979 and 1980 output per person-hour and output fell.

Mrs Thatcher's 'Productivity Miracle'

It may seem paradoxical, but there is evidence that a steep fall in demand and output can trigger an improvement in labour productivity. Between 1980 and 1981 output per person-hour in Britain's manufacturing industries rose very rapidly, by 4 per cent, though output was falling (Diagram 13.2(b). Another presentation of the movement of productivity is shown in Diagram 13.4. The path of output per person over four cycles is compared.[12] The important point is that output per person has risen during the 1979–83 cycle in spite of the steeper fall in output shown in Diagram

[12] The diagram was used in *Economic Progress Report*, January 1982. The indices start from cyclical output peaks.

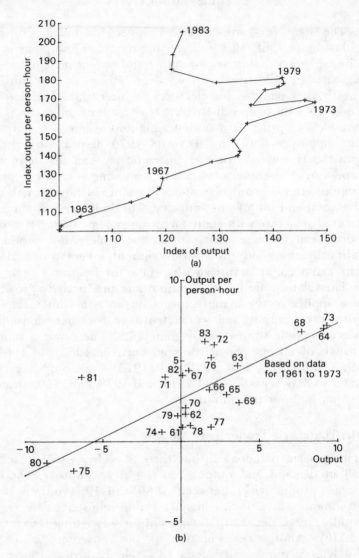

DIAGRAM 13.3   Output per person-hour and output for
manufacturing industries
(1960 = 100)

(a) Scatter diagram.
(b) Scatter diagram of year to year percentage changes;
    $Y = 2.64 + 0.47X, R^2 = 0.60$.

Sources: *ETAS* 1984, and *Economic Trends*, March 1984.

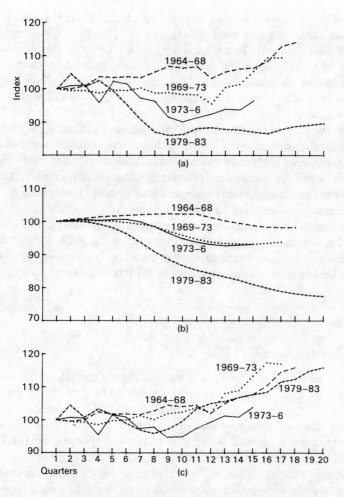

DIAGRAM 13.4   Manufacturing productivity
(A comparison of changes over successive cycles)

(a) Output.
(b) Employment.
(c) Output per person.

Sources: *ETAS* 1984, and *Economic Trends*, March 1984.

1964 Q4 to 1968 Q2 cycle	– – – – –
1969 Q2 to 1973 Q2 cycle	· · · · · · · · · · ·
1973 Q2 to 1976 Q4 cycle	———————
1979 Q1 to 1983 Q4 cycle	- - - - - - - -

13.4(a). To achieve this improvement employment has been reduced by 23 per cent. During the 1979–83 cycle firms did not hoard labour in anticipation of a recovery. But this was not the only factor explaining the productivity improvement. A fall in demand which leads to the closure of the least efficient factories (the Salter tail) raises average labour productivity. There were many closures in 1980 and 1981, and they were concentrated on the least efficient factories. Also, the severe *shock* to management caused by falling demand and high interest rates in 1980 made many of them seek ways of increasing efficiency and higher productivity. Employees moderated wage claims and co-operated to increase productivity to preserve some jobs.

Clearly there has been a step-up in productivity since 1979, but it is too early to judge the extent of any improvement to the long-term rate of growth of labour productivity —whether or not the *long-term* trend has been bent upwards.

Policy Implications

What are the policy implications of the relationships between the growth of output and productivity? The fact that a severe shock to industries, as in 1980 and 1981, increased productivity certainly does not carry the implication that governments should adopt a policy of perpetual intense deflation, because it results in a self-defeating increase in unemployment. Policies to maintain and boost demand *and* supply side policies should be used to take advantage of the effects of increasing output on improving labour productivity. But, though there is a place for demand management, and economies of scale are an important source of increased productivity, Britain's productivity problem does not stem from the slow growth of output and productivity caused by demand constraints alone. During the 1950s, and at times during the 1960s, demand for manufactures was buoyant but productivity growth was slow by international standards.

Methods of Tracing the Causes of International Differences in Productivity

There are two main approaches to understanding the forces affecting productivity and estimating their relative importance. The first is to analyse published statistics of output per person, output, etc. Salter's was an example of this approach. He emphasized the importance of technical change and economies of scale, but alone they are not convincing as explanations for the marked differences in the growth of labour productivity between advanced industrial countries, or between less developed countries, which emerged during the post-war period. New techniques were available to all firms, so why did productivity increase less rapidly in Britain than France or Germany, and why did productivity increase more slowly in Europe than Japan? If large scale was crucial, how did countries like Sweden and Switzerland achieve high levels of labour productivity? Salter recognized that factor substitution and the person efficiency of labour were 'important elements in increasing productivity, if not directly, at least in making effective productivity increases originating in technical change', but he had no means of estimating the impact of differences in the personal efficiency of labour, their intelligence, skills, and effort.

The second approach to studying productivity is to examine performance between and within industries and firms. At least it is possible to gain insights into the decisions which affect labour productivity in this way. The explanations for differences in performance given to the author by managers of international companies focused on the factors within the managers' control. Usually differences in product mix, production runs, and capital equipment between the operations of companies in different countries cannot be changed in the short-term, and managers are concerned to increase productivity within these parameters. Also, much of the information obtained from firms cannot be analysed rigorously, partly because there are too few observations for firms operating in the same industry.

It is possible to measure differences in inputs of some of the determinants (e.g. hours of work) of differences in labour productivity between firms. Differences in the application of some factors contributing to differences in output per person (capital equipment, training, competition) can also be measured, but their contribution to differences in productivity are difficult to assess. Finally there are some forces (effort) which often cannot be measured at all precisely. As the contribution of many of the forces determing differences in productivity cannot be assessed quantitatively, it is not possible to apportion the causes of differences in productivity; it is a matter of judgement.

Some Factors Contributing to International Differences in Productivity

In 1979 managers of international companies reckoned that they were getting a lower level of performance at their UK businesses than in Germany, France, and the USA. There was more slack, with more than 60 per cent of the companies considering their UK businesses over-manned. In part the differences were summed up by the claim that the labour force in other countries was better disciplined. Also, performance standards expected were in general higher overseas. People do not work at a calculated optimum pace, but at a pace set by tradition, circumstances, and rules, as well as their own idiosyncracies. Conventions accepted by managers and workers about the degree of effort expected from employees have often been lower in Britain. Put in these terms this conclusion is critical of the performance of the labour force, but differences in performance are the product of developments over many years which have affected attitudes and performance and have left many UK operations over-manned compared to our competitors. This conclusion mirrors that of Caves and Krause given earlier, that the origin of our productivity problems lies deep in the social system. It contrasts with Mr Prais's view, expressed in a comment on Caves's paper on productivity, that Britain's poor manufacturing productivity is to a substantial extent attributable to such specific matters as the frequency of strikes and the paucity of our vocational training.[13] In any

[13] R. E. Caves and L. B. Krause, *Britain's Economic Performance*, Washington, 1980, p. 198.

case the existence of this slack explains why the intense recession since 1979 could bring about an increase in productivity.

The second area for examination is the creation of internationally competitive giant firms. A feature of the successful advanced manufacturing countries is that they have internationally competitive firms—Boeing, Texas Instruments, IBM for the USA; Sony, Toyota, Nissan for Japan; Daimler Benz, GHH, Siemens for Germany; SKF, Volvo, Sandvik for Sweden. Britain too has internationally competitive firms such as Beecham and GEC, but Britain has fewer of them. During the 1970s there were no independent British motor vehicle companies in this class, and only one chemical company, while Germany had three chemical companies each the same size as ICI. It is fashionable to emphasize the importance of small and new firms, but while there is a clear need to encourage and foster their growth, it is only realistic to stress the importance of large companies. In 1978 twenty-two German companies accounted for nearly 40 per cent of German exports of manufactures. Exports by twenty-four British companies matched with them were one third of the level of the exports of the German companies, and accounted for about 30 per cent of Britain's exports of manufactures.

If the reasons why Britain has fewer companies in this class could be pin-pointed, then Britain's inferior post-war industrial performance may be explained. Such companies contribute directly to high productivity, and, by being able to pay high real wages, put pressure on other firms to do so too. The existence of these companies in an economy puts pressure on inefficient firms. What are the conditions for the creation and development of internationally successful firms? There is no single recipe, though the exclusiveness and/or high quality of products are usually ingredients. Technical superiority can be traced in many cases to an initial technical break-through, but a technical lead has to be protected by expenditure on research and development. Other ingredients are entrepreneurship and management skills to pick products and markets to develop, and large scale compared to competitors in similar lines of business to reap the economies of scale for research and development, production, and marketing, and to provide security and absorb mistakes. Achieving a high standard of production efficiency and marketing expertise are other factors which contribute to success. However, if one had to name the missing element for Britain, apart from the contribution of labour, it would be the relative weakness of entrepreneurship, of the absence of the industrial and financial genius and administrative know-how needed to create large competitive companies in industries where technical innovation is required.

The third group of forces highlighted as determinants of growth are those within the control of the state. Its role is more passive—to create the environment in which firms can succeed, and to support British firms in competition with overseas firms. The government determines the conditions on which Britain competes in overseas markets and at home by influencing the exchange rate and negotiating the terms on which Britain trades. The state finances much of the education programme, which is of fundamental importance in providing skills; it creates the legal environment within which firms operate; it sets the proportion of resources taken by public expenditure and taxes; and it holds the levers of Keynesian demand management. Governments also influence, as well as reflect, social and political attitudes.

It is the government's role in financing and controlling education about which there is most doubt over its contribution to the performance of the economy. Governments have not accepted full responsibility for determining the balance of education. In Britain the proportion of resources devoted to scientific and engineering education has been low, though this is less true in 1984 than 1960. The education authorities, which are in practice largely independent of government, have not put a high priority on providing pupils and students with vocational skills.

This survey of some causes of Britain's relatively dismal productivity performance has focused on the importance of the less tangible factors contributing to the growth of productivity. This reflects their importance. Britain's relatively low investment was described in Chapter 8. It is the forces discussed in this chapter which are primarily responsible for the low investment and slow growth of labour productivity.

Keynesian economists have emphasized the effects of the slow growth of demand and output of firms in Britain. In retrospect it is clear that demand for the output of British firms increased more slowly than demand for the output of Japanese, German, French, and Italian firms; but the initiating causes of the differences were the causes of slow growth of labour productivity in Britain.

14

Unemployment

The growth of unemployment in Britain and other advanced countries during the 1970s took economists by surprise. Most economists had come to believe that governments could regulate the economy by varying taxes and the money supply so as to maintain a high level of employment. As unemployment rose above levels that had previously been regarded as full employment, government unwillingness or inability to control unemployment was manifest.

The first challenge to economists posed by current levels of unemployment is to discover the causes of the increase. The second is to find effective ways of reducing unemployment, and the third is to persuade governments to implement solutions. Before dealing with these questions, the statistics of unemployment are reviewed in the first three sections of the chapter.

Trends in Unemployment

The estimates of unemployment shown in Table 14.1 and Diagram 2.3 are based on the number of people who claim benefits at Unemployment Benefit Offices. Since there is no compulsion to 'sign on', these figures are underestimates of the true levels of unemployment.[1] Another matter of definition is the inclusion or exclusion of unemployed school-leavers; they are excluded from unemployment for Table 14.1 and Diagram 2.3. The working population to which unemployment is related includes the self-employed.

Whatever the definition used, there is no doubt about the vast increase in unemployment since 1970. Moreover, the average duration of unemployment as well as the number of jobless has increased. More than 1.1 million people had

[1] See Appendix 14.1.

TABLE 14.1   *Unemployment*

	Average number unemployed[a]	Percentage of the working population[b]
	'000s	%
1950–9	330	1.4
1960–9	450	1.8
1970–9	940	3.7
1979	1,240	4.7
February 1984	3,000	11.2

Sources: *ETAS* 1984, and MDS, March 1984.

[a] Excluding school-leavers.
[b] Including the self-employed.

been unemployed for more than a year in 1984.[2] Between 1974 and 1983 unemployment rose by 1,000 per working day. There was a one-way ticket to the dole queue for many former employees, not a game of musical chairs in the labour market with the long-term unemployed representing a small percentage of the labour force.

An International Comparison

Britain is certainly not alone in facing the problem of growing unemployment, but as with most of the other bugbears of the Western economies, Britain has been affected very badly. Table 2.1, an international league table for six leading industrial countries, indicates that unemployment in Britain was around the average during the 1960s and 1970s, but Britain sustained the second highest international inflation rate. Deflation was not deemed necessary until the late 1970s, when unemployment in Britain outstripped all our major competitors. In 1984 no other major industrial country had as high a level of unemployment. With free trade between Britain and other EEC countries, and reduced

[2] See Appendix 14.2.

tariffs on imports from other countries, Britain may be likened
to a depressed area of a country in recession.[3]

Another international comparison is shown in Diagram
14.1; this time between the UK, the OECD, and Germany,
Belgium, and the Netherlands (GBN). The last group is included
as the economies which most resemble the UK in terms of industrial structure and circumstances, but like the UK they have
not adopted expansive economic policies, so the comparison
does not provide a test of alternative policies. Between 1976
and 1979 the levels of unemployment in the UK and GBN were
relatively steady, averaging 5.0 and 4.1 per cent. By 1981 the
UK level had increased by 80 per cent, and the GBN level by
34 per cent. By 1983 the increases from the 1976/9 base were
124 and 117 per cent. Until 1980 unemployment in the UK
was below the OECD average; since 1981 it has been 2 percentage points above it. Thus, using GBN as a basis of comparison, it

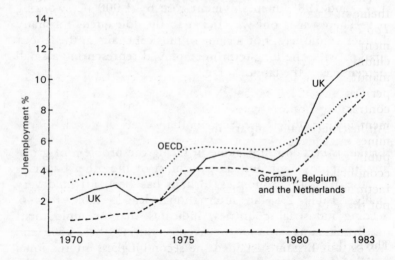

DIAGRAM 14.1   An international comparison of unemployment

Sources: OECD *Historical Statistics 1960–81*, and *Main Economic
Indicators*, March 1984.

[3] There are qualifications to this comparison. The recession is partly a result
of the deliberate adoption of monetarist policies by Western governments, and the
British government in particular. Britain could have reduced interest rates and
limited the rise in sterling in 1979 and 1980 to moderate the increase in unemployment, this option is not open to regions within a country. See Appendix 14.3.

can be seen that unemployment rose more rapidly in the UK between 1979 and 1981, but has since increased less rapidly. Compared to the OECD as a whole, Mrs Thatcher's unemployment record is dismal, but the USA and Japan have large weights in the total OECD average, and the circumstances of those economies are so different they do not provide a reliable basis for assessing the performance of the UK economy.

Regional and Sectorial Unemployment

The regional distribution of unemployment and the sectorial changes in employment are outlined in the Statistical Appendix.[4] Two-thirds of the reduction in employment between 1979 and 1981 was in manufacturing industries. The decline in employment in mechanical engineering, metal manufacture, textiles, and clothing has been massive.

The swing in employment away from manufacturing was a theme of Bacon and Eltis's work *Britain's Economic Problem. Too Few Producers*?[5] The trend has been away from employment in manufacturing towards the service industries, including services provided by the public sector. The share of manufacturing in GDP fell from 37 per cent in 1955 to 25 per cent in 1981. The fact that employment has continued to contract in the 'productive' sector since 1979, while employment in the public sector has simultaneously declined, undermines their main prescription—cutting back the growth of the public sector. The fundamental problem of the British economy has been the lack of competitiveness of the manufacturing sector which was discussed in Chapters 10 and 13, not the allocation of resources to the public sector.

The Relationship between GDP and Unemployment

What is the relationship between rising unemployment and the growth of GDP, and to what extent are available resources wasted? A close correlation between a change in the unemployment rate and a change in GDP was noted in America by Arthur Okun. An extra 3 per cent change in output, GDP, is

[4] See Appendix 14.4.
[5] London, 1978.

accompanied by an extra 1 per cent change in unemployment in the opposite direction. This empirical generalization came to be known as 'Okun's Law'. Unemployment does not respond in proportion to extra output; firms increase employment less than in proportion to a change in their output because of economies of scale and the utilization of spare capacity. Also, some of the change in employment is absorbed in unregistered unemployment. The implications of Okun's Law for the future are that high growth rates will be required to bring down unemployment, since much of the increased demand will be absorbed by existing capacity and higher activity rates.[6] Initially an increase in GDP of at least 2 per cent will be required to reduce unemployment by an extra 1 per cent. With productivity now increasing more rapidly, very high growth rates are required to cut unemployment.[7]

Okun's Law exaggerates the waste of resources represented by high unemployment. It would not be practical to raise GDP by the extra 20 per cent to reduce registered unemployment by 10 per cent. None the less, the waste of resources is immense at a time when there are latent private and public demands for many goods and services.

What is 'Full Employment'?

In the final analysis, the precise definition of full employment is unimportant. Unemployment is currently unacceptably high. Nevertheless, the term 'full employment' is often used. Full employment does not mean literally no unemployment at all. There will always be some frictional, seasonal, and structural unemployment however high the demand for labour. During the 1950s and 1960s experience of very low unemployment led to levels of unemployment of 2 per cent or less being regarded as full employment, and it was possible to maintain these levels of unemployment without accelerating inflation. Structural unemployment may have risen since 1970 for the reasons described below, and it is possible that frictional unemployment has increased because of the

---

[6] An activity rate is the proportion of a cohort of the population (an age-group) which is included in the working population.

[7] See Appendix 14.5.

post-war increases in social security benefits. The level of unemployment required to stabilize or reduce inflation has certainly increased, but the relationship between unemployment and wage increases is so uncertain that it is not possible to specify a level of full employment based on the inflation/unemployment trade off.

Lord Beveridge, writing in 1944, had a different perspective on unemployment.[8]

Full employment means that unemployment is reduced to short intervals of standing by, with the certainty that very soon one will be wanted in one's old job again or will be wanted in a new job that is within one's powers . . . [and] that unemployment in the individual case need not last for a length of time exceeding that which can be covered by unemployment insurance without risk of demoralisation.

He emphasized that the demand for labour and the supply of labour should be related qualitatively as well as quantitatively; in other words, structural unemployment is intolerable. For this reason, he put the maximum acceptable level of unemployment at 3 per cent. He concluded: 'For men to have value and a sense of value, there must always be useful things waiting to be done, with money to pay for doing them.'

It is to the causes and possible solutions for unemployment that we now turn.

Theories of Unemployment

'If the price of bananas is kept too high in relation to the price required to balance demand and supply, there will be a surplus of bananas. If the price of bananas is below the market-clearing price, there will be a shortage. The same applies to labour.'[9] This statement by Samuel Brittan opens up the question of why the pricing and demand and supply of labour should be different from commodities. If unemployment exists then wages are too high; the price mechanism operating through reductions in wages could restore the market equilibrium at the point of full employment.

In the *General Theory* Keynes was concerned with the

[8] Lord Beveridge, *Full Employment in a Free Society*, London, 1953, p. 18.
[9] Samuel Brittan 'Jobs and the Price of Bananas', *Financial Times*, September 16 1982.

impact of wage reductions on employment. Here the effects of increases in wages on employment are considered. Diagram 14.2(a) shows the relationships we would expect to operate in the banana market. In the short run the supply of bananas is rather inelastic, but demand for bananas responds to price; it is price elastic. Starting from a position of equilibrium at p_1, if the price of bananas were to rise, supply would exceed the reduced quantity demanded. In any case the important point is that supply and demand are pretty nearly independent; the price of bananas has only a slight effect on aggregate income and the price level and hence on the demand for bananas. When the price of bananas rises consumers buy less bananas because they substitute other products for bananas.

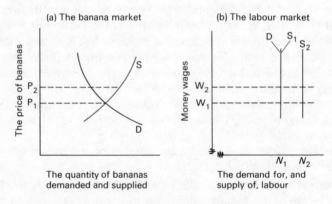

DIAGRAM 14.2

(a) The banana market.
(b) The labour market.

The demand for labour by a single firm is like that for bananas, price-elastic. A single firm which could lower its wages could reduce its prices and increase sales and employment. However, the aggregate demand for labour (the total demand for labour in the economy) is not necessarily inversely related to the level of wages. In aggregate, wages are the largest component for firms' costs and of personal income. We start by considering an economy with an accommodating money supply,[10] a proportional tax regime, and a floating exchange rate. If wages rise, then as a first approximation prices will rise at the same rate, workers' real income will not rise, and they will maintain their demand at the higher prices. Firms will maintain, but not increase, their demand for labour to meet the demand for their products. There will be no substitution of machinery for labour because the price of machinery will rise with the rise in wages paid by firms which make machinery and the firms which supply them. In brief, the aggregate demand for labour is independent of wages because changes in wages are passed on, and so prices increase at the same rate. Similarly, the supply of labour is independent of the level of wages; if prices change *pari passu* with changes in wages, the real wage and the supply of labour will not change. If the initial position were one of no widespread unemployment and with demand for, and supply of, labour unresponsive to changes in wages as illustrated by position W_1 N_1 and the lines D and S_1 in Diagram 14.2(b), unemployment would not emerge if wages rose. Alternatively, if the initial position was one of unemployment with more people willing to be employed at the current level of wages than demanded by firms, at W_1 N_2 in the diagram a rise in money wages would not lead to a change in employment and unemployment.

The first approximation of the effects of wages and hence prices rising is for the changes to cancel out, but it is an approximation only, since there are many subsidiary relationships which affect aggregate demand and the final outcome. Firstly, if it is assumed that the money supply is fixed in nominal terms and not accommodating, the real money supply will fall if wages and prices rise, causing some reduction in consumption and investment demand via the mechanisms described in Chapter 3. Similarly, if taxes are progressive, a rise in wages and prices will increase government revenue more than proportionately. There would be a reduction in the PSBR which would be contractionary unless the government reduced tax rates. If the exchange rate was fixed, not floating, the increase in wages and prices would

[10] A money supply which is moved up *or* down in line with changes in nominal income.

reduce exports and increase imports. Rising prices would also have effects on real income and wealth which were considered in Chapter 7. These would reduce consumption and aggregate demand.

So far it has been assumed that wages and prices rise at the same rate. If prices rise less than wages, and real wages do rise, then there could be positive net effects on aggregate demand in the short-term. The transfer of real income to wage earners could increase consumption by more than any consequential reduction in consumption and investment caused by the reduction in real profits and other incomes.

This essentially Keynesian approach to analysing the effects of wage increases, by considering their impact on aggregate demand, is facing renewed questioning. The Monetarist/Neoclassical economists see the labour market as more like that for bananas. Starting from a position of equilibrium at $\frac{W_1}{P_1}N_1$ in Diagram 14.3, if money wages rise then real wages will rise, though not by as much as money wages. If real wages rise to $\frac{W_2}{P_2}$ there will be unemployment. Prices rise more slowly than wages, so real wages rise and disequilibrium emerges. Possible examples of prices which increase more slowly than wages to allow the increase in real wages are those for raw materials.

Other possibilities which have to be considered very seriously following the experience of the 1970s are whether unemployment was created by a general failure or inability of firms to pass on higher wages, and whether there has been a fall in the equilibrium real wage. If firms are unable to pass on wage increases then real profits will fall. This would lead to a cut in employment as firms cut costs to restore profits and reduce investment.

The Causes of Unemployment

Why did unemployment re-emerge during the 1970s as a major economic problem? By definition it has been caused by a lack of effective demand which was analysed in Chapter 12. A major obstacle to expansionary policies identified in

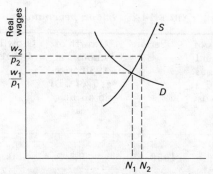

The demand for, and supply of, labour

DIAGRAM 14.3

Chapters 10 and 12 was the balance of payments constraint. Here this obstacle is considered from another perspective.

(a) International Trade

International trade provides opportunities for specialization and economies of scale, but it demands that countries adapt the structure of their industry continually. Adaptation requires industrial and financial enterprise and a labour force with relevant skills. Overseas firms have taken the markets of many British manufacturers who have then had to shed their labour force. Until entrepreneurs set up new businesses to supply goods or services, the potential output of the economy is reduced. One interpretation of the growth of unemployment is that the extent of adaptation required has outrun the capacity of Britain's entrepreneurs and labour force to make the changes required.

An indicator of the adaptation required of the economy is the growth of imports. Table 14.2 summarizes the changes in import penetration. In volume terms the increase in imports in each of the three decades distinguished represented about 10 per cent of GDP in the opening year of the decade. In spite of substituting North Sea oil for nearly half our oil imports, and much slower growth during the 1970s, imports cut into our market at a similar rate in the 1970s to that of the earlier decades.[11] These movements were exacerbated by

[11] North Sea oil, by causing an increase in the exchange rate, also raised imports.

TABLE 14.2   *Import penetration*

Imports of goods and services as % of GDP at factor cost		Period	Growth of Imports at 1980 prices as % of GDP in opening year	Growth of GDP	Percentage change in the price of imports relative to:	
					GDP	Exports
1950	27.0					
		1950–60	9.5	30	−22.1	−9.9
1960	24.3					
		1960–70	11.1	34	−7.4	−8.3
1970	25.4					
		1970–80	10.2	18	−3.6	−3.2
1980	29.4					

Source: *ETAS* 1984.

the change in the terms of trade being less favourable to Britain during the 1970s. Earlier the prices of imports fell relative to the GDP deflator and the price of our exports, especially during the 1950s. If the economy had grown more rapidly in the 1970s imports would have increased even more rapidly, and with them the requirement for adaptation to export to pay for the increased imports.

The forces requiring faster adaptation, which have been outlined, reduced the growth of potential output of the economy. Mr Callaghan and others have argued that Keynesian remedies for reducing unemployment do not work, that expansionary policies applied in the past have been followed after a lag by more rapid inflation and higher unemployment. In reality it is the need to speed up adaptation, or slow the requirement for adaptation by controlling imports, which has caused the unemployment; the main impact of expansionary and deflationary policies has been to determine the timing of the increase in unemployment.[12]

The alternative approach to explaining unemployment is in terms of movements of real wages and the natural rate.

[12] There are feed-backs in this process, a higher pressure of demand tends to maintain supply, and by increasing profitability might speed adaptation; but low demand can speed adaptation in other ways by putting pressure on firms to increase efficiency and to adapt.

(b) Increasing Wages

Money and real wage earnings rose by 325 per cent and 18 per cent respectively during the 1970s. To what extent did money wage increases cause the increase in unemployment? The increase in money wages was a cause, and an effect, of inflation which is dealt with in the next section. Here we are concerned with the question of whether rising real wages increased unemployment during the 1970s.

It is not possible to push the argument about the effects of rising real wages much beyond the earlier theoretical discussion. Diagram 14.4 graphs the trends in real wages, real wages per unit of output, and unemployment for manufacturing industry. Although real wages show a definite upward trend, it is worth noting that this is not so for real wages per unit of output. Real wages were not increasing faster than productivity. If rising unemployment is to be explained in terms of real wages being above, or rising above, the equilibrium real wage, it has to be couched in terms of the equilibrium level of real wages per unit of output falling; for example, because of the slow growth of world demand, intensifying international competition, and the oil price shocks.[13]

Alongside rising real wages in the 1970s, there was a sharp fall in real profits of industrial and commercial companies in 1974 and 1975 and again in 1980 and 1981, especially in manufacturing. This fall in profits was at least partly caused by the fall in demand rather than wage increases. The squeeze on profits reduced the financial resources available for investment and led to lower investment and hence lower aggregate demand, and in the long run to less capacity and employment. The positive link between profits and investment was shown in Chapter 8. The profits squeeze also caused firms to cut employment.

(c) Inflation and Unemployment

The extent to which inflation is to blame for high levels of unemployment is uncertain. Rapid price inflation led to some

[13] Also, the real wage per unit of output did not rise, partly because the increase in money and real wages from 1977 forced firms to increase labour productivity by reducing their labour force and increasing unemployment.

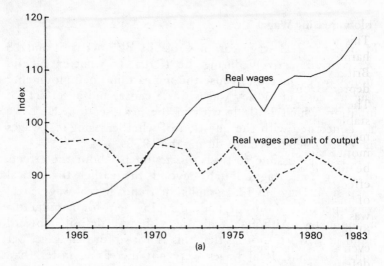

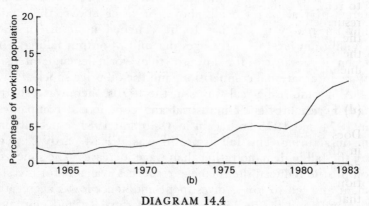

DIAGRAM 14.4

(a) Real wages and real wages per unit of output for manufacturing;
    (1970 = 100).
(b) Unemployment.

Sources: *ETAS* 1984, and *Economic Trends*, March 1984.

inefficiency because, for example, of the need to renegotiate
wages and prices more often. The rate of inflation was *uncertain*, so speculative buying may have distorted production
and price signals. These effects are difficult to measure and
assess.

In practice the effects of inflation were exacerbated by

slow adaptation of the tax system in Britain (and the USA). This at times sapped the post-tax profitability of firms, with harmful effects on investment; though the tax system in Britain has been very favourable to investment since free depreciation for machinery and plant was introduced in 1974. The manipulation of monetary and fiscal policy to maintain stable employment is, in any case, difficult. Even if a government wished to accommodate inflation by adjusting the money supply, its fiscal stance, and the exchange rate, it may be unable to do so in a manner which will even out the effects of inflation. For example, the acceleration of the rate of inflation in the 1970s increased personal saving, but this was not foreseen in advance, and it is doubtful if the effects of faster inflation on consumption can be forecast accurately even now. Once unemployment is allowed to build up as a defence against inflation, and for other reasons, it is difficult to reduce. The Salter tail of inefficient operations cannot be resurrected. The less skilled and employable have fallen into the pool of unemployed. The potential output or supply of the economy has been reduced. In monetarist terms, mass unemployment itself raised the natural rate of unemployment.

(d) Technology and Unemployment

Does Britain face an unemployment problem and an increase in the natural rate due to an increase in automation? If demand were stepped up would technology limit the reduction in unemployment? Layard has stated categorically that 'our abnormal unemployment since 1974 is not due to an abnormal burst of automation'.[14] None the less, the 'microchip revolution' has engendered a widespread fear that at least unskilled labour is becoming obsolete. The fear of technology is not supported by historical evidence. 'Inventions which reduce prices (for given wages) raise real purchasing power which makes it possible to sell more output', and in fact 'the industries in which employment has

[14] Richard Layard, *Unemployment in Britain: Causes and Cures*, LES, 1981, p. 1. If automation were causing the increasing unemployment then a rapid increase in labour productivity would be expected. There was no sign of this during the 1970s, but productivity has risen rapidly since 1979.

risen most tend to be those with most rapid productivity growth'. If Britain adopts new technology less rapidly than her competitors, this will leave us less competitive, and diminish employment opportunities in the long run. Countries with low unemployment, such as Japan and Sweden, have adopted new technology, not slowed its introduction.

Nevertheless, technology can create unemployment. We have no means of using macroeconomic statistics to show whether it is doing so, but we believe that it is. The fact that people have cried wolf about technological unemployment in the past, and been proved wrong, does not mean it cannot happen; there is no automatic economic law that people made redundant by technical advances will be re-employed. Even substantial cuts in wages will not necessarily bring forward extra job vacancies quickly. The pace of adaptation may be too slow and cut the increase in real purchasing power made possible by the new technology.

(e) Is there more 'Voluntary' Unemployment?

There is an argument, an echo from the 1930s, that high unemployment benefits, and changing attitudes towards them, have increased the incidence of voluntary unemployment and the natural rate. Gujarati tested whether any part of the upward trend in the registered unemployment rate after 1966 could be attributed to social security legislation passed in 1965 and 1966.[15] He found a definite divergence between the pre- and post-1966 trends. However, this does not prove the connection between work-shyness and the level of social security benefits. Diagram 14.5(a) shows that the number of vacancies has fluctuated less than unemployment levels since 1953, but it has fallen in times of high unemployment. Diagram (b) shows the pre-1967 relationship between vacancies and unemployment. (The relationship is not causal; both unemployment and vacancy statistics reflect the state of demand.) Diagram (c) shows how the pre-1967 relationship fits the post-1966 data: unemployment has progressively increased relative to the number of vacancies. There was a

[15] D. Gujarati, 'The Behaviour of Unemployment and Unfilled Vacancies', *Economic Journal*, 1972, p. 195.

further increase in 1981 and 1982 when Mrs Thatcher's government claimed to be restoring the incentive to work. The changed relationship may have more to do with changes in the demand for skills and indicate that technological advance is increasing the mismatch between the unemployed and vacancies. It is claimed that the numbers of unemployed not offering themselves for work has grown, but it is possible to assume that this is a result of high levels of unemployment, rather than a cause. The unemployed have been discouraged from looking for work by the high levels of unemployment. The rise in unemployment has not been caused by work-shyness.

Conclusions on the Causes of Rising Unemployment

It is true to state that unemployment is caused by a shortage of demand, but behind the failure to increase aggregate demand there are other causes of the rise in unemployment. These include increasing international competition, rapid inflation, and technological developments. Analyses of macroeconomic data cannot separate the contribution of each of these factors.

The Solutions

The mismatch of skills and the adaptation required in the economy mean that former ideas of full employment cannot be restored quickly. None the less, there are many methods of increasing employment. They may be considered in terms of demand-management/expansionist policies, supply-side policies, and action to reduce market imperfections. All these are aimed to increase employment; the other route for reducing unemployment is to share out more evenly the existing work-load, by a shorter working week, earlier retirement, etc.

The 'Keynesian' solution would be a boost to demand. The dangers associated with this are that inflation will accelerate, and that imports will increase and precipitate another balance of payments crisis. Incomes policies, devaluation, and import controls are prescribed for these dangers. The answer to the use of incomes policies is yes, but! The qualification is whether a long-term incomes policy can work

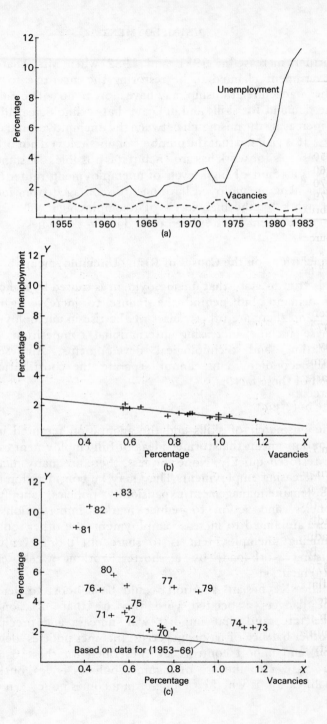

(a)

(b)

(c)

Based on data for (1953-66)

in Britain. Import controls could provide a solution to the balance of payments constraint and slow the rate of adaptation required by the economy, though for reasons given in Chapter 12 they are not an attractive option. There are also limits to the use of devaluation because of its effects on prices.

Even if the conventional Keynesian explanations for the emergence of mass unemployment were valid—that it was caused by allowing aggregate demand to fall below the level required to maintain full employment—the nature of the unemployment has now changed. Once factories have been shut, capacity reduced, and the skilled labour force redistributed with a high proportion of the unemployed being unskilled, an increase in aggregate demand will hit bottlenecks. It will not be possible to greatly reduce present unemployment by conventional economic policy instruments. This does not mean aggregate demand should not be expanded. If an increase in government expenditure was concentrated on the provision of services and construction, and subsidies to firms to increase investment and employment, a high proportion of the extra expenditure would result in extra employment in the UK and the initial import leak would be small. Alternatively, taxes could be reduced, but the import leak would be greater. Here we focus on the supply-side, and the problems of adaptation, since whatever view is taken of the deflationary policies of the Callaghan and Thatcher Governments, the results cannot be instantaneously reversed.

Supply-side Policies

Supply-side policies are not new. They are aimed to increase the output of, and employment in, the economy other than

---

DIAGRAM 14.5   Unemployment and vacancies
(as percentages of the working population)

(a) Time series.
(b) Scatter diagram (1953—66). Unemployment and vacancies as percentages of the working population; $Y = 2.76 - 1.51X; R^2 = 0.81$.
(c) Scatter diagram (1967—83)

Sources: *ETAS* 1984, and *Economic Trends*, March 1984.

by influencing demand. This leaves an extremely wide field. Much expenditure on education is designed to increase the skills of the labour force and so the potential output of the economy. Job training and subsidies to new firms are much more closely targeted to increasing the potential output of the economy. Supply-side policies include revenue-raising policies as well as expenditure policies. The distribution of taxes, within a given total, affects incentives for effort and risk-taking. Some supply-side policies affect neither government revenue nor expenditure. They consist of changing or influencing institutions.

The Keynesian orthodoxy was that increases in demand were required to increase output. However, where supply-side policies generate output which is exported without replacing existing British exports, or replace imports into the UK, they do create demand for the UK economy. Where the output competes with other British production some substitution or crowding-out occurs.

One argument against government supply-side intervention to speed adaptation is that it is unnecessary, that the market if left to itself will restore full employment. Plainly, however, the experience of the 1930s and the 1980s shows that the market solution operates slowly. Theoretical imperfections in the operation of markets can be claimed to support supply-side policies; private economic agents may take too short a view, and they do not take account of social costs. This may be true, but some government expenditure is misapplied. Subsidies are given for investments which would be made in any case, and some of the output of subsidized firms replaces that of more efficient home producers. In the end the level and direction of government aid must depend upon the competence of politicians and the bureaucracy, and be a matter for judgement.

Wage Cuts

The monetarist model is of a self-regulating economy in which markets clear. In practice, even at unemployment rates in excess of 10 per cent, wages are sticky in Britain: neither the general level of money wages nor the general level of real wages fall. This failure of the general equilibrium/ monetarist prescription for unemployment has been attributed to the monopoly power of unions and explicit and implicit contracts of employment which slow the adjustment of wages and salaries. The fact that most employees have information specific to the firms which employ them also limits the scope for their replacement by the unemployed at lower wages.

Whether general wage cuts would reduce unemployment is hypothetical because there seems no prospect of such cuts, but it is a solution for unemployment which is often suggested. It may seem paradoxical to argue that the rise in wages and inflation contributed to unemployment, but that a general fall in wages would not have any effect. It is not inconsistent. Instability, whether through rapidly rising or falling prices, damages confidence and hinders the efficient and effective operation of the economy.[16]

Although a general fall in wages and salaries seems unlikely, wage cuts for some groups are a possibility. The view of the labour market with wages wholly determined by monolithic unions and employers' associations is misconceived. There is a huge labour market where the laws of supply and demand still operate, and in which wages, especially for the unskilled, can fall. Changes in relative wages of this sort may generate an increase in demand for labour, particularly in the service sector for domestic help, waiters, etc. Changes restoring some earnings differentials eroded during the long period of full employment would provide incentives for the acquisition of skills for which there is a demand. These are the positive effects of wage cuts. There are offsets. If people do hire more domestic servants, etc. because of wage cuts, they will buy less of other goods or services. Nor do wage cuts go to the root of the problem. In most areas of the country there is a shortage of new jobs being created. There is no evidence that the creation of new jobs is very sensitive to wage levels. One explanation for this insensitivity is economies of scale and the advantages of established firms which have written off many costs of developing products and markets. Generally it is not economic to set up new firms

[16] See Appendix 14.6.

to make cars, petro-chemicals, machinery, or computers on a small scale. Even for microcomputers a new entrant has to have new ideas, and given those, the level of wages is not very important. Another explanation is the shortage of experienced managers to create new firms and expand existing firms. In any case, solutions for unemployment based on wage cuts are not appealing. Many already earn low pay.

Final Conclusions

Whichever Government had been in power during the 1974–84 period, and whatever conventional policies had been pursued, Britain would still be experiencing high levels of unemployment; it is an international malaise of the advanced Western economies. The tragedy is that the unemployment problem was exacerbated by anti-inflation policies during a time when it was destined to rise for other unconnected reasons.

Policies designed to improve the functioning of the market system are desirable; concentration on supply-side factors is justified and potentially beneficial. However, neglect of demand-management policy instruments is not justified. 'What experience and history teach us is this—that peoples and governments never have learned anything from history, or acted on principles deduced from it.'[17] We learnt from the Keynesian era the qualifications to erratic monetary and fiscal expansion. In the 1980s we should be better informed about the operation of the economy, and equipped to use expansionist policies in moderation to alleviate the most serious of all economic problems. In fact we seem not to have learnt from experience. Modern monetarists suggest perhaps technically superior, but basically identical, theories and policies. The government is taking a very similar line to the Conservative governments of the 1930s with the important exception that it is not using import controls. While the failures of the Keynesian era are used as an excuse for totally ignoring Keynesian remedies in the 1980s.

---

[17] G. W. F. Hegel, *Philosophy of History, Introduction*, translated by J. Sibree 1956 edition, p. 6.

15

Summary and Conclusions

During the 1950s and 1960s Britain had a low level of unemployment by historical standards, and a slow rate of growth in comparison to other countries. Governments believed they were regulating the output of the economy and controlling unemployment with Keynesian policies. They tried unsuccessfully to improve Britain's economic growth rate. During the 1970s the rate of inflation leapt, the growth rate slipped, and unemployment soared. Governments lost control of unemployment and finally Mrs Thatcher abandoned responsibility for it.

These events have been described, but the main purpose of this book was to provide a practical approach to understanding the operation of the economy. Using simple statistical techniques, the most influential economic paradigms of Friedman and Keynes have been contrasted. What conclusions may be drawn from this review of the operation of the British economy? The first reaction to surveying the development of the British economy during the 1970s and the economic relationships is one of uncertainty, of the absence of firm relationships. Nevertheless, it is possible to clear away some propositions about the working of the economy and reach conclusions which are now summarized.

Economic Paradigms

The monetarist and Keynesian models provide alternative basic frameworks for explaining the operation of an economy.

(a) The Monetarist Framework

The differences between the two models can be outlined in terms of elementary aggregate demand and supply relationships. The crucial assumptions for monetarists concern supply. In anything but the short-term (variously defined) they see the aggregate supply, or output, of the economy gravitating to the level corresponding to the natural rate of unemployment. If unemployment is at that level, an increase in the money supply will increase nominal demand and may increase output in the short-term, but prices and costs will rise and output will fall back to the natural level.

The relationship between changes in the money stock and prices was examined in Chapter 3. In Britain the growth of the money supply, as measured by $£M_3$, accelerated in 1972 and 1973, and rapid price inflation followed, but it was not possible to estimate the extent to which the growth of the money supply and prices were causally linked. There were alternative explanations for the price explosion. Data for Germany showed that accelerating inflation is not an automatic consequence of faster growth of the money supply. Nor was the relationship between the year to year growth of the real money supply and output close.

A cornerstone of the monetarist model is the attractively simple idea of the natural rate of unemployment. The relationship between unemployment and changes in wages was examined in Chapter 5. The monetarist explanation for the combination of faster inflation and increasing unemployment during the 1970s is that the natural rate greatly increased between the 1960s and 1970s because of the reduced incentives to work, the assertion of monopoly power by unions, and structural changes.

A related proposition concerns the ability of the economy to adjust if it is pushed off its equilibrium growth path with unemployment at the natural rate. The extreme rational expectations/monetarist claim is for rapid self-adjustment with all prices and wages flexible and markets clearing. What emerged in practice is the sluggish adjustment of the economy to shocks. According to the monetarist/neoclassical view, real wages should fall when unemployment rises. In fact real wages went on rising during the 1970s.

Robertson's summing-up of the role of money as the 'Old Policeman' is apt. If all else fails, *deflationary* policies built around high interest rates and fiscal contraction will slow the growth of the money supply and will reduce price inflation through a transmission mechanism involving a high exchange rate and high levels of unemployment. Mass unemployment is the 'Old Policeman's' baton.

(b) The Keynesian Model

Keynesians reject the monetarist/neoclassical ideas of price flexibility, especially for wages, and the effectiveness of wage flexibility to restore full employment. Initially Keynesians viewed aggregate supply as elastic up to the level of output consistent with full employment (or the onset of bottlenecks), beyond which supply was completely (or partly) inelastic. The Phillips curve formalized the relationship between unemployment and wage rates, and implied a smooth transition from elastic to inelastic supply at very low levels of unemployment. Since the collapse of the Phillips relationship during the 1970s Keynesians stress real wage resistance and the indeterminacy of wage increases. They see pricing as passive in the inflation process. A shock which reduces real income can lead to faster wage and price increases because of real-wage resistance. Also, for an open economy such as Britain's, a rise in output will increase imports, causing a fall in the exchange rate and lead to faster price and wage increases again because of real-wage resistance.

The 1970s

It has been suggested that new theories are required to account for the economic events during the 1970s. For the moment we leave the monetarist and Keynesian models, and summarize those events.

The statistical record was described in earlier chapters. Increases in British and world prices were accelerating before the first oil shock (Diagrams 2.2 and 2.5). The direct effect of the first oil price shock on domestic prices—4.4 per cent—does not account for the acceleration of inflation which preceded it, or by itself explain the further acceleration which followed. The alternative explanations for the collapse of the Phillips curve were described in Chapter 5. The decisive changes were social and political developments. Trade unions realized their power to increase wages in a period of low unemployment, and in the absence of firm resistance by the government and managements they exercised their power.

It is not difficult to account for the accelerating inflation during the 1970s. It is more difficult to assess the importance of inflation, particularly its impact on output and unemployment. In the context of the rational expectations model, Hahn has posed the questions; 'Why do people seem to hate [inflation]?', 'Why does it drive politicians to destructive frenzy?'[1] Some answers to these questions were given in Chapter 14. Rapid inflation contributed to the increase in unemployment. Even if a government wishes to accommodate inflation by adjusting the money supply, its fiscal stance, and the exchange rate, it is not practicable to do so in such a way as to cancel out the effects of inflation. In Chapter 12 it was shown that from the mid-1970s onwards governments in Britain did not accommodate inflation. Inflation and the political reaction to it slowed the growth of output and led to an increase in unemployment.

The second cause of the slow-down in the growth of output and the increase in unemployment was the balance of payments constraint, though this has been temporarily hidden by the present government's deflationary policies. Changes in trade created a need for rapid adaptation which was discussed in Chapter 14, if a high level of employment was to be maintained. Faster adaptation would release the tightening balance of payments constraint, and in this sense slow adaptation and lack of competitiveness are the underlying causes of the balance of payments constraint.

The Myth of the Stable Economy and Stable Relationships

The claim that the British economy is fundamentally unstable, that it does not automatically restore a high level of employment quickly once widespread depression exists, is far from new. Perhaps for many readers the most striking result of the survey is the extent of the instability of relationships. The savings ratio, whose stability and predictability

[1] Frank Hahn, *Money and Inflation*, Oxford, 1982, p. 101.

were important both for Keynesian theory and policy prescriptions, followed a trend increase in the post-war years, with substantial fluctuations about the trend. (In contrast, the American savings ratio has had a steady trend.) The velocity of circulation, stable and predictable in the monetarist model, has been erratic and unpredictable, admittedly during a decade of erratic monetary growth. The Phillips curve collapsed in the early 1970s, robbing policy-makers of that apparently simple trade-off between different combinations of inflation and unemployment. These results are not as negative as they may at first appear. We do not wish to imply that the economic system is no system at all; the aim has been to highlight the dangers of basing analyses and policies on simplifying assumptions concerning complex relationships which are prone to constant modification and alteration.

Social and Institutional Changes

The survey also illustrated the importance of institutional changes. Changes in British society and institutions are difficult to incorporate in economic models, but have been of fundamental importance in the post-war decades. They are not sudden destabilizing shocks like the first oil price

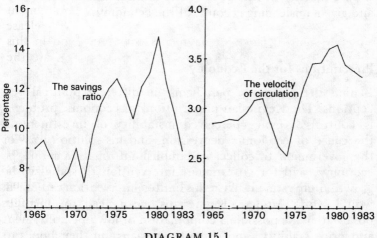

DIAGRAM 15.1

rise, but none the less have origins partly external to the economic system. Examples of such changes are scattered throughout this survey, but among the most significant were the introduction of Competition and Credit Control in 1971, a legal change which caused a soaring rise in $£M_3$, and the longer term rise of the pension funds, which contributed to the increase in the savings ratio. Incomes policies affected wage and price inflation. Changes in the tax rules allowing 'free depreciation' were an incentive for investment by firms on their own account and for leasing. Similarly, changes to tax rules had an impact on stockbuilding. In the international sphere, membership of the EEC changes the balance of payments, while the breakdown of the fixed exchange rate system in the early 1970s contributed to the volatility of sterling. The moves towards free trade and world industrial development set up intense pressures for adapting the economy. Some of these changes are reactions to economic pressures, but these pressures do not determine the extent of the changes, which are often jerky—major changes are made at infrequent intervals. The changes listed so far can be pinpointed. It is more difficult to assess changes in social and political attitudes—away from deference towards a more questioning self-assertive attitude—which underlay the pressure for increased wages during the 1970s. It is clear that simple models which ignore such changes will be inaccurate and give a misleading account of the economy.

Prescriptions for the Economy

Behind the economic paradigms lie different political perceptions. The Keynesian prescription for economic problems is controls. Keynes perceived instability of investment as the cause of economic depression, and his solution was for the government to collect and publish information about the economy, and for government intervention to stabilize the growth of investment. With this limited intervention capitalism would work. Modern Keynesians see a need for incomes policy to make possible a combination of low unemployment and price stability, and some Keynesians pin their hopes of removing the balance of payments constraint on re-imposing controls on international capital movements and imports.

Monetarists, and Friedman in particular, believe that in the long run freedom from controls, except controls required to regulate the money supply, will pay off. Friedman's views are at once appealing and repellent. They are appealing because they imply freedom from authority, meddlesome politicians, and bureaucrats, and that control of the economy is straightforward. They are repellent because we know that macroeconomic problems such as large-scale unemployment are complex, and that the costs of employing monetarist contraction are enormous.

Policy Implications for the Future

It is not the purpose of this book to map out the road to future economic success. Nevertheless, certain conclusions about future prospects and policy can be drawn. Clearly, the solution of what are commonly termed economic problems—inflation, sluggish growth, and unemployment—goes beyond the manipulation of economic variables. Three major problems which are crucial to future economic success lie outside the realms of economics alone. The first is the system of wage determination; the second, the problem of low and slowly improving labour productivity; and the third, to speed adaptation of the economy.

The rapid growth of money and real wages in the 1970s increased unemployment and provided an excuse for politicians *not* giving high priority to minimizing unemployment. While the danger of a wage explosion persists, the prospects for rapid growth and falling unemployment are bleak. There are two alternatives available for the control of wage settlements. The first is to leave their determination to market forces, with high levels of unemployment or other policies to reduce monopoly union and employee power. The second alternative, a far more acceptable one, is the implementation of an incomes policy. Britain's experience of incomes policies has not been encouraging, but other countries have had greater success. However, an effective tripartite incomes policy would require a change in attitudes by trade unions of which there is no sign. That leaves the government and management to impose an incomes policy. In some measure this is happening.

Low and slowly improving labour productivity in British industry are problems of long standing. Some of the explanations for this *malaise* were considered in Chapter 13. In Britain over-manning was commonplace in the 1970s, and Britain lacked the managerial and technical skills to create internationally competitive large-scale companies in industries where technical innovation was required. The productivity problem merges into the third one, which is to speed the rate of industrial adaptation to create and expand competitive businesses. Macroeconomic policies alone cannot solve problems of low productivity and slow adaptation. Creating mass unemployment, though brutal, has reduced inefficiency, but a new urgency in promoting supply-side policies, to encourage and speed the acquisition of skills, and investment in developing new and improved products to create new jobs, is needed. Though governments alone cannot provide a substitute for creative, skilful, and enlightened entrepreneurs, financiers, and managers, and skilled and co-operative employees, or coerce managers and workers into acquiring these attributes, governments in France, Sweden, and Japan have contributed to industrial success.

Final Conclusions

Erratic Keynesian expansionism damaged the economy in the early 1970s; dogmatic application of monetarism has damaged the economy still more dramatically in the early 1980s through its ruthless contractionary coercion on industry. No single model explains the operation of the economy or provides a recipe for economic policy. There are limitations on the power of governments to determine the development of the economy, but they influence the economy through an array of actions and policies including fiscal and monetary policy. Success depends upon governments' understanding of how the economy works and their judgement of the development of forces influencing the economy. It also requires understanding of the economy and co-operation by other economic agents.

Statistical Appendix

Introduction

I.1. Many series of statistics were revised by the CSO between preparation of *ETAS* 1984 and *Economic Trends* for March, 1984. Where series overlapped, data from *Economic Trends,* March 1984 were used.

I.2. *Regression Analysis*

The only statistical method used, apart from tabulating and graphing data, is regression analysis for two variables. Readers unfamiliar with this technique may refer to a statistics manual or simply take the regression lines, as in Diagram 2.1, to be lines of best fit to the data. They are lines calculated to minimize the sum of the squares of the deviations of the observations from the lines. For many relationships, R^2 is also given; this is an indication of the extent to which variations in the one variable about its mean (average) are explained by variations in the other variable about its mean. R^2 is the proportion of the variance (the sum of the squares of the deviations of the variable from its mean) explained by the regression line. R^2 varies between 0 and 1. If $R^2 = 1$, then the variations in one variable are completely explained by variations in the other variable. Regression analyses are used to estimate lines of best fit to data, and to summarize the closeness of the relationships between variables. Regression analysis does not indicate the direction of causation between variables, or whether any relationship is indirect — attributable to two variables being related to a third variable.

Chapter 2

2.1. *The data*

During the 1950s and 1960s much, though not all, statistical analysis was based on post-1950 data. Official estimates of national income commenced during the war, but data for the war years and early post-war period were discounted because of the controls and distortions which then applied. Estimates for the pre-war period were less reliable and in terms of the structure of industry, communications, international trade, and the level of unemployment, the period was so different from the post-war period that it was omitted from most statistical analyses which were intended to provide a basis for policy. The return of mass unemployment has weakened these arguments, and the 1950s and 1960s are in this respect unrepresentative. Nevertheless, it was decided to concentrate on data for the post-1950 period because of the greater availability and reliability of statistics for that period.

2.2. *Definition of Real GDP*

National income statisticians use the term Gross Domestic Product, or GDP, for the total output of the economy. If the value of GDP for each year is revalued in terms of a common set of prices, in this case 1980 prices, movements of the volume of GDP, or real GDP, can be compared.

GDP is estimated separately from three sources, expenditure, income, and output data. These estimates are averaged, and it is the average estimate which is shown in Diagram 2.1. The three estimates of the growth of GDP at 1980 prices between 1950 and 1980 are shown in Table A.2.1. For the first two estimates expenditure and income for each year are revalued at 1980 prices. For the output estimates measures of the volume of output are weighted by the value-added by each industry in 1980. The differences illustrate the lack of precision of national account data. The estimates of GDP in Diagram 2.1 are at factor costs; factor costs are market prices (the prices paid for goods and services) less indirect taxes, and with subsidies added back.

2.3.   The GDP deflator is an index of *home costs,* and is based on the expenditure estimates of GDP. It is derived by taking the estimate of GDP at current prices as a percentage of GDP revalued at 1980 prices. The index for each year is weighted by the pattern of expenditure in that year. A

TABLE A.2.1. *Growth of real GDP 1950 to 1980*
(at 1980 prices)

Method of estimation	Percentage increase 1950 to 1980
Expenditure data	105
Income data	107
Output data	92
Average	101

Source: *ETAS* 84.

comparison of estimates of the long-term increase in prices is shown in Table A.2.2. Prices for consumers' expenditure, measured by the deflator for consumers' expenditure, includes prices for the import content of consumers' expenditure. Prices of imports increased more slowly than home costs between 1950 and 1970, but faster between 1970 and 1980. Retail prices rose faster than prices for consumers' expenditure in both periods. The coverage of the index of retail prices is less comprehensive than for consumers' expenditure, and it is a base/moving-weight index which tends to exaggerate the increases in prices, because consumers take advantage of changes in relative prices and buy less of goods which increase most in price.

TABLE A.2.2. *Price inflation*

Index	Percentage increase 1950–70	1970–80
Deflator for GDP at factor cost	120	279
Deflator for GDP at market prices	128	269
Prices (deflator) for consumers' expenditure	109	247
Prices (deflator) for imports of goods and services	59	265
Retail prices	121	261

Source: *ETAS* 1984

2.4. *Trends*

The trend lines shown in the Diagrams are regression lines. The data used to calculate the equation for Diagram 2.1 were Y, the index of GDP (1980 = 100), and t (time: 1950 = 1, 1951 = 2 . . .). Where the Log (to the base e) $Y = a + bt$, the coefficient of the time variable gives the trend rate of growth 2.8 per cent p.a. compound.

2.5. To calculate the trend level of GDP in 1983 from the equation $Y = 3.858 + 0.0281t$: $t = 34$; $\log Y = 4.8134$; $Y = 123.1$. The index of actual GDP in 1982 was 103.5, 84.1 per cent of the trend level.

2.6. *Unemployment*

The definition of unemployment excludes school-leavers, while the working population includes members of the armed forces, the self-employed, and the unemployed.

2.7. *OECD* (The Organisation for Economic Co-operation and Development)

The GDP statistics include twenty European countries, the USA, Canada, Japan, and Australia. In 1975 GDP for the USA represented 38 per cent of the total.

2.8. *World Prices*

The World consumer prices index, calculated by the IMF, is a weighted index for more than one hundred countries.

2.9. *Claims on Growth*

Some growth is already spoken for. The 0.33 per cent p.a. increase in the labour force during, for example, the 1960s contributed to growth. If the labour force increases at 0.33 per cent, increases in wages and salaries will represent 0.25 per cent of output if rates of wages and salaries are unchanged. An important source of faster growth is the improved education and training of those entering the labour force. Entrants with qualifications expect and get higher relative rates of pay than those without qualifications leaving the labour force. This could account for a quarter per cent of growth per year. Similarly, growth requires investment. If investment had increased at the rate it increased during the 1960s, it would have taken an extra ½ per cent of GDP each year during the 1970s.

2.10. *Slow-down in Growth*

Other causes suggested for the slow-down in growth include

the years 1950–1973 being a period of exceptional prosperity for many countries. If growth had continued at the rate it reached between 1960 and 1973, resource bottlenecks may have developed. The first oil price explosion itself may have been a symptom of a bottle-neck in energy production. The slump in the 1930s and war-time disruption resulted in an acquiescent labour force in many industrial countries during the 1950s and 1960s, contributing to wage and price stability even at a high pressure of demand. Reconstruction after the war, the build-up of household, company, and bank liquidity during the war and the early post-war period, the use of Keynesian demand-management policies to expand demand, the expansion of the world money stock in the form of dollar balances created by American balance of payments deficits, and the freeing of regional world trade contributed to bouyant investment and the rapid expansion of demand and output. Growth of output was concentrated on some durable-goods industries which could use large numbers of unskilled employees.

2.11. *Energy Consumption*

Diagram A.2.1. shows a time series of UK energy consumption since 1965. Until 1973 energy consumption increased. It fell sharply in 1974 and 1975, rose then fell again in 1980, 1981, and 1982. GDP is a major determinant of energy consumption. Diagram A.2.2 plots energy consumption against GDP. To estimate the pre-oil shock relationship, data for 1960 to 1973 were used. The relationship is shown in the Diagram. For the post-1973 period, an estimate can be made of the effects of the oil-price explosion by comparing actual energy consumption and the expected level according to the relationship. In 1983 energy consumption was 18 per cent below the expected level.

The comparisons give a qualified indication, because GDP has grown more slowly since 1973 and there may be a trend for energy use to change through time (as more energy using processes are substituted for labour, or schemes for using energy more efficiently are invented and implemented), the composition of output may have changed (for example, away from energy-intensive manufactures) for reasons other

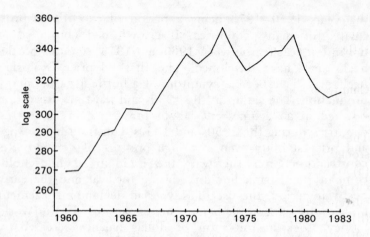

DIAGRAM A.2.1   UK energy consumption
(m. tonnes of coal equivalent)

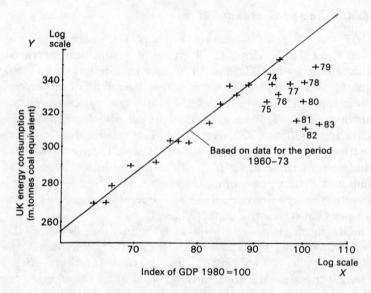

DIAGRAM A.2.2.   Energy consumption and GDP
Log Y = 2.65 + 0.71 Log X

than the rise in energy prices, and the system of weighting energy sources by their energy content does not exactly reflect the use of energy obtained from the sources.

Chapter 3

3.1. *Definition of the Money Stock*

The precise definitions of the main measures of the money stock used in the UK are:

(a) M_1 — a narrow measure consisting of notes and coin in circulation with the public plus sterling sight deposits — current accounts — held by the UK private sector.

(b) £ (Sterling) M_3 — includes notes and coin in circulation with the public, together with all sterling deposits (including certificates of deposit) held by UK residents in both the private and public sectors. The important distinction between M_1 and £M_3 is that the latter includes interest-earning deposit balances with banks.

(c) PSL_2 — which includes £M_3 plus other money market instruments and certificates of tax deposits (gross), plus building society shares and deposits, and other similar forms of 'liquid savings instrument').

3.2. Money stock figures in *ETAS* are for the end of each quarter. To estimate the average money stock for each year, the money stock at the end of the fourth quarter of the previous year and the four quarters of the year were averaged. The figure for the last quarter of the previous year and the last quarter of the year were given a weight of one each, and the first, second, and third quarters a weight of two each. This average centred on 30 June.

Chapter 5

5.1. *Wage-Rates and Earnings*

The divergence between the indices of wage-rates and earnings is termed wage drift, and occurs because nationally agreed wage-rates are supplemented at plant or factory level, and because of changes in the number of hours worked and the proportion of overtime which affect earnings but not wage rates. Also incomes policies may operate on wage-rates rather than earnings, which may include increases designed to avoid the guide-lines of incomes policy. Movements of the indices of wage-rates and earnings are shown in Table 5.1. There are sharp divergencies in some years, but over the 1970s these broadly cancel out, with the index of wage-rates increasing by 5.1 per cent relative to the earnings index. In Chapter 5 the index of wage-rates is used as the main indicator of movements of pay, because it is not affected by changes in the hours of overtime worked and it was used to derive the Phillips curve.

5.2. *Profits*

Estimates of profits earned in the UK are reported in *ETAS* and *National Income and Expenditure,* but they are subject to significant revision. Also, the movement of profits depends upon the definition used. During a period of inflation stocks appreciate in value. A firm which finances its stocks from its equity will need to retain, or plough back, stock appreciation if it is to maintain the real value of its equity capital. In fact, more stocks are financed with borrowed funds than with equity, and firms which borrow to finance stocks do not have to retain stock appreciation ot maintain their equity base. All stock appreciation is excluded from the profits shown in column 7 of Table 5.1.

5.3. *Unemployment Statistics*

Since Phillips estimated the Phillips curve, the historical statistics of unemployment have been revised. Feinstein's estimates,[1] which have been used elsewhere in this book, are lower than those used by Phillips. The effect of using the revised estimates would be to push the Phillips curve down and towards the Y axis.

[1] C. H. Feinstein, *National Income, Expenditure and Output of the United Kingdom 1855–1965,* Cambridge, 1972.

5.4. *Post-tax Real Income*

The CEPG (Cambridge Economic Policy Group) estimates of post-tax real earnings are:

1967	1968	1969	1970	1971	1972	1973	1974	1975	1976	1977	1978	1979
+ 2.8	+ 1.3	+ 0.3	+ 5.3	+ 2.5	+ 7.2	+ 3.1	− 1.8	+ 2.2	− 2.2	− 2.5	+ 6.5	+ 4.5

Source: *CEPG* Review, 1982, p. 49.

5.5. *The Natural Rate*

Examples of events which may alter the natural rate are changes in the composition of the labour force and the introduction of new technology. If youths are more fickle than adults about employment, then an increase in the proportion of youths in the labour force will increase the natural rate. An increase in the proportion of women in the labour force could have a similar impact. (The proportion of women in Britain's labour force did increase during the 1970s.) A speed-up in the introduction of new technology, requiring new skills and making old skills obsolete, also increases the natural rate, but is much more difficult to measure.

Monetarists claim that increases in social security benefits and increases in taxes relative to income have eroded the incentive to work, so the prospect of unemployment has been a diminishing check on wage claims. Certainly benefits did increase relative to earnings, and so did taxes. In 1961 unemployment benefit represented 42 per cent of *average* earnings of manual employees. In 1976 it represented 48 per cent of the average earnings of manual and non-manual employees, but with the earnings related supplement (ERS) the percentage was 66 per cent. The ERS did not exist in 1961 and has been stopped. (Earnings are after tax.) So far benefits have been related to average earnings. For those only able to earn less than the average, benefits form a higher percentage of potential earnings.

Although changes in the composition of the labour force and social security benefits might have caused some increase in registered unemployment in the absence of other changes, it is most improbable that they account for a significant proportion of present unemployment. The proportion of men in the age group 25—44 who are unemployed has greatly increased, and benefits have been cut since 1979.

Chapter 6

6.1. The estimates are unquestionably crude, but they reflect the ingredients of investment decisions made by fund managers and the determinants of bond prices. Expectations of the rate of inflation vary between fund managers, and there are factors apart from inflation affecting the rate at which rents increase.

6.2. The estimates of yields on shop property were obtained from *Evidence to the Committee to Review the Functioning of Financial Institutions*, vol. 3, HMSO, 1978, p. 152, for the period up to 1976. Estimates of yields made by a leading firm of estate agents were used for the period since 1976. Adjustments were made for the costs of managing shop property, which are greater than for bonds or equities, and the security of the money yields on government stocks; from 1960 to 1964 2 percentage points were added to the yield on bonds, from 1965 to 1969 1½ percentage points, and from 1975 1 percentage point. These arbitrary adjustments were reduced to reflect possible reactions to increasing inflation. Inflation replaced default as the source of risk of loss of the real value of investments, and reduced the relative importance of the secure money income on bonds. The year to year movements of the expected rate of inflation, as calculated, are affected by changing expectations of the growth of real rents as well as changing expectations of the rate of inflation. In 1973 a measure of rent control for commercial property was introduced as a part of an incomes policy. In 1974 there was a banking and financial crisis which affected yields on property and hence the estimates of the expected rate of inflation as calculated.

Chapter 7

7.1. *Saving by Other Sectors*

Chapter 7 focuses on saving by the personal sector, but the

government and company sectors also save (or dis-save). Table A.7.1 provides a summary of the capital account for the sectors in 1979. Section (a) shows gross saving and investment, before deducting depreciation and stock appreciation. It is gross saving that is used in the nominal savings ratio. Section (b) gives saving in net terms; the deduction of depreciation and stock appreciation (mainly from the company sector) leaves the personal sector as the main source of saving. This was not the case in 1972, as can be seen from section (d), which shows the change in the composition of net saving. Personal sector saving represented less than half the total in 1972. The final row of the table showing saving at 1972 prices indicates that real net saving has fallen. Section (c) of the table shows savings adjusted for gains or losses on the holding of monetary assets attributable to inflation. The personal sector has sustained losses from inflation, while the government sector and, on balance, the company sector have gained. The estimates of saving dealt with in sections (a) and (b) take no account of this real loss — income and savings are calculated before making any adjustment for the decline in the real value of monetary assets and liabilities.

The inflation adjustments were substantial for 1979. After deducting the real loss made on monetary assets saving by the personal sector was negative. This reflects the rapid rate of inflation in 1979, and could also explain at least some of the changes in the composition of saving shown in section (d) of the table.

7.2. *Inflation and Savings*

Two further explanations for the link between inflation and savings have been suggested by Buckley and Deaton. Buckley's theory predicts higher savings with anticipated inflation.[2] In practice, people make nominal wage agreements for a fixed length of time, say a year. The real value of the wage declines over the year, although (as inflation is anticipated) the effective *average* real wage remains constant. Thus towards

---

[2] G. Buckley, 'Personal Savings and Anticipated Inflation', *Economic Journal*, 1981.

TABLE A.7.1. *Summary of the capital account for 1979*

(a) Gross (before providing for stock appreciation and depreciation)

Saving	£bn	Investment	£bn
Personal sector	17.5	Fixed capital formation	34.9
Companies	25.3	Increase in book value of stocks	10.9
Public sector	3.4	Net investment abroad	− 0.7
	46.2		
Less residual error	− 1.1		
	45.1		45.1

(b) Net (less stock appreciation and depreciation)

Saving	£bn	Investment	£bn
Personal sector	12.3	Fixed capital formation	12.0
Companies	7.3	Value of physical increase in stocks	2.1
Public sector	− 5.0	Net investment abroad	− 0.7
	14.6		
Less residual error	− 1.1		
	13.5		13.5

(c) After adjustment for loss or gain on monetary assets attributable to inflation

Saving	£bn	Investment	£bn
Personal sector	− 2.0	Fixed capital formation	12.0
Companies	9.1	Stocks	2.1
Public sector	8.8	Net investment abroad	0.9
	15.9		
Less residual error	− 0.8		
	15.0		15.0

(d) Net Saving

	1972	1975	1979	1982
Personal Sector	2.9	6.5	12.3	13.3
Companies	2.8	1.2	7.3	5.1
Public Sector	0.7	− 2.4	− 5.0	− 5.1
In current prices	6.4	5.3	14.6	13.3
At 1972 prices	6.4	3.4	5.6	2.7

Sources: *National Income and Expenditure*, 1983, Table 1.7, and the *Bank of England Quarterly Bulletin,* June 1981, p. 233.

the beginning of the contract period (when the real wage is higher than average) people will save more, and towards the end (when the real wage is lower than the average) they will save less than if the real wage were constant over the period. If the anticipated rate of inflation is constant then aggregation over many individuals with overlapping contracts yields no extra savings. However, when anticipated inflation is increasing, the extra savings by those with recent pay awards will outweigh the lower savings of those coming to the end of their contract period. This will generate a higher savings ratio.

Deaton[3] has suggested a link between unanticipated inflation and higher saving. People buy goods sequentially. They interpret an increase in the price of each good as a temporary rise in its *relative* price, not as a rise in the average price level. Consequently they refrain from purchasing it, and saving rises. This explanation relies on the assumption that people take time to 'learn' about the rate of inflation. If rapid inflation continues for several years the lags may disappear as agents get used to inflation.

7.3. *The Permanent Income Hypothesis*

In order to test the Permanent Income Hypothesis (PIH) the savings ratio was related to a weighted average of current and lagged personal disposable income per capita, and then current, lagged, and future income; this assumes agents can and do forecast their income a year ahead. The results and the lags used are shown in Diagram A.7.1. Caution is required in interpreting the results. 1983 is excluded from (c) because future income is unknown for that year, and 1983 is an outlying observation for (a) and (b). These were crude tests of the PIH; income over a much longer time span might affect perceptions of permanent income, the methods agents use when forming their expectations of permanent income may have altered, and no allowance is made for the capital nature of expenditure on durable goods. When saving was lagged one quarter after income for (d) there was a very

[3] A. S. Deaton 'Involuntary Saving through Unanticipated Inflation', *American Economic Review*, no. 67, 1977.

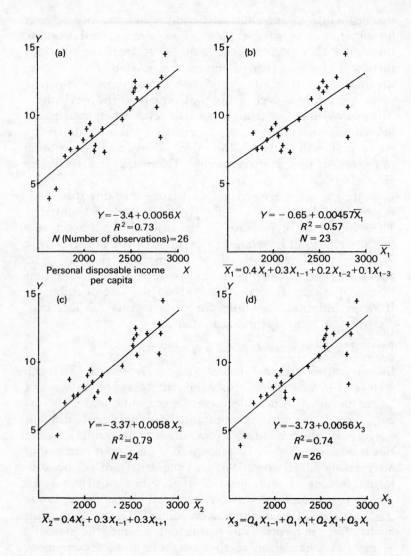

DIAGRAM A.7.1. *Savings Ratio and PDI*

(a) No lags
(b) Current and lagged income
(c) current, lagged and future income
(d) PDI lagged by one quarter.

marginal improvement in the fit of the equation; it would not be surprising if there were a lag of this type—agents' decisions on saving and consumption may be based partly on their income in the previous quarter.

7.4. *Personal Sector Net Wealth*

The net assets of the personal sector at the end of 1980 are listed in Table A.7.2.

TABLE A.7.2   *Personal sector net wealth* (at 31st December 1980)

		£bn
Physical assets		452.3
of which:		
Dwellings	300.7	
Agricultural and other land	30.7	
Consumer durables	80.0	
Financial assets		274.8
of which:		
Notes and coin	8.4	
Sight deposits at banks	14.2	
Other bank deposits	23.2	
Building society shares and deposits	49.6	
British government securities	11.3	
UK ordinary shares	32.5	
Equity in life assurance and pension funds	89.0	
Liabilities		81.7
of which:		
Bank loans and advances	14.8	
Hire purchase and other instalment debt	5.0	
Loans for house purchase	52.0	
Net wealth		645.4
Average net wealth per person		£11,500

Source: *Financial Statistics*, Feb. 1982.

7.5.   For years when the savings ratio was above the average for 1960/2, the excess saving was calculated $(S_t - S_{60/2} \times \text{PDI}_t)$. A deduction was made for indirect taxes and imports, and the remainder was added to the actual GDP at factor cost to estimate the hypothetical GDP if the savings ratio had remained at the average 1960/62 percentage. The deductions for indirect taxes and imports increased from 40 per cent in 1960 to 50½ per cent in 1983, to make an approximate allowance for the actual increases in indirect taxes and imports as proportions of consumers' expenditure.

Chapter 8

8.1.   There are problems for interpreting estimates of expenditure on plant and machinery at constant 1980 prices. This expenditure includes computers and similar equipment for which some relative prices have fallen in a spectacular fashion due to technical progress. As prices for a recent year, 1980, are used to weight expenditure the problems are not serious.

8.2.   It is possible that the National Income estimates of the capital stock do not allow fully for the scrapping of capacity which has taken place during the recession. The figures could therefore exaggerate the increase in the gross fixed capital stock.

8.3. In principle the price indices do take account of improvements in the 'quality' of products, they reduce price increases, but it is difficult, perhaps impossible, to measure changes in quality such as the introduction of numerical control to machine tools.

8.4.   Saving by industrial and commercial companies is undistributed income: it excludes stock appreciation and includes capital transfers (*ETAS* 1984, p. 182 col. 4 + col. 5 + col. 6 − col. 10). The definition of income excludes stock appreciation, but for firms which finance stocks by borrowing this is available for financing fixed investment. Saving and fixed investment were deflated by the deflator for fixed investment.

Chapter 10

10.1.   *Markets*

Table A.10.1 chronicles the increasing importance of trade during the 1970s for industry groups. Import penetration has advanced, but this increase has been uneven, being more

TABLE A.10.1 *Import penetration and export sales ratio for selected industries*

(1) Imports as percentage of home demand
(2) Exports as percentage of manufacturers' sales

	1974		1979		1980		1982	
	(1)	(2)	(1)	(2)	(1)	(2)	(1)	(2)
Food and drink	21	5	16	6	14	6	15	6
Chemical and allied industries	27	34	30	37	29	39	33	41
Mechanical engineering	28	40	31	40	32	45	35	47
Electrical engineering	29	29	37	37	37	38	49	45
Vehicles	26	42	41	41	39	43	45	46
Textiles	24	25	33	29	35	33	40	32
Total manufacturing	23.5	21.5	25.7	24.3	25.4	26.1	28.4	26.7

Source: *MDS* Oct. 1979, p. 134, and June 1983, p. 136.

marked for vehicles and textiles than chemicals or mechanical engineering. The food industry has even managed a reduction in import penetration. Similarly, exports as a percentage of manufacturers' turnover have increased.

One would expect the composition of trade to alter over time as markets and commodities change. Has the UK's disappointing export performance been caused by concentration on markets which have grown slowly? Even if this were the case prior to the 1970s, Table A.10.2(a) shows that the situation has altered markedly in recent years. The most notable feature is the substantial expansion of our trade with the EEC, which received 44 per cent of UK exports of goods in 1983, as compared with 29 per cent in 1970. It was also the source of 45.6 per cent of UK imports (27 per cent in 1970). The proportion of export trade with North America declined and recovered during the 1970s, while exports to other developed countries (including the old Commonwealth) as a percentage of the total have declined. One surprising feature is the fall in the proportion of exports to OPEC states between 1975 and 1979, although this was reversed by 1983. The reduction in imports from OPEC can be explained by the increasing production of North Sea oil.

TABLE A.10.2 *Composition of UK trade in goods*

(a) Groups of countries (FOB) Percentage shares by area

	1970	1975	1979	1983
	FOB	FOB	FOB	FOB
Exports: EEC	29.2	32.2	43.0	43.8
Rest of West Europe	17.0	16.9	13.7	12.4
North America	15.3	11.7	11.8	15.4
Other developed countries	10.0	9.4	6.1	5.2
Oil-exporting developing countries	24.9	11.4	9.0	10.1
Non-oil-exporting developing countries		14.6	13.2	11.0
Centrally planned countries	3.3	3.3	2.9	1.8
	CIF	CIF	CIF	CIF
Imports: EEC	27.0	36.4	44.5	45.6
Rest of West Europe	14.7	14.7	15.3	15.8
North America	20.3	13.3	13.2	13.7
Other developed countries	8.0	7.6	6.5	7.8
Oil-exporting developed countries	25.6	13.5	6.8	4.2
Non-oil-exporting developed countries		11.0	10.9	10.3
Centrally planned countries	4.0	3.1	2.5	2.3

(b) Groups of commodities Percentage distribution by commodity

	1970	1975	1979	1983
	FOB	FOB	FOB	FOB
Exports: Food, beverages and tobacco	6.4	7.1	7.2	7.0
Basic materials	3.4	2.8	3.1	2.6
Fuels	2.5	4.1	10.6	21.7
Total manufactures	84.4	82.6	76.0	65.9
	CIF	CIF	CIF	CIF
Imports: Food, beverages and tobacco	22.7	18.1	13.9	11.9
Basic materials	15.1	9.2	8.9	7.2
Fuels	10.5	17.8	12.3	10.7
Total manufactures	50.5	53.1	63.3	68.0

Source. *MDS*, April 1984, June 1983, and earlier issues.

A notable aspect of Britain's trade is the favourable balance with developing countries. But how significant is this — could Britain replace its Western European markets by more trade with developing countries? It is more of a curiosity; our exports to non-oil-exporting developing countries represent only a fifth of our exports to Western Europe, and oil importers might demand balanced trade with oil exporters if protectionism were to spread, so oil-exporting-developing countries could be unreliable customers for Britain.

10.2. *Commodities*

The destination of UK exports changed during the 1970s, and so has the broad commodity composition as shown in Table A.10.2(b). The percentage share of fuels has increased since North Sea oil came on stream to 21.7 per cent of exports of goods. It is clear that the UK no longer conforms to the popular view of a country which exports manufactures and imports food, materials, and fuels — dependence on foreign fuels has decreased, while food and basic materials constituted only 19.1 per cent of total imports in 1983.

10.3. *The Invisible Balance*

Invisibles include receipts from (credits) and payments for (debits) shipping, aviation, and financial services, and interest, profits, and dividends. In recent years an increasing charge in the invisibles sector has been for the profits of overseas-based oil companies in respect of their North Sea oil operations. Although exports of 'financial and other services' have increased since 1965, as shown in Table A.10.3, they represent only a quarter of exports of manufactures in 1983. There is therefore no prospect of these exports totally replacing Britain's export trade in manufactures.

Chapter 11

11.1. The breakdown between employment, income, and profits used in Table 11.1 is based on average relationships. Marginal increases in output lead to larger than average increases in profits, and lower than average increases in income from employment. (At the margin, firms are likely to change employment less than proportionately to changes in output for reasons described in Chapter 14.) No allowance has been made for the diversion of exports to meet increased home demand.

11.2. Another important modification which could be

TABLE A.10.3   *Trade in invisibles as percentages of GDP at market prices*

	Transport and travel	Financial and other services	Interest, profits, and dividends	Total invisibles
Credits (exports)				
1965	3.1	1.7	2.8	8.1
1970	4.1	2.5	2.8	10.0
1975	4.4	2.9	2.7	10.9
1979	4.3	3.0	4.1	12.3
1983	3.2	3.0	3.8	11.2
Debits (imports)				
1965	3.3	0.9	1.6	7.5
1970	4.1	1.0	1.7	8.3
1975	3.9	1.4	2.0[a]	9.1
1979	3.7	1.1	3.6[a]	10.8
1983	3.4	1.0	3.6[a]	10.3

Sources: *ETAS* 84, and *Economic Trends,* March 1984.

[a] Earnings of foreign oil companies in the UK rose from a negative amount in 1975 to £3.0bn. in 1980, and were £3.1bn. or 1 per cent of GDP in 1983.

made to the multiplier concerns changes in stocks. Initially a change in demand for goods will be met from stocks. Only when the stocks are replenished will output rise. However, if as was shown in Chapter 8, firms relate their stocks to sales, a continuing injection will lead to an increase in stocks and thus increase the multiplier.

11.3.   At times of high general unemployment, output responds to increased demand. Even so, long-term crowding-out may occur if resources cannot be switched back to the private sector when it revives. This depends in part on the sources of an increase in the government's deficit. Increased current expenditure on, say, health service care for the elderly may be difficult to reverse, extra expenditure on rebuilding could be reversed.

11.4.   If the injection takes the form of increased social security benefits it would not create a future flow of income.

Chapter 14

14.1   There have been significant changes in the practice of registration as unemployed. In particular, until the mid-1970s many married women did not register because they could not claim unemployment pay. The administrative practices have also changed; 'signing-on' has been separated physically from employment exchanges.

14.2.   This understates the increase in long-term unemployment, because the recent increases in unemployment are still working their way through the periods distinguished.

14.3.   Another feature of international comparisons of employment and unemployment is that the proportion of the population which is available for work (the working population and those counted as unemployed) − the 'activity rate' − is higher in Britain. In 1979 the UK average was 74.5 per cent of the population aged from 15 to 64 'active', compared to the EEC average of 66.3 per cent; this represents an extra 3 million people in the UK labour force. In Britain a higher proportion of women work.

14.4.   *Regional and Sectorial Unemployment*

The regional pattern of unemployment since 1965 is shown in Table A.14.1. In 1983 the South East was the only region with an unemployment rate below 10 per cent, while the West Midlands has had the worst increase in unemployment.

Table A.14.2 shows the changes in unemployment by industrial sectors since 1970. Although employment declined in some service sectors between 1979 and 1981, the loss of jobs was concentrated on manufacturing industries. The insurance, banking, and finance sector actually expanded employment, although by only 7,000, over this period.

14.5.   Some caution is required when using these relationships. A higher proportion of any change in employment does affect registered unemployment at high levels of unemployment. Initially, cuts in employment are concentrated on employees over or near retirement age, and will not be fully reflected in the unemployment figures. The scope for

TABLE A.14.1   Regional unemployment[a]

	Prosperous[b]					Middling[b]		Depressed[b]		
	South East	East Anglia	West Midlands	East Midlands	South West	North West	Yorks and Humberside	North	Wales	Scotland
1965	0.8	1.2	0.6	0.8	1.5	1.5	1.0	2.4	2.4	2.8
1970	1.6	2.1	1.9	2.2	2.8	2.6	2.8	4.5	3.7	4.1
1975	2.7	3.3	3.8	3.4	4.5	5.0	3.8	5.5	5.3	4.9
1979	3.3	4.1	4.9	4.2	5.2	6.2	5.2	7.9	6.9	7.0
1983	9.1	10.2	15.0	11.3	10.9	15.0	13.4	16.4	15.3	14.1
Change in percentage points 1979 to 1983	5.8	6.1	10.1	7.1	5.7	8.8	8.2	8.5	8.4	7.1

Sources: *ETAS* 1984, and *Economic Trends*, March 1984.

a Numbers unemployed, excluding school-leavers, expressed as a percentage of the appropriate mid-year estimate of total *employees* (employed and unemployed).
b The analysis is based on unemployed percentages in 1970.

TABLE A.14.2 *Employees in Employment Mid-year estimates*

Employees in employment	1970 (000's)	1979 (000's)	1981 (000's)	1970–79 Change (000's)	1970–79 Percentage change	1979–81 Change (000's)	1979–81 Percentage change
	22,479	22,920	21,198	+ 441	+ 2.0	− 1,722	− 7.5
By industry:							
Agric., forestry and fishing	466	367	360	− 99	− 21.2	− 7	− 1.9
Petroleum and nat. gas	410	346	338	− 64	− 15.6	− 8	− 2.3
Other mining and quarrying							
Manufacturing	8,341	7,176	6,060	− 1,165	− 14.0	− 1,116	− 15.6
Construction	1,339	1,292	1,130	− 47	− 3.5	− 162	− 12.5
Gas, electricity and water	391	346	338	− 45	− 11.5	− 8	− 2.3
Transport	1,136	1,070	1,006	− 66	− 5.8	− 64	− 6.0
Communication	436	424	446	− 12	− 2.8	+ 22	+ 5.2
Distributive trades	2,675	2,827	2,642	+ 152	+ 5.7	− 185	− 6.5
Insurance, banking, finance, etc.	956	1,233	1,240	+ 277	+ 29.0	+ 7	+ 0.6
Public admin. and defence	1,482	1,620	1,561	+ 138	+ 9.3	− 59	− 3.6
Professional, scientific and miscellaneous services	4,845	6,219	6,077	+ 1,374	+ 28.4	− 142	− 2.3

Source: *National Income and Expenditure*, 1982, p. 15.

such reductions in the labour force has now passed for most firms. Also, if unemployment is to be reduced quickly (though it is not clear how this can be achieved) it will be impossible to accumulate capital to provide the additional employees with new equipment, so after the initial expansion, unemployment may fall more quickly in relation to any rise in output — the productivity improvement component could be smaller than during recovery from shallow recessions.

14.6.   A *once over* general fall in wages, or a slow decline in wages, could have some advantages. Firms may be able to increase their profit margins, and falling prices would encourage the government to use expansionary policies. If the exchange rate did not rise in line with the fall in wages, that would lead to an expansion of exports and contraction of imports, but in practice falling UK prices might well make the UK a magnet for overseas funds and force up the exchange rate.

Index